Towards a Methodology for Comparative
Studies in Religious Education

Waxmann Verlag GmbH
Steinfurter Straße 555, 48159 Münster
info@waxmann.com

Religious Diversity and Education in Europe

edited by

Cok Bakker, Hans-Günter Heimbrock,
Robert Jackson, Geir Skeie, Wolfram Weisse

Volume 24

Globalisation and plurality are influencing all areas of education, including religious education. Moreover, education about religious diversity for all citizens has become an issue in individual countries and in the policies of European institutions such as the Council of Europe and the Organisation for Security and Co-operation in Europe. The intercultural and multi-religious situation in Europe demands a re-evaluation of the existing educational systems in particular countries as well as new thinking at the broader European level. This book series, started in 2006, is committed to the investigation and reflection on the changing role of religion and education in Europe. Books in the series are concerned with empirical research with young people, teachers, teacher trainers and policy makers. The series also includes works contributing to scholarship and theory, which reflect on fundamental issues and develop new perspectives for better policy making and pedagogy, especially in relation to classroom practice.

The publishing policy of the series is to focus on the importance of strengthening pluralist democracies through stimulating the development of active citizenship and fostering greater mutual understanding through intercultural education. It pays special attention to the educational challenges of religious diversity.

The Religious Diversity and Education in Europe series originally published books produced by two European research groups, in which scholars were engaged in empirical and theoretical research on aspects of religion and education in relation to intercultural issues:
* **ENRECA: The European Network for Religious Education in Europe through Contextual Approaches**
* **REDCo: Religion in Education. A contribution to Dialogue or a factor of Conflict in transforming societies of European Countries?**

Although the series will continue to publish books from REDCo and ENRECA, it now includes texts from a wider range of sources, including revised versions of European doctoral theses, edited collections of essays, and reports from national or European research projects. The series is aimed primarily at teachers, researchers and policy makers. It is committed to involving practitioners in the research process. Most books are published in English, but manuscripts in German are also considered.

Book proposals should be directed to one of the editors or to the publisher.

Oddrun M. H. Bråten

Towards a Methodology for Comparative Studies in Religious Education

A Study of England and Norway

Waxmann 2013
Münster / New York / München / Berlin

Bibliographic information published by die Deutsche Nationalbibliothek
Die Deutsche Nationalbibliothek lists this publication in the
Deutsche Nationalbibliografie; detailed bibliographic data
are available in the internet at http://dnb.d-nb.de.

Religious Diversity and Education in Europe, volume 24

ISSN 1862-9547
ISBN 978-3-8309-2887-4

© Waxmann Verlag GmbH, 2013
Postfach 8603, 48046 Münster, Germany

www.Waxmann.com
info@Waxmann.com

Cover Design: Pleßmann Design, Ascheberg
Printed on age-resistant paper, acid-free as per ISO 9706

Printed in Germany

All rights reserved. No part of this publication may be reproduced, stored in
a retrieval system or transmitted in any form or by any means, electronic,
electrostatic, magnetic tape, mechanical, photocopying, recording or
otherwise without permission in writing from the copyright holder.

Foreword
by Robert Jackson

I first had the pleasure of meeting Oddrun Bråten (then Oddrun Hovde) at the Nordic conference on religious education held in Iceland in 1999 (Gunnarsson 2000). We had several conversations about issues in religion and education in Norway and England, and her ideas were creative and challenging. We continued to stay in contact after the conference, and to share our conversations with Dr Geir Skeie, who was then based full time at the University of Stavanger in Norway.

In 2002, Oddrun registered to conduct research for a part-time PhD at the University of Warwick under my supervision, and we invited Geir Skeie to act as co-supervisor. Oddrun had raised a number of issues about the complexity of comparing 'religious education' systems and practices across national boundaries, and she proposed exploring these general issues both through a discussion of theoretical issues and a specific comparative study of England and Norway. Additional inspiration for the research came from the work of Frederick Schweitzer, who has eloquently stated the need for well-developed methodologies for comparative study in the field of 'religious education' (Schweitzer 2004; 2006). Oddrun Bråten's degree was awarded in 2010, following much research, a marriage (and a name change), maternity leave and the arrival of a beautiful son and daughter (with a second daughter arriving post thesis and pre-book).

Oddrun Bråten's PhD is a groundbreaking study in the methodology of comparative religious education and I was not surprised that it won the award for Outstanding Research Student of 2009-2010 in the field of education at the University of Warwick, presented by Professor Ann Caesar, Pro Vice Chancellor, at a ceremony at Warwick University in October 2010. The thesis has been revised and updated for publication as a book in the Waxmann series *Religious Diversity and Education in Europe*.

Oddrun's PhD set out to utilise and test her methodology for comparative religious education (Bråten 2010; see also Bråten 2013a & b). This synthesises three sets of ideas. The first includes supranational, national and subnational processes. *Formal supranational processes* refer to international (educational) policymaking in international organisations. *Informal supranational processes* include secularisation, pluralisation and globalisation. Comparison in RE includes exploring the influence of supranational processes on national processes. *Subnational processes* refer to variations between regions within a country.

The second set of ideas from Oddrun's thesis concerns the societal, institutional, instructional and experiential *levels of curriculum*. They are affected by supranational, national and subnational processes. In discussing the *societal level*, attention needs to be given to the histories of religion, state and school in each country. Research at the *institutional level* involves analysis of relevant policy documents and legislation in each country, while research at the *instructional level* involves analysis of how teachers interpret, plan and teach the curriculum (including ascertaining factors that teachers identify in decision making), while the *experiential level* researches how students interact with one-another and with teachers to develop their own understanding. Historical and documentary studies lend themselves especially to research at the *societal* and *institutional* levels, while ethnographic and survey methods are particularly appropriate for the exploration of the instructional and experiential levels.

The third set of ideas includes Bråten's use of Schiffauer and collaborators' concepts of *social/national imaginary* and *civil enculturation* (Schiffauer et al. 2004). The *social imaginary* is the dominant national self representation of a nation state, a central feature being the relationship between state and religion, decisive for what kind of religious education develops in specific countries. *Civil enculturation* is 'the process by which an individual acquires the mental representations...and patterns of behaviour required to function as a member of (civil) culture...' through education. The concepts of *social imaginary* and *civil enculturation* help in grasping the historical and sociological depth of national traditions.

The publication of Oddrun Bråten's book is timely in relation to developments in the field of religion and education in educational systems and schools in different parts of the world. Speaking personally, it is especially relevant to my own recent work, involving the dissemination of a Europe-wide Recommendation from the Committee of Ministers of the Council of Europe concerning teaching about religions and beliefs in the Council's 47 member states (Council of Europe 2008; Jackson 2009, 2013). By way of background, the Council of Europe, based in Strasbourg, France, is an international organisation promoting co-operation between European countries in the areas of human rights, democratic development, the rule of law, cultural co-operation and legal standards. It was founded in 1949, and its member states have over 800 million citizens. Education is a major priority in the Council of Europe's work.

The Council of Europe aims to encourage the development of Europe's cultural identity through protecting human rights, pluralist democracy and the rule of law. It also aims to find common solutions to various challenges facing European society and to consolidate democratic stability in Europe. At the same time as promoting and encouraging the development of Europe's cultural identity, cultural *diversity* is also valued highly. The Council of Europe recognises that each state has its own history and cultural traditions, its own language or languages and its own religious traditions. Thus, there is a creative tension between developing a European cultural identity based on shared human rights values whilst preserving distinctive cultural traditions. Moreover, no state is homogeneous culturally. Some states have long established ethnic and religious minorities with very long histories, sometimes preceding the formation of the state. Many states have substantial ethnic and religious minorities as a result of migration from other countries within Europe and beyond, mainly during the 20th and current centuries. Diversity within states is complex and connects with global as well as regional, national and local issues.

The Council of Europe has sponsored various projects on topics such as intercultural education, education for democratic citizenship and human rights education. For quite a long period, the Council of Europe took the view that religion was largely a private matter, and that each member state was responsible for its own policies, related to its particular history. General debate about the place of religion in the public sphere began to change that view, against a shifting background of globalisation in which religion was often a factor. The events of 9/11 in the United States of America were a symbol of the entry of religion into general public discussion, both within and beyond individual states (Jackson 2008).

As a result of the migration of peoples, and as a consequence of other features of globalisation, European states have become more religiously pluralistic, and more alert to religion as a phenomenon of both local and global significance. The issue of social cohesion – of living together in harmony within diverse democratic societies – has been complicated by these factors. However, currently, education about religious diversity, and about non-religious worldviews, is very varied across Europe. Some states have educational systems in which religious education is understood primarily as the *transmission* of religious beliefs and values from one generation to the next. Some have no specific provision for teaching about religions in the curriculum of the school. Others include some teaching about religions, or teaching about religions and non-religious worldviews as part of the curriculum for all students.

The Council of Europe aims to encourage member states to develop appropriate teaching about religions in order to increase understanding of religious diversity in Europe and more widely, and to encourage genuine dialogue between people having different religious and non-religious worldviews. The ethos of the Recommendation is inclusive and democratic. It is concerned to provide an education about religions and non-religious convictions in the context of intercultural education. This form of education is logically distinct from forms of religious education which aim *specifically* to nurture children and young people in a particular faith tradition. However, if the Recommendation is followed through, the form of intercultural education suggested should be *complementary* to many forms of faith-based education, and could be adapted to many faith-based contexts.

The Recommendation acknowledges diversity and complexity at local, regional, national and international levels, and encourages connections to be made between 'local' and 'global'. It also advocates the exploration of issues concerning religion and identity, and the cultivation of positive relations with parents and religious communities, as well as organisations which relate to non-religious philosophies. The intention is to introduce young people to a plurality of positions and debates in an atmosphere of mutual tolerance.

The Recommendation was published in December 2008 and circulated to member states. To explore the extent to which the Recommendation had been discussed by stakeholders, the Director of Education at the Council of Europe and the Director of the European Wergeland Centre (http://www.theewc.org/) set up a joint committee of experts in 2011 to encourage utilisation of the Recommendation across the 47 member states (Jackson forthcoming). There was no intention to impose the Recommendation, but rather to produce a 'road map' or 'travel guide' enabling users to engage with the Recommendation in their own particular national or regional contexts, and to encourage developments relevant to particular settings.

Initially, the committee decided to design a questionnaire to be completed by national representatives on the Council of Europe's Education Committee. Some important general points emerged from the responses to the questionnaire. First, there was general support for more discussion of the Recommendation. Second, it was clear from responses that there was some confusion and misunderstanding due to different shades of meaning given to terminology such as 'religious education' and 'non-religious convictions' across different countries, and sometimes even within the same country. This issue includes discussion of the relationship between religious education seen as a means of deepening young people's understanding of religion(s), whatever their background, and religious education understood as initiating young people into a particular religious way of life. Third, quality of teaching was an issue referred to frequently, a point having implications for the development of pedagogy and didactics as well as teacher training. Fourth, there was a general concern about how to integrate or address non-religious worldviews alongside religions, or even whether it was appropriate to address this area alongside religion. Fifth, there was a concern with media representations of religions (through television and the internet, for example) and how to deal with these critically in the classroom. Sixth, the point was made that the Recommendation should be seen not only as having relevance to the classroom, but also to whole school policies on diversity and contact with the community and with schools more widely; the view was presented that the Recommendation was relevant to the ethos of schools, and not just to curriculum subjects. Seventh, some respondents referred to human rights issues such as freedom of expression and the rights of minority pupils (including wearing religious symbols) (Jackson, forthcoming).

The questionnaire responses provided valuable material for use in writing the 'roadmap', which will be complemented by feedback from consultations at national and international conferences, and by findings from recent European research. Following the completion and distribution of the roadmap, there are likely to be further dissemination activities perhaps including some action research in selected member states and various courses and conferences for stakeholders.

Clearly Bråten's framework will be highly relevant to the analysis of any developments at national and regional level resulting from the utilisation of the 'roadmap' in different contexts. The formal supranational process of the development and distribution of the roadmap will interact with expressions of social imaginary and civil enculturation at national levels, and it will be interesting to see the extent to which any effects of this interaction are primarily 'top down', resulting from policy development, or 'bottom up', growing from the work of teachers in collaboration with students, and from teacher trainers and other stakeholders.

Oddrun Bråten's book is clearly relevant to the example of the Council of Europe Recommendation and 'roadmap' outlined above. It is equally relevant to the analysis of developments in the field of religion and education in any particular country within or beyond Europe, and I am sure that Bråten's framework will be used extensively and creatively in many future national and comparative studies.

Robert Jackson
is Professor of Religions and Education at the University of Warwick, UK and Professor of Religious Diversity and Education at the European Wergeland Centre in Oslo (http://www.theewc.org/). He is one of the founding editors of the Waxmann Religious Diversity and Education in Europe series.

References

Bråten, Oddrun M. H. (2010) *A comparative study of religious education in state schools in England and Norway*, Unpublished PhD Thesis, University of Warwick.

Bråten, Oddrun M. H. (2013a) 'Comparative Studies in Religious Education: The Issue of Methodology', *Religion & Education*, 40:1, pp. 107-121.

Bråten, Oddrun M. H. (2013b) 'Comparative Studies in Religious Education: The Issue of Methodology' in Joyce Miller, Kevin O'Grady and Ursula McKenna (Eds.) *Religion in Education: Innovation in International Research*, New York and London: Routledge, pp. 182-196.

Council of Europe (2008) 'Recommendation CM/Rec(2008)12 of the Committee of Ministers to member states on the dimension of religions and non-religious convictions within intercultural education', available online at: https://wcd.coe.int//ViewDoc.jsp?Ref=CM/Rec(2008)12&Language=lanEnglish&Ver=original&BackColorInternet=DBDCF2&BackColorIntranet=FDC864&BackColorLogged=FDC864 (accessed 4 March 2013).

Gunnarsson, Gunnar (Ed.) (2000) *Kundskab og Oplevelse*, Reykjavik, Islands Paedagogiske Universitet.

Jackson, R. (2008) Teaching about Religions in the Public Sphere: European Policy Initiatives and the Interpretive Approach, *Numen: International Review for the History of Religions*, 55 (2/3), pp. 151-182.

Jackson, R. (2009) The Council of Europe and Education about Religious Diversity (Editorial), *British Journal of Religious Education*, 31 (2), pp. 85-90.

Jackson, R. (2010) Religious Diversity and Education for Democratic Citizenship: The Contribution of the Council of Europe, in K. Engebretson, M. de Souza, G. Durka, and L. Gearon (Eds.) *International Handbook of Inter-religious Education*, Volume 4: *Religion, Citizenship and Human Rights* (Dordrecht, the Netherlands, Springer Academic Publishers), pp. 1121-1151.

Jackson, R. (2013) Why Education about Religions and Beliefs? European Policy Recommendations and Research, in Gareth Byrne and Patricia Kiernan (Eds.) *Toward Mutual Ground: Pluralism, Religious Education and Diversity in Irish Schools*, Dublin: Columba Press, pp. 41-53.

Jackson, R. (forthcoming) The Development of European Policy on Religious Diversity and Education: the Work of the Council of Europe, *Journal of Beliefs and Values*.

Schiffauer, W., Baumann G., Kastoriano R. and Vertovec S. (2004) *Civil Enculturation. Nation State, School and ethnic difference in The Netherlands, Britain, Germany and France*, New York, Oxford Berghahn Books.

Schweitzer, Friedrich (2004) 'Comparative Research in Religious Education: International-Interdenominational-Interreligious', in R. Larsson and C. Gustavsson (Eds.), *Towards a European Perspective on Religious Education*, (Stockholm, Sweden: Artos & Norma), pp. 191–200.

Schweitzer, Friedrich (2006) 'Let the Captives Speak for Themselves! More Dialogue between Religious Education in England and Germany', *British Journal of Religious Education* 28, no. 2, pp. 141–151.

Contents

Acknowledgments 15
Abstract 16
Abbreviations 17

1. Introduction 21
   1.1 A systematic approach to comparative studies in Religious Education 21
   1.2 The cases: RE in England and Norway 22
   1.3 Different school systems 25
   1.4 Scope and limitations 26
   1.5 Main research questions 27
   1.6 Summary and Conclusion 28

2. Towards a Methodology for Comparative Religious Education 29
   2.1 Introduction 29
   2.2 Comparative studies in related fields 29
   2.3 Pioneering work in the field of RE 34
   2.4 Challenges in comparative studies in RE 37
       Classification of RE 37
       Problems of terminology 39
       Why comparative studies? 39
   2.5 Methodological considerations 40
   2.6 Is this a new methodology? 42
   2.7 National imaginaries and supranational processes 42
   2.8 Three dimensions in comparative studies 44
   2.9 The supranational dimension 47
   2.10 A template for comparative studies in RE 52
   2.11 Summary and Conclusion 54

3. Societal Level: Themes within Academic Debates
   about Religious Education in England and Norway 56
   3.1 Introduction 56
   3.2 The contribution of 'secular' religious studies to the development of
       multifaith approaches to RE in England and Norway 57
   3.3 The institutional basis for RE research 63
   3.4 Can we talk about 'traditions' for pedagogy of RE? 65
   3.5 The reading of two 'power texts' by looking for
       characteristics of academic debate in England and Norway 69
   3.6 The supranational dimension in academic debates on RE today 79
   3.7 Summary and conclusion 82

4. Institutional Level: Legal and Policy Developments in England and Norway 83
    4.1 Introduction 83
    4.2 The Legal Framework 83
    4.3 Law regulating RE in state schools 84
    4.4 Laws regulating the right to opt out 87
    4.5 The Norwegian law suits 88
    4.6 Religion in laws regarding schooling in general 89
    4.7 Comparative discussion on legal issues 90
    4.8 Introducing QCA 2004 and UD 2005 95
    4.9 QCA 2004 96
    4.10 UD 2005 98
    4.11 Comparative remarks regarding layout and structure 100
    4.12 The place in the school curricula 101
    4.13 Comparative points 102
    4.14 Structure and content of RE in England and Norway exemplified through QCA 2004 and UD 2005 103
    4.15 Comparative discussion regarding structure and content 108
    4.16 Concluding discussion 110
    4.17 Summary and Conclusion 114

5. Religious Education in Practice: Introduction to Case Studies from England and Norway 115
    5.1 Introduction 115
    5.2 Representation and national imaginaries 115
    5.3 Different styles of civility in the school systems 118
    5.4 Characteristics of the schools 123
    5.5 Location of the schools and characteristics of the school populations 126
    5.6 Do classroom activities reflect different national styles? 127
        The pupil population 127
        Organisation of teaching rooms 128
        Topics covered 129
        Teaching methods and styles 130
        Dialogue in the classroom 131
        Different styles? 132
        Visiting Christian believers 133
        Pupils' interest in the topics taught 134
    5.7 National styles and civil enculturation 136
    5.8 Reflecting on the empirical studies in the methodology 136
    5.9 Summary and Conclusion 138

6. Instructional Level: Teachers' Perspectives 139
    6.1 Introduction 139
    6.2 The teachers and their contexts 140
    6.3 Describing their school and its RE 141

6.4	Aims of RE	143
6.5	The importance of RE	144
6.6	National aims and local adjustments	148
6.7	Text books and schemes of work	150
6.8	Content of teaching	152
6.9	Social enculturation gives nationally distinctive patterns in teaching?	154
6.10	Learning about and from religion	155
6.11	Reflecting on multifaith RE as integrative RE	158
6.12	Is RE creating otherness?	160
6.13	How is 'Norwegianness' and 'Englishness' imagined?	161
6.14	Summary and conclusion	162

7. Experiential Level: Pupils' Perspectives 166

7.1	Introduction	166
7.2	The pupils and their context	167
7.3	Which modernities?	170
7.4	Aims of RE	174
7.5	Content of learning	177
7.6	What can explain the difference in quality of factual knowledge?	178
7.7	Religion in Britain? Norwegian religion?	180
7.8	Learning about and from religion	183
7.9	What kind of imaginary would be inclusive?	186
7.10	Summary and conclusion	189

8. Concluding Discussion 192

8.1	Introduction	192
8.2	A systematic approach to comparative RE	192
	A model	192
8.3	Is this a general model, a template for comparative studies?	193
8.4	Obstacles and limitations	195
8.5	Results: Examples of findings	196
8.6	Different national styles	198
8.7	Inclusive RE and construction of otherness	202
8.8	Summary and conclusion	207

Appendix 1: Interview Schedules 210

Schedule for interviews with RE teachers	210
Questions	210
Backgrounds	210
Aims	210
Contents	211
Learning from and about	212
Respect	212
Personal growth	212
Interview schedule for group interviews with pupils	212

    Questions 213
    Aims 213
    Contents 213
    Learning from and about 213
    Respect 214
    Personal growth 214

Appendix 2: Norwegian Legal Texts 215

    The law on KRL prior to the change in 2005 215
    Christian object/ purpose clause – the school law preamble before 2008 215
    The Bolstad Committee's suggestion for a new school law preamble 216

Appendix 3: The Teachers' Educational Backgrounds 219

References 221

Acknowledgments

This book is based on my PhD at the University of Warwick entitled *Comparative studies in Religious Education in state schools in England and Norway*. I want to thank Bill Gent for his excellent proof reading and Beate Plugge at Waxmann Verlag for her work on this publication. It represents many years of hard work, inspired and made possible by my supervisor, Professor Robert Jackson, and the team at WRERU at the University of Warwick. It is an honour to be associated with the work done at the unit. The high quality of the research carried out at WRERU and the standards which Bob Jackson sets have made me stretch my own limits.

Thanks, also, for important contributions from my co-supervisor Professor Geir Skeie whose comments had a way of making me rethink it all. I am grateful to Bob and Geir for having invited me into important networks and seminars such as IS-REV and ENRECA. I have especially appreciated the Viste Seminars organized by Geir Skeie, where meeting others who were doing PhDs in RE in Norway provided a great opportunity to bond and network. A special thanks to Lars Laird Iversen, Trine Anker and Marie von der Lippe for becoming special "friends in the trade".

Further, I want to thank the leaders I have had at Sør-Trøndelag University College, Department for Teacher Education and Deaf Studies. I thank Torunn Klemp for hiring me (in 1998) and thus giving me the opportunity to both teach and do research. I am also grateful to Geir Botten who decided to give me a grant to study in Warwick, and, later, Arnulf Omdal, who also gave me support. Special thanks go to my closest colleagues in the RE department, Ola Erik Domaas and Camilla Stabel Jørgensen, for being genuinely good people and, in the final and crucial month of my studies, for doing my teaching and thus making it possible for me to submit in time.

Last, but not least, I want to thank my family for keeping up with me during the years of my studies. Special thanks go to my husband, Anders E. Bråten, for helping me draw the model in chapter 8 (!), but, more importantly, for keeping our home going in the absence of mommy. Further, I must express gratitude to my three children, Brage (10) and Idunn (6) and Jenny (2), for giving life meaning outside the crude but seductive world of academia. Thanks also go to my mother-in-law, Gerd Inger Nilsen, and my mother, Marit O. J. Hovde, for occasionally filling in for me at home and making it a little easier to complete a PhD and getting it published, whilst also being a mother of small children. I hope you will continue to keep up with me: I love you!

Abstract

In this book, I develop a methodology for comparing religious education internationally. This is done through a systematic comparison of religious education in state schools in England and Norway. Comparative studies in related fields and pioneering works in comparative RE informed the formulation of a methodology, essentially a template for comparative religious education. This is a synthesis of two sets of ideas. The first is an idea of *three dimensions in comparative education*: supranational, national and subnational processes. In *supranational processes*, I distinguish between *formal* and *informal* processes. *Formal* processes refer to formal international (educational) policymaking which takes place in international organizations. *Informal* processes include social and/ or political developments which take place both in and through the formal processes but also outside them and, partly independently of them – such as secularisation, pluralisation and globalisation. My perspective is that comparison in religious education is about the study of the impact of supranational processes on national processes. *Subnational processes* refer to variations between regions within a country.

The second set of ideas is *levels of curriculum*: societal, institutional, instructional and experiential. The chapters of the book explore these levels, examining how they are affected by supranational, national and subnational processes. In discussing the *societal level*, the focus is on academic debates. The *institutional level* is represented mainly by relevant legislation plus key policy documents, the Non-Statutory National Framework for RE (QCA 2004) and local agreed syllabuses in England, and the Norwegian National Curriculum for RE (UD 2005). The *instructional level* includes how teachers plan and deliver the curriculum and the *experiential level* corresponds to how learners receive it. The *societal* and *institutional* levels are explored through theory and documentary studies, while empirical studies are part of the material for the chapters concerning practice. *Civil enculturation*, *social imaginaries* and *national imaginaries* are important analytical concepts that are drawn upon. The suggested methodology and some central findings are discussed further in a concluding chapter.

Abbreviations

BBC	British Broadcasting Corporation
BJRE	British Journal of Religious Education
Cand. Mag.	Candidata Magistrata (lower university degree)
CD-ROMs	Compact Disc Read-Only Memory
DCSF	Department for Children, Schools and Families
DfE	Department for Education
DES	Department for Education and Skills
DCSF	Department for Children, Schools and Families
EDC/HRE	Education for Democratic Citizenship and Human Rights
EU	European Union
ES1	English School 1
ES1-P	English School 1 – Pupils
ES1-T	English School 1 – Teacher 'Sally'
ES1-PG1	English School 1 – Pupil, Girl 1
ES1-PG2	English School 1 – Pupil, Girl 2
ES1-PB1	English School 1 – Pupil, Boy 1
ES1-PB2	English School 1 – Pupil, Boy 2
ES2	English School 2
ES2-P	English School 2 - Pupils
ES2-T	English School 2 – Teacher 'Vicky'
ES2–PG1	English School 2 – Pupil, Girl 1
ES2–PG2	English School 2 – Pupil, Girl 2
ES2-PB1	English School 2 – Pupil, Boy 1
ES2-PB2	English School 2 – Pupil, Boy 2
ES3	English School 3
ES3-P	English School 3 - Pupils
ES3-T	English School 3 – Teacher 'Ruth'
ES3-PG1	English School 3 – Pupil, Girl 1
ES3-PG2	English School 3 Pupil, Girl 2
ES3-PB1	English School 3 – Pupil, Boy 1
ES3-PB2	English School 3 – Pupil, Boy 2
GCSE	General Certificate of Secondary Education
HEF	Humanetisk Forbund (Norwegian Humanist Association)
IAHR	The International Association for the History of Religion
ICT	digital tools (Computer Technology)
IKO	Institutt for kristen oppseding (Institute of Christian Upbringing)
ICCS	Inter-European Commission on Church and School
IMER	International Migration and Ethnic Relations (the Norwegian Research Councils initiative to fund research into migration)
ISREV	International Seminar on Religious Education and Values
KIFO	Stiftelsen Kirkeforskning' (Church Research Foundation), a church related sociology of religion institute
KRL	**1997-2002:** Kristendom med Religions og Livssynsorientering ('Christianity with orientation about Religions and Life views') **2002-2008:** Kristendom, Religion og Livssynskunnskap (the meaning of the acronym was changed to 'Knowledge of Christianity, Religion and Life views')
KUF	. Det kongelige kirke-, utdannings og forskningsdepartementet/ Kir-

	ke-, utdannings og forskningsdepartementet
KUF 1996	Det kongelige kirke-, utdannings og forskningsdepartementet (KUF) 1996) – The 1997 Norwegian National Curriculum
LA	Local Authority (from 2007 replacing the term 'LEA')
LAS	Local Agreed Syllabus
LEA	Local Education Authority (until 2007)
LS	Læringssenteret
LS 2002	2002 National Curriculum for RE in Norway
NoReFo	Norsk religionspedagogisk forskningsforum (Norwegian forum for research on pedagogy of religion)
NOU	Norsk Offentlig Utredning
NOU 1995: 9	Norsk Offentlig Utredning 1995:9 *Identitet og dialog* (Identity and Dialogue)
NOU 2007: 6	*Formål for framtida: Formål for barnehagen og opplæringen* (Purpose/ object for the future: purpose/ object of kindergarten and education
NEKRIF	Nettverk for forskning på kultur, religion og identitet I en flerkulturell kontekst
NS1	Norwegian School 1
NS1-P	Norwegian School 1 – Pupils
NS1-T	Norwegian School 1 – Teacher 'Jon'
NS1–PG1	Norwegian School 1 – Pupil, Girl 1
NS1–PG2	Norwegian School 1 – Pupil, Girl 2
NS1-PB1	Norwegian School 1 – Pupil, Boy 1
NS1–PB2	Norwegian School 1 – Pupil, Boy 2
NS2	Norwegian School 2
NS2-P	Norwegian School 2 – Pupils
NS2-T	Norwegian School 2 – Teacher 'Ingunn'
NS2-PG1	Norwegian School 2 – Pupil, Girl 1
NS2-PG2	Norwegian School 2 – Pupil, Girl 2
NS2-PB1	Norwegian School 2 – Pupil, Boy 1
NS2-PB2	Norwegian School 2 – Pupil, Boy 2
NS3	Norwegian School 3
NS3-P	Norwegian School 3 – Pupils
NS3-T	Norwegian School 3 – Teacher 'Oline'
NS3-PG1	Norwegian School 3 – Pupil, Girl 1
NS3-PG2	Norwegian School 3 – Pupil, Girl 2
NS3-PG3	Norwegian School 3 – Pupil, Girl 3
NS3-PG4	Norwegian School 3 – Pupil, Girl 4
NTNU	Norges Teknisk Naturvitenskapelige Universitet
OECD	Organisation for Economic Co-operation and Development
Ofsted	The Office for Standards in Education, Children's Services and Skills (Her Majesty's Inspectorate)
OSCE	Organization for Security and Co-operation in Europe
OSCE (2007)	*The Toledo Guiding Principles on teaching about religions and beliefs in public schools*
Ped.Sem./ PPU	Pedagogisk Seminar/ Praktisk Pedagogisk Utdanning ('Educational Science')
PGCE	Post-Graduate Certificate in Education ('Educational Science')
PhD	Doctor of Philosophy
PSHE	Personal, social and health education
RE	Religious Education

REDCo	Religion in Education. A contribution to Dialogue of a factor of Conflict in transforming societies of Europe. The EC REDCo Project is a large comparative EU funded project launched in 2006 involving eight European countries
RI	Religious Instruction
RLE	Religion, Livssyn og Etikk (Religion, Life views and Ethics)
SACRE	Standing Advisory Council on Religious Education
SCAA	School Curriculum and Assessment Authority
Shap	The Shap Working Party on World Religions in Education
USA	United States of America
UD	Utdanningsdirektoratet (the Norwegian Directorate for Education and Training)
UD 2005	The KRL book 2005: Knowledge of Christianity- religions- and philosophies of life: Curriculum for $1^{st} - 10^{th}$ grade: Curriculum-guidance and information
UD 2008	The new National Curriculum for RE from 2008 in which the name was changed to Religion, Life views and Ethics (RLE)
UK	United Kingdom
UN	United Nations
VS.	Versus
WRERU	Warwick Religions and Education Research Unit
WTO	The World Trade Organization
QCA	Qualifications and Curriculum Authority
QCA 2004	The Non-Statutory National Framework for Religious Education

1. Introduction

1.1 A systematic approach to comparative studies in Religious Education

There is always a relationship between religion and society, but what that relationship is will change over time and be different from place to place. What is that relationship at a given time and place and why is it different or similar in other places? This is a sociological and historical question, and to answer it one needs a comparative approach. Different actors will have different views about what this relationship is, descriptively, but especially about how it ought to be, normatively. This has serious bearings on the question of how religion and life views should be taught in school, a question which is both pedagogical and political.

This book sets out to make some comparisons between religious education (RE) in fully publicly-funded community schools in England and state schools in Norway. It follows Professor Schweitzer's plea for systematic comparative work in the field of RE (Schweitzer 2004). Schweitzer and others argue that the increasing importance of the supranational context to education in general and to RE in particular, creates a need for comparative studies. While Schweitzer makes a plea for more comparative work he also notes that a more systematic approach to this is needed. In this book I suggest and try out a new methodology for comparative work in RE.

In chapter 2 I present a suggested template for comparative RE which I try out in the rest of the study. Comparative studies in related fields and pioneering comparative works in RE inform the underlying rationale of this methodology. It is a synthesis of two sets of ideas. The first is an idea of three dimensions in comparative education: *supranational, national* and *subnational* processes. My perspective is that comparison in RE is about the study of the impact of *supranational* processes on *national* processes. *Subnational processes* refer to variations between regions within a nation.

The second set of ideas is of four levels of curriculum: *societal, institutional, instructional and experiential*. The chapters of this study explore these levels by looking at how they are affected by supranational, national and subnational processes. The *societal level* is seen as political, and includes public as well as professional debates about RE, but the focus here is on the latter. The *institutional level* in England is represented by the law, the Non-Statutory National Framework for RE and local agreed syllabuses, while in Norway it corresponds to the law, the National Curriculum, and local work in schools. The *instructional level* includes how teachers plan and deliver the curriculum and the *experiential level* corresponds to how learners receive the curriculum and make it personal. The relationship between these levels is also considered.

The societal and institutional levels are explored through theory and documentary studies; while empirical studies are part of the material for the chapters in which the instructional and experiential levels are discussed. *Civil enculturation, social imaginaries* and *national imaginaries* are important analytical concepts. The suggested methodology and the central findings of the comparison are discussed in a final chapter (8). I suggest that this template provides a framework for capturing different levels of national processes within a supranational context.

1.2 The cases: RE in England and Norway

To make sure that comparative studies in RE are meaningful, it is necessary to narrow the focus to specific themes. The cases should also share some basic similarities (Lijphart 1971: 687). England and Norway have state-run schools which must be considered (informal) 'public spheres' (Habermas 2006); both offer RE as a separate subject (as opposed to France, for example) and have non-confessional multifaith approaches to RE (as opposed to Germany, for example) (Jackson et al. (eds.) 2007). It is a basic similarity that the main aims of RE in public schools are educational and not religious, and also that *multifaith* RE has developed in response to supranational processes such as secularisation, pluralisation and globalisation.

Differences as well as similarities between the two countries' state school RE will be dealt with in more detail in the chapters of this book, but here at the outset I shall discuss some immediate differences and similarities. One essential point is that both countries attempt a *non-denominational* and *non-confessional multifaith* (inclusive/ integrative) RE in state schools.

The term *non-confessional* here connotes a form of RE which aims to be free of religious instruction or nurture into a particular faith. It is necessary to point out that this is not the same as *non-denominational*. In the Norwegian language, the word 'konfesjonelt' covers both 'denominational' and 'confessional'. In England, Religious Instruction (RI)[1] in state school was always non-denominational. However, until 1988 it had a confessional element. It was a form of non-denominational Christian instruction – a generic, mainly Bible-based form of teaching, derived from Protestant sources (Copley 1997), which could also be described as civil religion (Davie 2007).

Different Christian denominations such as Catholics and Methodists have had a strong presence in British society besides the established Anglican Church (Protestant). However, Roman Catholics have often sent their children to state-funded Catholic Voluntary Aided Schools, so they have taken little part in policy making and syllabus construction for RE in fully state-funded community (formerly County) schools (Jackson 2004a).

In Norway, by contrast, Christian denominations other than the Norwegian State Church (Protestant) have been more marginal in society. RE in state schools was until 1969 instruction into the faith of the Norwegian State Church (Haraldsø 1989). Alternatives to the state schools have been close to non-existent.

From 1969 till 1997, RE in Norwegian state schools was, in theory, a *non-confessional* but still *denominational* Christian Education, emphasising Norwegian

---

1 In legislation, the name was changed from Religious Instruction to Religious Education in 1988.

Lutheranism. As in the English situation, this could be seen as civil religion. In practice it was to a great extent perceived as still being instruction in the Norwegian State Church religion (Haakedal 1995: 9). This can be argued based not only on what we know about how the subject was practised, but also on the continued existence of the school law preamble ('formålsparagrefen' see chapter 4), § 1-2. This preamble stated that the overall purpose of education as such in Norway was to aid parents in the Christian upbringing of their children.² Confessional and denominational has in practice been two sides of the same coin in the Norwegian context and has come to mean the same in the language ('Konfesjon' = denomination, 'bekjennende' = confessional).

In other words, while there has been an important difference between *confessional* and *denominational* in the English context, in Norway there has not really been a difference. This is an example of the way in which elements which, at first glance, may appear to be similar, will reveal important differences when studied in more detail. In the course of my study there were many examples of this. An important insight is that in a comparative approach one needs to consider what the national contexts mean for the ways in which concepts are understood.³

It is, for instance, an interesting difference that English RE was *confessional* but *not denominational*, while Norwegian RE was *denominational* but not *confessional:* and an interesting historical question, which will not be pursued further here, is how much difference this made in practical teaching. Did it, for instance, mean that a certain style of civil religion was what was really on the curriculum, in both cases? If this is the case, this difference may reveal some interesting similarities.

With reference to English and Norwegian RE, by *multifaith* RE I mean descriptively a kind of RE where all children in school, regardless of faith background, are taught together; where the content of the teaching includes material from and about different religions (and life views and philosophy); and where the methods of teaching should be such that the intention is not to nurture children and young people into a specific faith.⁴ This has been the aspiration of Norwegian state school RE since 1997 and of English state school RE since 1988 (and in some places before this, due to the system of locally agreed syllabuses).

From 1997 to 2008, RE in Norwegian state schools was a subject called 'KRL'. From 1997-2002 this acronym referred to 'Christianity with orientation about Religions and Life views' (Det kongelige kirke-, utdannings og forskningsdepartementet (KUF) 1996). From 2002-2008, however, the meaning of the acronym was changed to 'Knowledge of Christianity, Religion and Life views'.⁵ The KRL cur-

---

2 The preamble was changed in 2008, see chapter 4.
3 See Schweitzer (2006: 8) on the different meanings of confessional and denominational in England and Germany.
4 Alberts (2007) calls this kind of RE integrative RE. Her choice of concept enhances the contrast to 'Separative approaches' where children are not taught together about religion, but where children's RE is seen as the responsibility of the specific denomination/ religion they or their parents belong to, as in Germany.
5 1997–2002: Kristendomskunnskap med Religions og Livssynsorientering, 2002–2008: Kristendom, Religion og Livssynskunnskap.

riculum, which is national, was revised in 2002 (Læringssenteret (LS) 2002) and 2005 (Utdanningsdirektoratet (UD) 2005).

In 2008, the name of the subject was changed to 'Religion, Life views and Ethics' (RLE). Changes made in 2005 coincided with a general revision of the National Curriculum in 2006, but the changes in KRL were advanced because the authorities needed to address a criticism from the United Nations' (UN) Human Rights Committee that KRL was in violation of the convention for civil and political rights. The changes in 2008 resulted from addressing a verdict along similar lines in the Human Rights court in Strasbourg (Utdanningsdirektoratet (UD) 2008) (more details on this in chapter 4).

From 1997, Norwegian state school RE was intended to be a subject in which pupils with different religious and non-religious backgrounds could learn about religions, ethics, philosophy and secular life views together. It is important to distinguish this clearly from religious groups' own RE, where the nurturing of children in faith is the aim (Norsk Offentlig Utredning (NOU) 1995: 9, KUF 1996).

In England a similar open and plural type of RE had been developing locally, through the system of local agreed syllabuses since the 1970s, the Education Reform Act of 1988 formally recognizing this development (Jackson & O'Grady 2007). In England, the term 'religious education' has changed in meaning over time. In current usage, in relation to the subject in fully state-funded community schools, the subject involves both learning *about* religions and providing the opportunity for pupils to learn *from* them. It is not about the transmission of religious culture.[6]

In being inclusive of different religious faiths, RE in the two countries is similar, but there are also some significant differences. One is that Norwegian RE includes secular life views as an important part of the subject, even in the subjects' name, while in English RE secular life views have been marginal. In some Local Education Authorities (LEA until 2007/ Local Authorities (LA) after this date) something about secular life views had been included in some local agreed syllabuses, but this has not been very common (Copley 1997). There is no strong tradition of teaching secular life views in English schools but, in the Non-Statutory National Framework for RE, launched in late 2004 (Qualifications and Curriculum Authority (QCA) 2004), secular humanism was included.

Another difference is that in English RE Sikhism is included in the religions usually represented; while in Norway Sikhism is marginal. Philosophy and ethics are important parts of Norwegian RE, and ethics is also an important aspect in English RE. Religions other than those five or six which are considered 'major' are marginal both in the Norwegian and English curricula and syllabuses. This includes, for instance, ethnic religions, nature religions, new religious movements and archaic religions.

---

6   On the ambiguities of 'religious education' and other terms, see Jackson (2008a).

1.3 Different school systems

The school systems in England and Norway are different in many important ways. For instance, in England there is a variety of types of school within the state system, while this is not the case in Norway. The four main types of English state schools are[7]: Community schools, Voluntary Controlled schools, Voluntary Aided schools and Foundation schools. In addition, there is also a significant number of independent schools.[8] Schools with a religious character are supported within the state system in England even though this is a contested issue (see Jackson 2004a: 39-57). The development of the English school system must be understood in the context of "the dual system": where the establishment of schools for important part of the history was done in cooperation between the state and religious groups included the Church of England.

In Norway there is only one type of state school, independent schools being very marginal, providing only for about 2% of school children (Skeie 2007). The Norwegian school is called 'enhetsskolen', which in this study will be referred to as the unitary school. Telhaug (1994) describes the unitary school as four dimensional: 1. The resource dimension: that there should be equality in availability of resources (economically and otherwise). 2. The social dimension: the school should include all pupils within a geographical area coming together in heterogeneous groups. 3. The cultural dimension: pupils should acquire subject culture; in their subject learning, shared traditions, values and knowledge should be emphasised as a common frame of reference. 4. The dimension of difference: unitary school ideology includes respect for difference and plurality of backgrounds among its pupils. The education should be adjusted to their individual needs so that all receive education according to their different abilities.

In European educational debate, the issue of social cohesion is a frequent topic, and in several countries, including England, citizenship education has been introduced. In the Norwegian context there has not yet been a real debate about this, and I think one reason for this is the unitary school ideology. This school tradition already works towards social cohesion and Østberg (1998b), for instance, has argued that the unitary school ideology is one important factor for explaining why multifaith RE was introduced in 1997. It needed to be one common subject for all.

Differences between the school systems turned out to be an important source for explaining the differences between English and Norwegian RE. However, to avoid twisting my focus towards comparing the school systems, differences between the educational systems as such are as a rule only addressed where it is directly relevant to the analysis of differences in RE. In chapter 5 there is an exception to this. Here, differences between the educational systems as such are focused on through some illustrative points.

---

[7] This was so up to the general election of May 2010. But since then, the coalition government has been introducing a wider range of schools such as 'academies' and 'free schools'.
[8] See http://www.inca.org.uk/england-system-mainstream.html

1.4 Scope and limitations

It would be impossible to compare every possible variable affecting RE within the two education systems. In this book, the scope, the range of domains and examples covered are limited in the following ways:

Firstly, the bulk of the study concentrates on recent developments, here meaning from the 1988 Education Reform Act in England when multifaith RE was sanctioned nationally, and the 1997 Curriculum Reform in Norway when multifaith RE was introduced. These are the points in time when multifaith forms of RE were sanctioned in law.

Secondly, the range of examples selected for comparison is deliberately selective. The framework for selecting examples is based on Goodlad and Su's ideas of 'levels' of curriculum: that there is a societal, institutional, instructional and experiential level (Goodlad & Su 1992). Within these levels, particular examples have been selected for comparison. *Academic debates* relate to the societal level (chapter 3); educational policy relates to the institutional level (chapter 4). For those two chapters the source material consists of documents and texts. Educational practice, including *teachers' perspectives*, relates to the instructional level (chapter 6), while *pupils' perspectives* relate to the experiential level (chapter 7). In the case of the 'instructional' and 'experiential' levels, particular use is made of empirical case studies conducted by the researcher in secondary schools in England and Norway, but I also refer to other empirical studies.

I have also made use of grounded theory (Glaser & Strauss [1967] (2008)). This is not *a* theory but a method for generating theory from empirical data, contrasted to the 1960's view of using empirics for testing pre-existing theory. It is research aiming at generating new theory that fits the facts. It can be contrasted with 'grand theories', but once a category is abstracted from the facts at hand, it can be used for theorizing on a more general level.[9] I went to the field with certain questions but, where I found interesting elements in the comparison, I have discussed those as findings. As I was looking for explanations for similarities and differences, I wanted to look for themes that emerged from the material (see chapter 8).

The study concentrates on the domain of culture, and I have an interest in looking for and comparing examples of ways in which RE has come to be perceived as contributing to students' cultural understanding. This is sometimes expressed as RE's contribution to 'multicultural' or 'intercultural' education.[10] Relevant here too are perceptions of RE as contributing to education for democratic citizenship or as

---

9   Using grounded theory can mean a detailed systematic method (coding, see Robson 2002: 492ff.), but it can also be applied more generally (Robson 2002: 495). 'It is, of course, possible, to design a study which incorporates some aspects of grounded theory while ignoring others' (Robson 2002:193).

10 Although multiculturalism can be understood differently, as group plurality (see McIntyre 1978, Gravem 2004), others have more flexible and malleable ideas of multiculturalism (Baumann 1996, Jackson 1997, 2004, Hylland Eriksen 1993, Davie 2007). In political rhetoric in the UK (and in the White Paper on Intercultural Education from the Council of Europe) as well as in Norway and other European countries, multicultural education is seen in a negative light as something to leave behind in favour of *intercultural education*, which allows more easily for cultural change and cultural interaction.

a tool for promoting social or community cohesion (Jackson (ed.) 2003) or, in the case of Norway, generic formation ('buildung', see chapters 3 and 4).

That grounded theory is based on data means it is dynamic and open to change when new data challenge the findings. '(…) so the published work is not the final one, but only a pause in the never ending process of generating theory' (Glaser & Strauss 1967: 40). This quotation aids the way that I think about the findings presented in this book. On occasions I theorise from certain facts, but the theory is open to change in meeting with new facts, for example more representative documentation of how RE is practised (see chapters 6 and 7).

1.5 Main research questions

My main research questions were 'What are the main similarities and differences in English and Norwegian state school RE?' and 'How do we account for these?' This was broken down into sub-questions for each main chapter. Through the levels that I have chosen to use as basic categories for the comparison, I move systematically from the general to the specific (see chapters 3-7).

Thus, my sub-questions are: What principles should be applied in comparative studies in RE? (Chapter 2): What are main similarities and differences in academic debates about RE in England and Norway? How do we account for these? (Chapter 3): What similarities and differences exist between English and Norwegian laws concerning religion and school? How do we account for these? (Chapter 4): What are the main similarities and differences between English and Norwegian policy as expressed in *the Non-statutory National Framework for RE* (QCA 2004) and *The KRL book 2005: Knowledge of Christianity- religions- and philosophies of life: Curriculum for 1st – 10th grade: Curriculum-guidance and information* (UD 2005)? How do we account for these?

Further, for chapter 5 the main question discussed is: How does the empirical research fit into the overall methodology as outlined in chapter 2? Following this I proceed to chapter 6 with the questions: What are important similarities and differences between the instructional level of curriculum in England and Norway as expressed by teachers in this sample material? How do we account for these? And how do we account for these with reference to the other levels (the institutional and societal) of curriculum? For chapter 7 the main research question was: What are similarities and differences between the English and Norwegian curriculum's experiential level as expressed by pupils in this sample? How do we account for these? And how do we account for these with reference to the other levels of curriculum?

I would like to stress that I am not comparing between the countries based on the six cases, but use each national context as a frame of reference for analysing and suggesting explanations for findings in these cases. For the final chapter 8, my question was: What are important findings? How could this methodology be used further? This adds up the four chapters which explore the methodology (chapters 3, 4, 6 and 7) and the two chapters which discuss methodological issues explicitly (chapters 2 and 5)). Hence, there is a movement between discussion of the methodology and trying it out, making the question about methodology very much central to this study.

1.6 Summary and Conclusion

In the introduction to this book I have outlined the basic ideas behind the suggested methodology for comparative studies in RE which is presented and tried out in this study. Further, I have set the scene by presenting some immediate similarities and differences between English and Norwegian RE. The scope and limitations are made clear, and I have also presented the main research questions.

Besides bringing out issues relating to the particular national situations of England and Norway, this book will also inform wider debates about European policy regarding RE. But, most importantly, I hope my study will contribute to discussions about methodology for the field of the comparative study of RE.

In chapter 2, which now follows, I will proceed to discuss comparative studies in RE in more detail, presenting the background arguments for my suggested methodology.

2. Towards a Methodology for Comparative Religious Education

2.1 Introduction

How can comparative studies in related fields, comparative religion and comparative education, illuminate and help formulate a view on comparative RE? Insights from these two fields together with experiences from pioneering work in the field of comparative RE forms the background for suggesting that in comparative RE there should be an awareness of supranational processes, European as well as global, at the national level, and also at the local level. Based on this and on Goodland's theories of levels of curriculum, I suggest a template for comparative studies in religious education that both takes account of the international complexities like international trends and politics, and different levels of history, law, politics and practice nationally.

In this book the main focus is on national factors, but I will also take account of supranational factors, such as the trend towards the recommendation of studies about religions, as part of education throughout and beyond Europe (for example Organization for Security and Co-operation in Europe (OSCE) 2007; Council of Europe 2007). For the chapter at hand my research question is: What principles should be applied in comparative studies in religious education?

2.2 Comparative studies in related fields

At a conference in Lund, Sweden, in March 2004, Friedrich Schweitzer made a plea for more comparative research in RE and pointed to the fields of comparative education (Schweitzer 2004: 198) and comparative religious studies (Schweitzer 2004: 192-193) as especially relevant. Comparative studies in RE are not about comparing religions, but education concerning religion, including education about religions. In a sense it is therefore closer to the field of comparative education than to comparative religious studies. Nevertheless, insights from both fields are valuable in so far as they illuminate comparative RE. An aspect where comparative religious studies and comparative studies in RE particularly share interests is in relation to the question of how adherents of the religions deal with the next generation, and how new generations respond to the expectations or even demands of older generations (Schweitzer 2004: 195).

In the development of these two disciplines one can recognise general developments in academia as well as in society. These move from grand universal theories in the 1950/60s through a period of dispute and contest in the 1970/80s, to a post-modern eclectic, reflexive, inter-textual and pragmatic orientation in the 1990s, with an ambivalent nostalgia for certainty and delight in diversity (Paulston 1994: 924). It follows the pattern of development from modern to post-modern/ late modern society. 'Comparative educators and their texts are becoming more reflexive and eclectic' (Paulston 1994: 932). This could be said about recent trends in comparative religion as well, although the different positions, on the ways religions are represented in the late modern context, are complex (see for example the sophisticated but rather different stances of Flood and Fitzgerald discussed by Jackson (2008b)).

Since the origin of religious studies[11] in the 1850s, there has been a tradition of comparison: 'He who knows one knows none' (Müller 1873: 16)[12]: he who only knows one religion, his own, does not even know that, because he does not know what is unique or what is similar to elements in other religions. This could also be claimed for RE. Through comparing RE in different school traditions one will gain new perspectives on developments in RE in one's own country.

Comparative education originated in 1808 when Basset called for exchange of educationalists so that they could become free from national and methodological prejudice (Epstein 1994: 918). In RE too, comparison between different countries' RE could lead to new ideas which potentially could challenge set national perspectives on RE. With Alberts (2007), this is also an explicit goal of her comparative work. Comparison makes us think of questions which do not occur in our own context (Schweitzer 2004: 193).

For many years there has been an extreme self-criticism in comparative religious studies. Typically researchers would not claim enough of an overview of more than one area to conduct valid comparisons (Stausberg 2006). With reference to his cooperation with Osmer (Osmer & Schweizer 2003) Schweitzer also warns that 'this study could not have been done in a similar way by one researcher alone, (…) because of the required in-depth familiarity with two different contexts, locations, and traditions' (Schweitzer 2004: 199). He recommends inclusion of representatives of different countries in comparative studies as a joint enterprise.

In the EC REDCo Project comparative studies are conducted as joint efforts involving scholars from eight European countries (see below), but there are also examples of comparative studies in RE carried out by single authors (Haakedal 1983, 1986, Alberts 2007). I take the view that it is important to be self-critical in RE as well, but not to the point that researchers refuse to attempt comparative studies, and that it is possible even for single scholars but that cooperation's between scholars being experts on the different contexts would be beneficiary.

One point in the self-criticism in religious studies has been an awareness of the dangers of ethnocentric and biased comparison. Comparing religions have had different aims and goals, including being polemical towards other religions than one's own, and in an evolutionist paradigm judging other religions as primitive.[13] Con-

---

11 The discipline goes by many names: Religious Studies, Science of Religion, Comparative Religion, Phenomenology of Religions, and History of Religion.
12 He argued that what Goethe had said about studying languages was also relevant for the study of religion. The Comparative Indo-European Study of Languages served as model.
13 Much of the criticism of early comparisons in the discipline had to do with using the Darwinist evolutionary paradigm where religions were ranked according to how primitive or evolved they were, where the religions most like Christianity; those who had holy scriptures and only one god, were considered less primitive (Sharpe 1975: 47-71). The phrase 'primitive religions' still lingers in the language, often with not very helpful 'quotation marks'.

siderations so as to avoid biased and polemical foci are also relevant to comparison in RE.

Schweitzer (2006) responds to an article about RE in Germany and England (Hull 2005) with the criticism that this did not have a mutual two-way perspective, and stresses the importance of contextuality in comparative analysis. On the one hand Schweitzer is convinced that it is 'more and more important to work towards international agreements about basic criteria for what should be considered quality religious education' but, on the other hand, he stresses that this can only be achieved through a mutual critical dialogue (Schweitzer 2006: 141-142).

Schweitzer points to a number of contextual factors, like for instance different legal systems, different histories of relationship between state and church and degree of Church 'control' of RE in school. Schweitzer argues that a thorough contextual comparative analysis would be open to the possibility that what would seem in the first instance like similarities might be differences and what appears in the first instance to be differences can turn out to be more similar (Schweitzer 2006: 148). He gives the example that, if two countries both have 'non-confessional' RE, this would be at face value a similarity. Since the term 'non-confessional' might have different meanings in different countries, however, important differences might surface if this is explored in more depth. I take Schweitzer's point, and have in chapter 1 also discussed how the terms 'non-confessional' and 'non-denominational' can easily be a source of confusion in a comparison of RE in England and Norway.

Further, in my comparison between English and Norwegian RE I see it as inappropriate to use examples from the English context in order to be polemical towards Norwegian RE and vice versa. It is important to be sensitive to contextual reasons for differences. This does not mean that any insight from one context could not be used in the other, but it is important to keep the comparison impartial and to understand differences in light of nation-specific histories and school traditions. However, Alberts (2007), a German like Schweitzer, uses the comparative perspective to make points of criticism about RE in Germany. This brings out the point that comparative perspectives can also be a source of critique of national processes.

Comparisons, like all other kinds of academic studies, will always be guided by interests. It includes a relation between the two items being compared, and the specific interest of the researcher (Smith 1990: 51 in Stausberg 2006: 34). This means that, even if I attempt not to be biased in my comparison, the examples of RE from both contexts are represented through my choice of foci and interpreted through my research questions and analysis. Because of the awareness that no comparison can be neutral, I would argue that today comparison also needs to be more contextual, strategic and reflexive.

A comparison of religions, Stausberg (2006: 40) claims, 'is always an interpretation and to a certain extent also an explanation'. In comparative studies in RE as well it is important to have an awareness of the interests and cultural backgrounds and values of the researcher conducting the study. In my case this is a curiosity about English RE from the perspective of a Norwegian religious studies graduate coming into teaching RE to teacher students at a time when the revolutionary KRL replaced traditional teaching of Christianity in Norwegian state schools. Even though to a certain extent all approaches are biased, I will attempt to be interpretive rather than normative or purely descriptive.

In comparative religious studies it has been essential to establish valid comparative categories. One did not try to compare, for instance, all of Islam with all of Christianity, which would be impossible, but to limit the comparison to certain categories, like for instance rituals, concept of 'god' etc. (Sharpe 1975). In comparative education, Kandel (1933) also argued that comparative approaches should use certain common concepts (Epstein 1994: 920). Examples of such concepts are church and state, rural education, adult education, higher education. To make sure that comparative studies are meaningful, according to Lijphart (1971: 687) it is necessary to narrow the focus to specific themes and also to find cases which share some basic similarities.

In comparative RE as well it is not possible to compare every aspect of, for instance, RE in England with every aspect of RE in Norway. It is necessary to choose categories or themes to focus the study. Phenomena which are being compared must have something in common; they must be genuinely comparable. There is no point in comparing a cat to a dog, if you want to know more about different kinds of cats.[14] In comparative religious studies there has been a distinction between typological and hermeneutical approaches. The typologists only wanted to categorise while the hermeneutists also wanted to make interpretations (Sharpe 1975: 220-250).[15] In comparative studies in RE the interpretive aspect is important. Analysis would set out to find possible explanations for differences and similarities.

Paden (1994: 1-12) points to two poles in the perspectives on comparison in religious studies while arguing for the possibility of a middle way. One pole relates to the traditional preconceptions for doing comparison in religious studies, a focus on similarities: generally speaking that there is an essence to 'religion' as such and that all religions therefore essentially are the same type of phenomena and therefore comparable.[16] The most radical critique of this led to almost abandoning comparisons as a strategy in religious studies, in favour of a focus on differences: generally speaking that religious traditions are completely unique phenomena which cannot be compared to each other.[17] In RE there is god reason as well to raise the question as to whether the systems for RE of two different countries are really comparable, or completely unique.

In the light of this kind of critique, Paden (1994) explores the possibilities of doing valid comparisons through taking account of the uniqueness of the different contexts. He argues that the comparative should not be understood as an alternative to historical and contextual knowledge, but as a supplementary perspective. '(...) comparison is not an end in itself. It yields comparative perspective, the process by which overreaching themes on the one hand and historical particulars on the other get enriched by the way they illuminate each other' (Paden 1994: 4).

---

14 In the words of Schweitzer (2004: 192): apples are not oranges.
15 For the typologists the problem was how to compare without adding their own subjective interpretation while for the hermeneutics the question was how interpretations could be made.
16 This has a reference to essentialist theories of religion sui generis, religion as such.
17 This perspective has reference to a contextual postmodernist view.

It is important in RE to acknowledge a position between the two poles of essentialism and particularism, and consider comparative studies as complementary to close up studies of RE in one context. The specific contribution of comparative studies would be the possibilities of adding overreaching perspectives and explanations that can only be found in the supranational dimension (see below).

Paden's (1994) emphasis on context is evident in his main comparative concept: 'religious worlds'. He underlines that where similarities are pointed out, one must not think of this as identical but similar phenomena. Because of the uniqueness of the contexts they are not the same. Paden also points out that if the plural nature of the phenomena compared is to be maintained in the analysis, differences should be as much focused as similarities. In the same manner, for instance, the similarity that both England and Norway have a non-confessional multifaith approach to RE in state schools would also have to be understood in light of the different contexts, including school history and school systems, and the differences must be considered just as interesting to the analysis as the similarities.

Sadler, in a lecture delivered in 1900, stressed that comparative education required examination not only of schooling itself but also of the social context within which the schools functioned (Epstein 1994: 919). After the 2nd World War the social sciences came to play a paramount role in comparative education, and the discipline was refocused as a social science activity (Epstein 1994: 920). The field now views schools as integral parts of culture and social change. This makes demands on education and comparativists can study how these demands produce different results among societies (Epstein 1994: 922). Perspectives from social science are also important in comparative RE. For example, changes in RE across countries are closely linked to social changes such as secularisation, pluralisation and globalisation. The fact that these social changes are of a supranational character makes comparative studies/ perspectives necessary for those seeking to understand developments even in one country.

Some claim comparative education should include actual comparisons between two or more countries, and Alexander's book 'Culture and pedagogy: international comparison in primary education' (2000) is an example of this. Alexander compares systems, politics and history as well as schools and classroom activities in France, Russia, India, the United States and England.

Alexander is concerned with globalisation as a context and, for instance, warns about borrowing educational politics from countries which are successful economic competitors as a political 'quick fix' for perceived weaknesses in a country's educational system (Alexander 2000: 2). The need for informed international educational comparison is now inescapable, he argues. In RE as well one should be cautious of borrowing elements from one country without an understanding of contextual differences, and also, in relation to RE, one could argue that thorough international comparative analysis is necessary now, because exchange of ideas is happening and we need to have better knowledge of this phenomenon. Schweitzer (2004: 194) also argues that comparative work in the field of RE is needed today because it potentially adds a theoretical level to on-going international exchange (see also Alexander's (2000) discussion: 531ff).

Rather than seeing comparative education as a comparison of certain aspects of education in two or more countries, it is more common among comparative educationists now to have a broader definition (Halls 1990 in Buk-Berge 2005: 274). International developments that transcend traditional nation state borders have given the discipline a new focus. In RE, international developments have led to the establishment of international networks, seminars and recently some international and comparative research. Comparative education is often described as the study of international problems in education (Epstein 1994: 922). Comparativists' interest is to explain why educational systems and processes vary and how they relate to various social factors. Comparative RE too could be seen as the study of international problems in the subject – the study of how RE varies across countries and reasons for this.

In religious studies today the comparative perspective is more than the explicit comparison of two or more religions. There is more awareness now of the inner diversity in religions (see for example Said 1993) and that even the study of one religion is a comparative project. In RE as well a comparative project could just as well be a comparison between elements of RE in different parts of a county or region within a country, differences between rural areas and city areas or, for instance, between different political or religious interests regarding RE in one country.

Comparative education is not simply a process of comparing two educational systems, but may be an exploration of developments in one country in an international context. It could also be a study of how international processes affect various educational systems. The point would then be to offer interpretations and explanations of global phenomena on a national level, like for example Karlsen's (2006) book about Norwegian educational politics in an international perspective. This approach could also be applied to comparative RE: it could be seen as an analysis of the developments in one country's RE in an international context.

R. Jackson's (2004a) Rethinking Religious Education and Plurality: Issues in diversity and pedagogy, for instance, does not explicitly compare two countries, but it compares different approaches to RE in England in light of social developments which are international, especially pluralisation. It is in a sense a study of how international trends affect one country's RE, but his discussions have proved internationally relevant. One example of this was when a panel at the American Academy of Religion, inspired by Jackson's book, focused on the challenges of pluralism and religious diversity for RE in Europe and the United States.[18]

2.3   Pioneering work in the field of RE

Haakedal (1983)[19] is an early Norwegian comparative study in RE which compares English RE and Swedish Life Views Education with the purpose of appreciating

---

18   The papers from this session were published in a special edition of the journal Religion and Education, spring 2005. See especially the papers by Grelle, Nord and Moore, all written from an American perspective.
19   A Norwegian master's thesis in Pedagogy of Religion: Kristendomsundervisning, religionsundervisning, livssynsundervisning. En systematisk drøfting av problemer innen Engelsk re-

the elements from these in relation to the Norwegian context. At the time Norwegian state school RE included Christian Knowledge, which predominated, and the subject of Life Views as a more secular alternative. One point she makes is how different developments in the societies nationally have led to the kinds of RE which she finds there (Haakedal 1983: 2). Following this initial comparative work, Haakedal later wrote a booklet, a reader for the study of Pedagogy of Religion at the Norwegian School of Theology (Haakedal 1986)[20]. This builds on her master's thesis (Haakedal 1983) and includes additional perspectives from West Germany and Denmark in an expanded comparative analysis.

Haakedal's comparative work (1983, 1986) is written in a context where the problem at hand in Norway is seen to be secularisation rather than pluralisation.[21] A central question in her work is whether pedagogy of religion should be based on theology or pedagogy, and whether RE (in Norway) should be confessional/ denominational or not. One of the things she considers is the significance of the emancipation of the education systems as such from the Churches, and the general development in educational systems towards becoming more of a secular public enterprise (Haakedal 1993: 1). Despite the emergence of the KRL in 1997 this question is still relevant to the discussion of RE in Norway, especially in light of the Strasbourg verdict and the reasons for it as well as the consequences. Especially relevant is the discussion of and changes in the school law preamble, the school object clause: 'formålsparagrafen' (see chapter 4).

Haakedal's (1983, 1986) comparative perspective also presents the problems of whether aims in RE should include addressing plurality, especially through the English material (Haakedal 1986: 188). She discusses the grounds for and the reasons given for RE in the different contexts as well as the different aims, content and form (methods and approaches). Haakedal's analysis is thorough in taking seriously the different context of RE in the different countries' religious and school traditions. At the same time, her argument for doing comparative analysis is that:

(...) in spite of national differences one can see that there is a general development in Western European countries which means that several challenges in religious education are the same (Haakedal 1986: 1).[22]

---

ligionspedagogikk i sammenligning med svensk religionspedagogikk. My translation into English: Christian Education, Religious Education, Life Views Education. A systematic discussion based on questions within English Pedagogy of Religion in comparison with Swedish Pedagogy of Religion.

20 Trends in Pedagogy of Religion related to the development of education in Christianity, Religions and Life Views in some western European school systems in the 1960s and 1970s (my translation into English). Original: Religionspedagogiske tendenser med hensyn til utviklingen av kristendoms-, religions- og livssynsundervisning i noen vesteuropeiske skolesystem under 1960- og 1970-årene.

21 An English publication preoccupied with this same issue is Edwin Cox (1966).

22 My translation into English, original: "Men på tross av nasjonale forskjeller kan en snakke om en generell vesteuropeisk samfunnsutvikling, og følgelig er mange av de problemer og utfordringer som religionsundervisningen i de forskjellige land står overfor, sammenfallende".

Despite its modest booklet (unpublished) form, in my opinion Haakedal's comparative analysis is an impressive piece of early comparative work, raising questions which are still central to comparative work in the field, and giving arguments for doing comparative research which are still valid. In the Norwegian context it is of particular interest that her titles include "Christianity, Religions and Life views", referring to Norwegian (Christianity), English (Religions) and Swedish (Life views) RE, because this, 'Christianity, Religions and Life views', was the title of the revolutionary new RE, the 'KRL' which came about 10 year after these works.

In the second of these texts, Haakedal (1996: 187) distinguishes between confessional/ denominational types of RE (Germany, Norway, Finland), and non-confessional/ denominational types of RE in her material (Sweden, Denmark, England). With the 1997 reform, Norway, at least in theory, shifted from being in the group supporting confessional/ denominational types of RE to being in the group embracing non-confessional/ denominational types of RE.

Twenty-four years after Haakedal's comparison of English and Swedish RE the German scholar Alberts (2007) publishes a thesis which also compares English and Swedish RE. Alberts is also taking account of RE in some other European countries, namely Norway, Germany and the Netherlands. An interesting similarity to Haakedal's work is that they both at the time of writing were situated in countries with predominately confessional Christian RE in schools, and from such a position choose to compare English and Swedish RE. Apart from that, I would say that their works are quite different. While Haakedal is interested in discussing whether pedagogy for RE should be theologically or pedagogically based, Alberts wants an 'Integrative' RE which is a study-of-religion-approach.

Alberts (2007) defines Integrative RE as identical to multifaith RE (Alberts 2007: 1), but prefers to call it Integrative since this does not emphasise a specific aspect of religion (faith). Initially she uses the term Integrative RE descriptively as opposed to Separative RE, i.e. when children are not taught together but receive confessional RE in separate settings, like in most German schools. Then she sets out to investigate what she considers to be existing models of Integrative RE. The models she investigates, described as academic concepts of religious education, are evaluated as useful or less useful for Integrative RE.

For example, with regard to the Westhill Project, she asks whether its aim of the spiritual development of children is an acceptable aim for Integrative RE (Alberts 2007: 112). The 'Gift to the Child' approach she considers not acceptable, because it favours a religious life view over a secular one (Alberts 2007: 127). The Interpretive Approach she says '(…) reflects recent developments in the study of religions' and is evaluated as useful for Integrative RE and promising for further developments in the subject (Alberts 2007: 161). She also considers Andrew Wright's critique of contemporary liberal consensus to be helpful (Alberts 2007: 171). In my view this makes Integrative RE something other than a descriptive term, as it is clearly something different to those existing models that she is investigating. One of its defining criteria is that it is a study-of-religions approach (Alberts 2007: 353ff, see further discussions in chapters 6 and 8 of this book).

In addition to Haakedal's and Alberts' comparisons of English and Swedish RE, I consider three further pioneering works in comparative RE:

Kuyk et al. (2007)[23] is the latest of three versions of a book with Religious Education in Europe in its title which present information to educators about arguments for RE in different European countries. These books have been central in the gathering of information on RE across the various educational systems in Europe, important for gaining a basis for comparative analysis.

Osmer & Schweitzer's (2003) *Religious Education between modernization and globalization: New perspectives on the United States and Germany* must be considered a pioneering analysis in the field. Osmer & Schweitzer's study presents modernisation, globalisation and postmodernism as a key framework for focusing on different styles and methods for teaching religion in two countries. Their interest is to see how these international trends affect RE in Protestant churches in Germany and the USA.

Religion in Education: A contribution to dialogue or a factor of conflict in transforming societies of European Countries? The EC REDCo Project is a large comparative EU-funded project launched in 2006 involving eight European countries (Weisse 2007: 10).[24] This is the most ambitious pioneering project in comparative RE yet, and among other things it aims at opening up the emerging field and to encourage further research (Weisse 2007: 23).

2.4 Challenges in comparative studies in RE

Classification of RE

In comparative attempts it is common to make distinctions and try to classify different types of RE in Europe. With reference to Hull, Schreiner (2007: 9) makes the distinction between educating into, about and from religion and also between 'Religious Studies approaches', of which he considers Norwegian KRL to be an example, and 'Denominational or Confessional' approaches which RE in Germany would exemplify (Schreiner 2007: 11). However, Schreiner warns against labelling different countries' RE too quickly.

Alberts (2006) distinguishes between Integrative RE which is based in religious studies and Separative/ confessional, which is based in theology and then adds that there are other kinds of RE which are 'some kind of mixture' (Alberts 2006: 267). She considerers Norwegian RE to be a 'half way house' between the two (Alberts 2007: 326). In addition to these kinds of distinctions, Jackson (2007a: 29) points to a third possibility, of geographical categorisation of difference in types of RE in southern and northern European countries.

---

23 The book presents information about RE in different European countries. It is published by the organisation Inter-European Commission on Church and School (ICCS) and the 'Institut for Kristen oppseding' (IKO): Institute for Christian upbringing.
24 REDCo is connected to the EU program "Citizen and Governance in the knowledge based society" section for "Values and Religions in Europe" and involves ten projects from the following eight European countries: Germany, Great Britain, France, Netherlands, Norway, Estonia, Russia and Spain. http://www.redco.uni-hamburg.de/web/3480/3481/index.html

Willaime (2007) initially made the distinction between confessional religious instruction and non-confessional religious education, and adds the third alternative which is unique to France: no religious instruction in schools (Willaime 2007: 60). However, he nuances this initial classification by noting that certain processes, which are supranational, like secularisation and religious pluralisation, have led to developments in all countries regardless of RE being formally confessional or non-confessional. In the case of secularisation, this has led to seeing RE as a school rather than a church project even when a confessional frame for RE is kept. In the case of plurality, developments in all countries go towards taking account of religious plurality in whatever kind of RE is offered in school.

I agree that it is important to be nuanced in considering 'types' of RE, and it is possible to argue in line with the critique of comparative religion (see above) that each single example is a unique type. However, some type of classification is necessary in attempts at comparative analysis, but I think one should be careful about making theory out of comparative studies which is not sensitive enough to contextual difference.

Schreiner (2007) underlines the importance of considering the reasons for particular types of RE in particular countries; the relationship between state and church, for instance (p. 10). Sometimes schools are secular public places, as in France, but church schools or faith-based schools are also very common, in England and the Netherlands for instance, and are sometimes part of a state system. Schreiner (2007) enhances the significance for RE of differences in the educational systems, including the role and place of RE in that system, a point which became very significant in this present study.

Willaime (2007) considers how goals of education in general often include a religious dimension, of which the preamble to the Norwegian school law (the 'formålsparagraf') and the obligation to have an act of worship in the English school are examples (see chapter 4). Willaime (2007) notes three current main developments across Europe, one being a growing integration of religious education with overall educational goals (Willaime 2007: 62).

Schreiner (2007: 14), Haakedal (1986) and others point out that the traditions for RE, even though rooted in complex situations in each country, are now challenged by common international developments. Schreiner (2007: 11) claims there is a general tendency in the development of RE across Europe that it moves from confessional to non-confessional approaches because of the need to reflect the increasing plurality of cultures and religions.

Willaime (2007: 57) also claims that RE across Europe is converging. Even where confessional approaches are maintained, focus can no longer be exclusively on one faith tradition because it is challenged by radical changes in society due to issues related to secularisation, pluralism and globalisation (Schreiner 2007: 13). Willaime gives two types of explanations for this convergence; the first relates to sociological developments in society which challenge RE, and the other to legal arguments of non-discrimination on religious grounds, based on Human Rights principles especially.

Problems of terminology

Schreiner (2007) warns that obstacles to comparative studies may include problems of terminology, because our conceptualisation of what RE is will be shaped by the background and history of RE in our different countries (see chapter 3). Schreiner (2007) also warns that there will be problems of language and cultural barriers. In European countries we carry different cultural baggage, and 'linguistic communities correspond to cultural communities shaped by a common history' (Kuyk et al. 2007: 15). In an article, Schweitzer (2004) also warns that comparative studies can be particularly demanding because of language barriers and different use of terminology (Schweitzer 2004: 197).

Variation in meaning of 'confessional' and 'denominational' is the example Schweitzer (2006) chose to illustrate this problem. In the introduction to this book (chapter 1) I too have noted the differences in meaning of 'confessional' and 'denominational' RE in the case of England and Norway. These two concepts are often used in classifications of RE in Europe (Haakedal 1986, Schreiner 2007, Jackson 2007, Willaime 2007).

'To use the same term in different languages is either to change its meaning or to equivocate' (Murphy 2000: 183). This point is one which immediately occurs in comparative studies involving different languages, cultures and traditions. It is especially important to pay close attention to the meaning of concepts in different contexts/ languages in comparative work, or else one might overlook differences as well as similarities, and miss differences and similarities which are not immediately apparent (Schweitzer 2006).

> *'To begin with a simple fact: two languages, by their very two-ness, are different languages. To explain in English how something is said in German is to speak German in English. The words, or signifiers, may be identical but they are not spoken in the same language. Here, it is English which speaks German'* (Murphy 2000: 183).

In my work I have come to the conclusion that sometimes it is impossible to translate a Norwegian concept without adding English preconceptions; for example, the word 'inspection' is in itself easily translatable (Norwegian: inspeksjon), but when it is used in this study to refer to school inspection, misunderstandings could easily occur because the kind of inspections that are conducted in English schools are so different from the kind that occur in Norwegian schools that it would be unreasonable to use the same concept for it (see chapter 5). When this problem occurs I sometimes choose to use the Norwegian word in the text instead of an English translation and then explain its meaning in its context. This is to make the significance of the different contexts evident so that readers are not confused or misled.

Why comparative studies?

Osmer & Schweitzer (2003) discuss religious education in the context of Protestant churches in Germany and USA, which is quite distant from the kind of multifaith

RE in state schools which is my interest. But even though, from a Norwegian point of view, there are good arguments for viewing church/ faith-based RE and (multi-faith) state school RE as separate fields, internationally the two are intertwined both in school practice in most countries as well as in research (see chapter 3).

Our reasons for doing comparative work do, however, overlap since I am also interested in how the same basic international trends (modernisation, globalisation and postmodernism) affect English and Norwegian state school RE. We are also both interested in investigating how and why comparative studies are useful in RE today.

Osmer & Schweitzer (2003: 23-28) argue that the comparative perspective is necessary because different countries are affected by the same international trends, and that it is therefore necessary to study more than one country to understand the development in each of the countries separately. Although I had already initiated this comparative study when I encountered their argument, I saw this as an encouragement to pursue a comparative study, and this argument as central for doing comparative work today.

In comparative work the point of reference must go beyond the particular educational practice or theory, and be based on processes which countries share, such as pluralisation. Osmer & Schweitzer's (2003) research question was, for instance, how RE has responded to and dealt with the challenges of modernisation and globalisation in both countries. At the same time there is also the aspect of national histories to be considered.

In the different contributions to the first publication in the EC REDCo Project (Jackson et al. 2007), a variety of supranational challenges to RE are mentioned, for instance globalisation (Jackson 2007: 28) and international policy-making (Jackson 2007: 33-43), secularisation and pluralisation (for example Willaime: 100), integration (for example Knauth 2007: 251). The international nature of these challenges makes it appropriate to address them in a comparative project. I see that both Osmer & Schweitzer (2003) and also the various authors in the REDCo publication (Jackson et al. 2007) have this dynamic sense of the international and national processes that are at work. This is maintained in the three dimensional model for comparative RE which I suggest below.

2.5 Methodological considerations

In comparative studies different methodologies are used (Schweitzer 2004: 192). Comparative education today is a multidisciplinary field using theories and methods from a range of scholarly disciplines (Adams & Keeves 1994: 949). As Adams and Keeves say, 'There is a need for using a multiplicity of methodological approaches' (Adams and Keeves 1994: 956). Thus, the generic consideration of qualitative vs. quantitative methods is of concern to comparativists as it is to other researchers.

Both approaches are valid and they may be complementary, as indeed it is in the EC REDCo Project.[25] A comparative design may well use a mix of qualitative and quantitative methods, but I have chosen a qualitative approach.[26] In addition to comparing elements at the macro/ national level, I also have an empirical element where I have gathered information about the micro/ practice level in six schools, three in England and three in Norway (see chapter 5, 6 and 7).

Schweitzer (2004) warns about one-to-one empirical comparisons between one school in one country and one school in another, because variations between schools within a country are too large, and that 'it will not stand the test of educational practice' (Schweitzer 2004: 198) and will have limited validity. Rather, Schweitzer recommends more comprehensive comparisons (Schweitzer 2004: 98-199), which I attempt in chapters 3 and 4.

However, Alexander (2000) argues that it is also important to include the level of practice in addition to the systems in comparative education. This does not mean that he does not acknowledge the difficulties of undertaking such a task. Alexander (2000) criticises comparative education research for having focused more on macro/ national levels than on the practice of teaching and learning and stresses the exploratory nature of his undertaking (Alexander 2000: 5) when he set out to correct this.

I have no illusions about the intellectual risks of going where relatively few ventured: five countries rather than one or two, the classroom as well as the system, practice as well as policy. To do this kind of work makes heavy demands on an individual's capacity to garner, understand and synthesize material from very different sources, disciplines and of course cultures (Alexander 2000: 3)

This was a strongly felt risk of my own undertaking as well, and even though there are other pioneers in the field of comparative research in RE[27], there are very few models to consider, and the discussions in the field are in their infancy. Discussions in related fields must therefore be seen as very relevant.

For instance, in Ragin's (1987) account of qualitative method in comparative education he claims that the schools of thought that use quantitative methods are interested in variable oriented causal models of whole populations while the qualitative oriented researchers, on the other hand, focus on complexity. While quantitative methods start with simplification, qualitative methods 'starts by assuming maximum causal complexity', and one still makes a choice about whether to 'mount an assault on that complexity' (Ragin 1987: preface).

It is fair to say that at the outset of this qualitative comparative analysis, I did assume maximum complexity. I fully acknowledged the difficulty of the task, but I

---

25 http://www.redco.uni-hamburg.de/web/3480/3481/index.html (Accessed 24.07.2009).
26 This limitation is mainly due to the need to limit the project to what one person can do in the amount of time available for a PhD, but with regards to chapters 5-7, where I make use of field research, I have considered also some data from both the qualitative and quantitative parts of the REDCo study.
27 Several of whom have been conducting their researches simultaneously to my own work, like Alberts (2007) and the EC REDCo Project.

still make the choice to 'mount an assault on that complexity' (see also Bråten 2009).

2.6 Is this a new methodology?

It follows from the discussion above that I fully recognise that in comparative studies different methods should be used. I need, therefore, to address the question of whether what I suggest in this chapter and in this book is a new methodology for comparative studies in RE. No new methods are developed specifically for comparative studies, but a combination of known methods is used in a specific design. This design takes account of a number of concerns regarding comparative studies which are discussed in this chapter.

In formulating this design, I have looked both at related fields and at pioneering work in the field of RE. One could call it a design, an approach or a template, but I will argue that, in a certain sense, this is also a new methodology being suggested for the field of comparative RE. Certain elements could be altered within it, as long as the core of it is maintained. This core is the combination of three dimensions and four levels, which will be further elaborated below. This is my approach to comparative studies in RE which I will apply and discuss further in the following chapters of this book.

2.7 National imaginaries and supranational processes

Schiffauer et al. (2004)[28] is a large published comparative study with an educational perspective, set in a social science framework focusing on integration of immigrants in schools. Even though it is not explicitly about RE, its research interests makes it is very relevant to RE. It is an empirical comparative project involving one school in each of the four countries, so it could be argued that this study has fallen into the trap that Schweitzer (2004) warns about, in attempting to compare one school from each country.

However, the authors attempt to make up for this through being clear that they are aware of this as a limitation of the study, but also through constructing a very sophisticated conceptual and theoretical framework and analytical tool. Their core concepts are: civil culture, national imaginary and civil enculturation (Schiffauer et al. 2004: 1-18). On the one hand, I will be very aware of the dangers of generalising from a limited sample in my fieldwork, and thus take Schweitzer's (2004) warnings very seriously, but I will also make use of the terminology in Schiffauer et al. (2004) as I see these terms as very useful analytic tools in comparative studies (see chapter 5).

The comparative aspect of Schiffauer et al. (2004) is based on the question of how two conflicting international trends in European history influence education in

---

28 The book is entitled Civil Enculturation: Nation State, School and ethnic difference in the Netherlands, Britain, Germany and France.

these different countries. The first is the development towards Nation States from the 1870s. The idea of the Nation State is seen as dependent upon the creation of a national imaginary to which citizens tie their identities (Schiffauer et al. 2004: 8) – for instance, a certain view of history, but one that must not be mistaken for what really happened.[29] The second is the growing multiculturalism in Europe as a result of immigration starting in the 1950s/ 60s.

I see Schiffauer et al.'s concept of national imaginary as useful in grasping the historical and sociological depth of national traditions. A central feature of this national imaginary would have to be the relationship between state and religion, which in turn is decisive for what kind of RE has developed in a specific country. The growing multiculturalism as a supranational trend across European country is the one factor which challenges RE in European countries the most (Haakedal 1986, Schreiner 2007, Jackson et al. 2007, Weisse 2007, Willaime 2007), so this makes Schiffauer et al.'s analysis very relevant to comparative studies in RE.

Schiffauer et al. (2004) show how integration of immigrants in the different countries in their sample – Germany, France, the Netherlands and the United Kingdom – take on different styles reflecting the national imaginary. I would be interested to ask how national imaginary shapes what kind of RE is possible in the different countries when the challenge to each is the same. But, also, vice versa: how are these international trends and the whole context of globalisation (see below) challenging the national imaginaries and the traditions for RE which reflects those imaginaries? (See chapter 8.)

The central aim of Schiffauer et al. (2004) is to offer insights into 'the changing dynamics of nation-state civil cultures in multicultural societies' (back cover). A key research question is 'How do Nation State-schools manage to maintain and update their old links with the national imaginary despite there being so many school pupils who are not nationals or else not ethnically recognizable as such?' (Schiffauer et al. 2004: 10). I think this is very closely related to the central problem of how RE can contribute to social cohesion and citizenship education (for example Jackson (Ed.) 2003, 2007a), or, in the case of Norway, to generic formation ('building') (see chapters 3 and 4).

In the EC REDCo Project, Weisse points out that in a plural society religion has an ambivalent potential for contributing to dialogue and social cohesion on the one side and conflict and social tension on the other (Weisse 2007: 9). Despite anticipation that religion would disappear from the public sphere, the opposite has happened, and religion is today an important factor in the public sphere (see below). Since the events in the USA on September 11th 2001, the dangers arising from religious isolation and confrontation have become clear to a wider public (Jackson 2007).

Since this danger is a common European challenge, it transcends the national borders and needs to be addressed in a comparative study. The main aims of the REDCo project were to 'establish and compare the potentials and limitations of

---

29 Schiffauer et al (2004) refer to Andersons (1991) Imagined communities, which is also a main reference for Taylor (2004) Modern Social Imaginaries, which he according to the introduction to this book had to stop and write up as a separate book before he could finish his work on A Secular Age (Taylor 2007).

religion in the educational fields of selected European countries and regions' (Weisse 2007: 10) and 'to look at the challenges facing religious education in the context of current change in European societies and its importance for dialogue and mutual understanding without disregarding potential problems' (Weisse 2007: 12) and making religion in education a factor promoting dialogue in the context of European development.

Both in design and research interests, this project has strong similarities to my own, though the difference in size and ambition is huge. Methods chosen for the EC REDCo project is text analysis with reference to hermeneutic methods combined with some empirical methods,[30] which is basically what I have done. The basic questions evolve around the historical background in each country, legal institutions and frameworks as well as teachers' and pupils' perspectives on religion and plurality (Knauth et al. 2008, Valk et al. 2009, van der Want et al. 2009). These all are elements included in what I have studied and compared in the case of Norway and England. The main methodological stimulus is R. Jackson's interpretive approach (Jackson 1997) to the study of religious diversity (Weisse 2007: 17), and this is a main inspiration for me too. This huge comparative project launched four years after I started and financed by the EU (Weisse 2007:10) shows the wider relevance of what I have been interested in doing in my own study.

2.8 Three dimensions in comparative studies

In a publication about 'Supranational regimes and national educational policy' (Kallo & Rinne 2006), Dale (2006: 27ff) discusses 'policy relationships between supranational and national scales', and he points to a 'widespread recognition that the relationships in the area of educational policy between supranational and national organizations have become more and more common, extensive and more complex' as a result of globalisation and the development of a 'knowledge economy' (Dale 2006: 27). This is especially true within the EU. To focus on what Dale considers as being the fundamental template of education governance, he suggests a 4x4 matrix (funding, provision, ownership, and regulation vs. the state, the market, the community and the household (Dale 2006: 32-33)). However, and this is the central point here, to take account of globalisation he adds a third 'scale', including supranational, national and subnational factors.

After the analysis of comparative studies in related fields and pioneering work in the field of comparative RE above, it became increasingly clear to me that comparison in RE should include awareness of these three dimensions:

1. Supranational processes
2. National processes
3. Subnational processes

---

30 Though they use a wider range of empirical methods, both qualitative and quantitative, including participant observation, semi-structured interviews, questionnaires, videotaping, and triangulation.

The notion that comparison in religious education is about the study of the impact of supranational processes on national processes is an important reason for this conclusion. The central point is that what are basically considered to be the same processes are met differently in different cultural contexts (Karlsen 2006, Haakedal 1986, Schweitzer 2004, 2006, Jackson et al. 2007). This is the dynamics of supranational processes meeting national and subnational contexts, and relates to globalisation as a problem area. According to Leganger-Krogstad (2007: 99), 'global understanding is considered to be a main objective in contextual approaches'. The global is also seen as part of the school context, in addition to factors such as local geo-culture and the national context (see chapter 7). All dimensions would include both historic and current processes.

In these dimensions I distinguish between formal and informal processes.[31] By formal processes I mean processes of formal educational policymaking which can be found locally, nationally as well as on the supranational scene. Formal processes are going on in various international organisations such as the World Trade Organization (WTO), the United Nations (UN), the European Union (EU), the Council of Europe, and the Organisation for Security and Co-operation in Europe (OSCE) (Karlsen 2006, Jackson 2007). Informal processes include social and/ or political developments which go on both in and through the formal processes but also outside them and, in part, independently of them. Included here, for instance, are the processes of secularisation, pluralisation and globalisation (for example Osmer & Schweitzer 2003, Jackson et al. 2007).

Regarding the *formal supranational processes* one should be aware of both *general educational policy* and *specific RE policy*. Dale's model only takes account of general educational policy. The policy specifically regarding RE is, of course, the most relevant for comparative studies in religious education, but there may be elements in general educational policies which are also important to consider (Karlsen 2006). Movements in general educational policy internationally may influence the whole curriculum nationally, and thus the curriculum or system of RE in the country. For example, changes in curriculum policy in Norway adapting the concept of 'basic skills' also affect Norwegian RE (UD 2005) (see chapter 4).

Regarding specific RE policy some inter-governmental organisations, which have developed stances on general educational policy, have for many years avoided the sensitive field of religious education and left this to the particular national educational systems. In the case of religion, partly as a reaction to the events of 9/11 and their consequences, this has been changing (Jackson 2007). International politics regarding RE is now emerging: in the EU, The Council of Europe (Jackson 2007) and OSCE (2007) with The Toledo Guiding Principles, for instance.

In the national dimension, *formal* and *informal* processes would refer to formal national educational policy on the one hand and informal processes in and about the national education system on the other. Regarding *formal* national educational policy, one should also here distinguish between *general* educational policy and *specif-*

---

31 Habermas' (2006) distinguish between the formal and informal public political sphere and school is seen as part of informal public sphere: making it acceptable to discuss religion(s) here (see chapter 4).

45

ic RE policy within the national educational system. Both are relevant even though the specific issues of RE policy are most relevant.

The third dimension which refers to subnational processes would be relevant in a comparison between national regions (Dale 2006: 33). One could argue that the dimension of the subnational processes would perhaps be especially important for decentralised education systems, like the German system or the one in the USA. However, it will also be important to catch subnational variations in strongly centralised educational systems, like the Norwegian or French system. This third dimension would be particularly relevant when empirical studies are included in comparative work because this will inevitably bring subnational factors into the analysis (see chapter 5-7).

Supranational processes influence *national processes*, and this is a central argument for the relevance of comparative studies: to study how supranational processes affect national systems. I would, however, also argue that *national processes* influence *supranational processes*: since processes in national policy are likely to be the origin of ideas exported to an international arena.

For example, the concept of 'basic skills' was introduced in the new National Curriculum in England in connection to the 1988 Education Act, and may have been exported from this and other national contexts to the international arena: in OECDs definition of key competences (DeSeCo)[32], for instance. There is also the possibility of one particular country having a specific influence on another, of course. This process is sometimes referred to as 'policy borrowing' (see Spreen 2001, Phillips 2005, Phillips and Ochs 2004, Steiner-Khamsi 2004). In connection to the 1988 Education Reform in England and Wales, for example, policies were borrowed from other countries such as the concept of 'basic skills' being borrowed from educational politics of the USA in the 1980s.

There is a certain dynamic in the relationship between the dimensions. For instance, Karlsen (2006) shows that recent developments in Norway are influenced by supranational processes. At the same time, these influences are also shaped nationally with reference to Norwegian history and school traditions. Both Karlsen (2006) and Dale (2006) discuss how, when national educational politics are influenced by supranational regimes, this might sometimes be seen as an imposition and raise resistance nationally. This resistance towards international influences may have many reasons; however, one possibility is that they originated in a nation or in nations with quite different histories and school traditions, and with different *national imaginaries*.

This underlines the importance of having a cultural contextual perspective in comparative RE. However, this must not lead to deterministic attitudes that change is not possible or desirable. Alberts (2007) is clearly looking for arguments for changing the general approach to RE in public schools in Germany. Indeed, changes are frequent, and they are often linked to international developments, even if international imposition is also resisted at a national level (Karlsen 2006). An important spur to do more comparative studies is that policy borrowing and imple-

---

32 http://www.oecd.org/dataoecd/47/61/35070367.pdf (downloaded 18.03.2012).

mentation of international policies could be carried out but based on a better awareness of the significance of contextual national factors.

2.9 The supranational dimension

The national dimension is the main focus in this work, but here I will take the opportunity to expand a little on the supranational dimension as outlined above. In relation to *informal* supranational processes, I mentioned especially secularisation, pluralisation and globalisation. These are processes that run through but are also, in part, independent of *formal* political processes. Globalisation is perhaps especially in a limbo between informal and formal processes.

Informal: Habermas (2005, 2006) talks about religion in the public sphere, with reference to Berger (1999) (Habermas 2005: 1, 2006: 1), where Berger radically shifts from his earlier widely acknowledged theories of secularisation and now talks about a desecularisation (resacralisation) of the world. In other words, the world is not seen as secularised in the sense that religion is a declining phenomenon in it. Rather, the process of secularisation is seen as referring to changes in the role of religion in society.

The word 'secularisation' was first used to describe the transfer of property from churches to secular authorities (Wilson 1987: 159): in the twentieth century 'Sociologists have used this word to indicate a variety of processes in which control of social space, time, facilities, resources, and personnel was lost by religious authorities' (Wilson 1987: 159). Wilson refers to secularisation as an international phenomenon, a historical process which was considered a global phenomenon. However, it has lately been argued, for example by Berger (1999), that secularisation in this sense has in fact been a marginal historical phenomenon limited to aspects of 'the western world' (Habermas 2005: 4).

Based on this, I do not see secularisation as a single global process but, in western modernity, as the process of the changing role of religion in society. In view of Taylor's (2007) point that in today's world many modernities coexist (see chapter 7), this would mean, for example, that some people could be seen as living in a secular modern world, while others could be seen as living in a non-secularised modernity. It is possible to be religious and modern at the same time.

Habermas' (2006) concern is the degree to which there can be communication between the secular and the religious, and the reason for this concern is that he sees religion as very much present in today's societies, something that the events on September 11th 2001 made overtly apparent. Habermas suggests, for example, that this is possible in schools, as he sees schools as an informal public sphere (see chapter 4).

A point here is also that I see the process of secularisation – understood as the process of the changing role of religion in (modern western) societies – as intertwined with developments towards the individual's right to religious freedom. Though there is difference between how exactly the right to religious freedom developed in England and Norway (see chapter 3), this right has now materialised itself into informal as well as formal supranational processes: most importantly in the international declaration of Human Rights, which makes religious freedom a 'globalised' right, or value.

The individual right to religious freedom made possible the radical religious pluralisation that took place in western European countries from the 1950s - 60s on. Before this there had been a plurality of Christian belief in the western world, often leading to conflicts, but after the 1950s there has been a radical increase in the number of non-Christian religions. Contrary to the traditional (pre-Berger 1999) view that secularisation was a process that was threatening to religion, it may actually now be argued that secularisation leading to pluralisation is a process that has strengthened rather than weakened the role of religion in society. This presupposes that 'religion' also includes individual spirituality of the kind often found in new age/ alternative spirituality networks, and the more traditional religions that are not new as such, but has a new presence in the western world as a result of globalisation (including migration).

In her account of recent developments in sociology of religion, Davie (2007) distinguishes between European secularisation theories which have seen secularisation as a threat to traditional religion, and therefore as a 'loss', and American rational choice theory which, inspired by economic thinking, sees the plurality that is a consequence of secularisation as strengthening religion because of the competitive situation in the plural context (Davie 2007: 67 ff).

In western (post)modernity, a radical individualisation of personal spirituality is seen as characteristic of the way people relate to religion. An early description of this kind of spirituality is offered by Bellah (1985) who studied hippies in California: 'Sheilaism' is described as Sheila's personal 'pick and choose' spirituality/ religiosity (see also chapter 7). Lately, however, it has been argued, by Heelas & Woodhead (2005) for instance, that a modern western process of sacralisation, as opposed to the idea that the modern western world is desacralised, is a process which is characterised by this kind of individual spirituality. This view suggests that this individualistic spiritual approach is increasingly characteristic of the way modern western people relate to religion.

It is interesting to see this in relation to Taylor's (2007) point that many modernities coexist in today's world, and in chapter 7 this view becomes important in my analysis of the way individual children describe themselves as religious or not; they exist in different modernities.

Skeie (1995) distinguishes between *traditional* plurality and *modern* plurality. *Traditional plurality* refers to new groups in the social fabric that have come with recent immigration from non-western countries and cultures. Skeie argues that the coexistence of distinct cultural groups in a society is not confined to our time and our society: 'If we want to grasp the specific modern and western situation, this concept of plurality is not enough' (Skeie 1995: 86). The *modern plurality* refers to an individual level; the way that each of us relates to the plurality of ideas that is available in the post modern/ late modern globalised world.

This is interesting in relation to the way that Heelas & Woodhead (2005) propose that individual spirituality is what is most characteristic of the way people in (post)modern/ late modern western world relate to religion today. Modern plurality has to do with individualisation, privatisation of religion and debates about modernity and late post/ late modernity (Jackson 2004a: 9). Focusing on individual differences also brings forward the inner diversity and contestability in religions/ religious traditions, which is central in the research undertaken at the University of Warwick and their development of pedagogy of religion (Jackson 1997, 2004a). Still, however, the concepts of the religions as wider traditions are regarded as important, a view that I share as this is something that, for instance, children relate to in their relationship to religion.

I see the processes of secularisation and pluralisation, both traditional and modern, as intertwined and, together with the globalisation process, decisive for the place of religion in society today.

Globalisation is in a kind of limbo between *informal* and *formal* supranational processes. As informal it is a description of a central characteristic of late modernity with its increased travelling activities, free trade and exchange of capital, developments of global mass media and communicative computer technology leading to increased contacts and cooperation globally (Karlsen 2006: 47). These processes are subject to attempts to regulate them by various international organisations such as the EU or OECD. Their policies are formal supranational processes. The increasing influence of supranational organisations on national policy is one effect of globalisation (Dale 2006: 27).

It is generally acknowledged that at the heart of globalisation is the liberal global market economy (Karlsen 2006: 47). The logic of global capitalism challenges the independent government of nation states, for better or for worse. Habermas (2000), for instance, claims that the politics of today are drained of vision because politics are reduced to adjusting to the international global economy.

Globalisation is conceptualised in different ways. The word globalisation is commonly used about a variety of cultural and economic processes. One definition may be that 'Globalisation is the process through which local happenings are influenced by distant events which, in turn, are shaped by local events' (Jackson 2004a: 10). While some say that globalisation is an inevitable process and focuses the possibilities of development and international problem-solving (for example Giddens 1990, 1999), others are concerned that the spreading of western culture that is happening through the globalisation process is a kind of cultural imperialism. In reference to the global economy, therefore, all have to play by the rules of the western style / of ideals for a global economy, or else suffer poverty. In reference to education, it means that the increasingly standardised western education system is spread, including certain ideas about what count as valid knowledge (Karlsen 2006, Alexander 2000: 564).

Delors (1996: 41) points out that economic globalisation also leads to a globalisation of human activities. If economic rationality is used in the field of education, education becomes important because it may give advantages in the global economic competition. In fact, there is a knowledge economy developing and, for instance, a European educational sector is developed and runs in parallel with national educational sectors (Dale 2006: 46, Karlsen 2006).

Hakovirta (2006) makes the distinction between globalisation and problem-based globalism. He loosely defines *governance* as something between the management of international problems and a vision of global government. He sees the

UN as the seed of such a world government (Hakovirta 2006: 368). Global problems are problems which are dominated by global aspects; that are spread from one country or are common internationally shared problems; that cause world scale threats and which need a worldwide sense of responsibility to solve.

Examples would be global climate change or global poverty (Hakovirta 2006: 362- 363). These problems seem to cluster with each other and almost always have a social character. He raises the question of what kind of educational politics best contributes to solving global problems (Hakovirta 2006, 354). A central global problem in relation to RE is exactly that which Weisse (2007: 9) describes as religion's ambivalent potential for dialogue and social cohesion as well as social conflict.

The world is in a process of globalisation which manifests itself in many ways, including ways having to do with religion and education. Religion's potential for conflict is hardly news, but it has become obvious to a wider public after the events of September 11th 2001 in the USA: this has been described by some as globalisation fighting back. This has raised the place of RE on the agenda of educational politics both locally and internationally.

In European countries the systems for RE are diverse and reflect each nation state's history, religious traditions and culture. Contextual factors are historic tradition: history of Church/ State relations, the nature and degree of 'multiculturalism' in society, geographical position (north, south, east, west), socio-political/ economic systems, international/ global influences, general educational values and aims (Jackson 2009). More often than not, a kind of confessional RE is found in (state) schools in Europe still today (Willaime 2007). Basically, it is in Scandinavia as well as in England and Wales that a non-confessional multifaith type of RE is found.

The motivation for having a form of multifaith RE has to do with wishing to promote tolerance and respect, knowledge, social cohesion and dialogue in a plural society. These ideas are spreading both in non-confessional and confessional systems of RE across Europe. The motivation for having this kind of RE is overlapping with motivations for promoting Intercultural Education, Citizenship Education, Peace Education and Education in Human Rights. This is currently triggering political processes on a European as well as on a wider international level. At the same time, local traditions are strong, and religious bodies' motivation for preserving and strengthening traditional religious nurture is triggered by that same pluralistic challenge (see chapter 3).

Formal: In relation to formal political processes internationally, I will mention three examples of this development: 1. developments within *the Council of Europe*, 2. the *Toledo Guiding Principles on teaching about religions and beliefs in public schools* by the OSCE (2007), and 3. the funding of an EU research project on religious education in Europe: *Religion in Education: A contribution to Dialogue or a factor of Conflict in transforming societies of European Countries* (REDCo).

1. The Council of Europe has a project in *Education for Democratic Citizenship and Human Rights (EDC/HRE)*[33]. It has led to citizenship education in various

---

33 http://www.coe.int/t/dg4/education/edc/default_EN.asp? (08.08.07).

forms being established all over Europe (Jackson 2003, Jackson 2007: 30). It includes elements of human rights education, civic education, peace education, global education and intercultural education and issues of religious diversity and discrimination. *The New Challenge of Intercultural Education: Religious Diversity and Dialogue in Europe* is another project aiming more precisely at raising awareness about the implications of the religious dimension of intercultural education among decision-makers, educators and teachers. Intercultural and interfaith dialogue is now to be made one of the major axes of the Council of Europe development.

A key condition for having a public policy about religious education is that, in this context, religion is seen as a cultural fact. This was the lowest common denominator with which all states in the Council of Europe could work in an educational context (Jackson 2007: 27). There are widely different views about the place of religion in education in the member countries, but all could agree that religion is 'a cultural fact' and that 'knowledge and understanding of religion at this level is highly relevant to good community and personal relations and is therefore a legitimate concern for public policy' (Jackson 2007: 37). This is neither an epistemological stance nor a secular assumption, but a strategy for dealing with religion and religious education publicly at a political level in Europe (Jackson 2007: 44).

These reasons given by the Council of Europe for having RE in state schools are in many ways a contrast to traditional reasons for RE which has been a wish to nurture children into a particular faith. 'Changing Aims in Religious Education' was the title of a book published in Great Britain in 1966 (Cox 1966). It was about how RE should be adjusted to meet the reality of a secular society, and this is also a theme in Haakedal (1983) (see above).

Today, the aims of RE are changing mainly for reasons having to do with societies' change towards religious and cultural plurality (Willaime 2007). This calls for including teaching about faiths other than Christianity and for methods encouraging tolerance and respect in order to lower the level of religious conflict in plural societies. It also reflects a shift in focus, from the need of religions to teach and preach to the needs of children to learn.

Now, the focus is more on what children need to learn than what the religions would like to teach them. At the same time, the need for religious groups to nurture children into their own particular faith is strengthened rather than weakened by that same plurality, so what kind of RE is best suited for the situation is disputed in most countries today. The need for cultural cohesion has been a part of the motivation for having RE traditionally, and is also today part of the argument for having RE. However, since society is now plural, RE also needs to be plural in its approach (for example Skeie 1998, Jackson 2004: 161ff).

2. The *Toledo Guiding Principles on teaching about religions and beliefs in public schools* by the OSCE (2007) are meant to be a tool for the 56 OSCE participant states in implementing existing principles and commitments 'on freedom of religion or belief, tolerance and education' (…) and 'to ensure that teaching about religion is carried out in a fair and balanced manner' (OSCE 2007: 10).

The guidelines are restricted to teaching *about* religion as the lowest common denominator for RE in the public sphere in this international European context. At the same time, it gives Human Rights arguments for the availability of religious nurture as well (OSCE 2007: 12). The basic human right of respecting freedom of religion or belief is central to the document (OSCE 2007: 13, 16). The production of this document by a panel of experts on Freedom of Religion and Belief together with scholars and experts in other relevant fields is seen in the context of the OSCE's conflict- preventing role in response to the growing presence of religion in the public sphere (OSCE 2007: 11).

It is a basic assumption that 'it is important for young people growing up today to acquire a better understanding of the role that religion play in today's pluralistic world' (OSCE 2007: 9). Sixteen key guiding principles are formulated, and number one and two include respect for human rights and commitment to religious freedom.

Arriving at international standards such as these would have to lead to the identification of expectations towards RE which would be acceptable across borders, and this requires a comparative perspective. This is, for example, reflected in the emphasis on 'religious facts': this was something that all could support despite the different traditions for RE in different countries.

3. *Religion in Education. A contribution to Dialogue or a factor of Conflict in transforming societies of European Countries:* 'The EC REDCo Project' is described above. In this context I only want to enhance the point that, while it has previously proven difficult to get funding for research on religious education from the EU (Jackson 2004b: 26), the funding given by the EU to this historically large project on comparative RE (or RE in general) is also a token of the new focus on policy regarding religious education.

2.10 A template for comparative studies in RE

This present study of two countries' RE in state schools aims to illuminate and exemplify the significance of contextual perspectives in comparative studies. Therefore, the national dimension (see above) is emphasised in the methodology and in the chapters 3-7. It is my view that comparison needs to move underneath superficial common features and look at national cultural and historical factors. It is important not to underestimate the significance of both the national or the subnational contexts. At the same time, the supranational dimension remains an important factor in the analysis. When two countries are being compared with regard to RE, a supranational dimension is implied.

In the field of curriculum theory I found a tool for capturing national processes, including the reality of what goes on in schools (practice). Widely differing phenomena are viewed as 'curriculum', and it is therefore necessary to have different definitions.[34] In a Norwegian context, the most immediate association is the National Curriculum, but this will not be the case in countries which do not have

---

34 Goodlad & Su (1992) suggest these definitions: 1. A design or plan of institutionalised education, 2. The actual learning opportunities provided at a given time or place, 3. An instrument for bringing about behaviour changes in learners as a result of their activities in an educational institution, 4. All the educational experiences that learners have under the guidance of the school.

school systems as centralised as this, like, for instance, Germany or the USA or England prior to the reforms of 1988. In England, RE remained in a special decentralised arrangement outside the National Curriculum but is still a part of the basic curriculum (Education Act 1988, section 2.1).

If we take a broader view and include other countries, we will find varying history and practices, and different ideas of what the term curriculum implies, even if there are varying ideas of curricula nationally as well. A quotation which sums this up is: 'The curriculum is in the eye of the beholder. And so there are many curricula perceived simultaneously (...)' (Goodlad 1979: 30).

In Goodlad's writings (for example *et al.*1966, 1979, 1986) and in the literature, different versions of levels of curriculum can be found,[35] but the guiding idea seems to be to classify curriculum according to its remoteness from the learner. I have chosen to use Goodlad & Su (1992) as I see this as an especially useful and meaningful version of his theories in relation to the comparative work of this thesis, because both English, Norwegian and other ideas of curricula for RE fit into it. Although Goodlad's work is specifically about the curriculum, I extend his notion of 'levels' to include different historical experiences, specifically the different histories of Church and state in Norway and England, which make an impact on current education in general in both countries, and on RE in particular. These levels are as follows:

A. The *societal level* is the level most remote from the receivers. This includes the socio-political processes involved in determining what subjects and topics should be studied in schools, and what materials should be used. Actors on this level are politicians, special interest groups, different kinds of administrators and professional specialists, and the general public. In both England and Norway, the *societal level* would be the political, public as well as professional debates about the curricula/ syllabuses for RE in schools. One could see this as the process prior to a new curriculum or syllabus being given a written form. One could, however, just as well see it as an on-going process, in England in relation to local agreed syllabuses which are being renewed every fifth year, and in Norway in relation to the frequent revisions of the National Curriculum for RE. The theme *academic debates* (chapter 3) relates to this level.

B. The *institutional level* is the curriculum derived from the societal level but specified by the state or province and modified by the school board. Central questions on this level are how much of it should be commonly required for all and to what degree students' interests should be considered, whether subjects should be

---

35 In Germeten (1999), a report which is a part of the evaluation of the Norwegian reform in 1997, she builds her theory on Goodlad (1986). Goodlad (1986) is an English article by Goodlad in Gundem, B. (Ed.) Om læreplanpraksis og læreplanteori. Germeten talks of Goodlad dividing the field of curriculum theory into three areas: 1. The substantial area: the content, 2. The social-political area: the battle of what the curriculum should contain of, and 3. The technical-professional area: how the curriculum is put into practice by professionals on different levels. These three areas, she says, Goodlad links to six different levels of curriculum: 1. The curriculum of ideas, 2. the formal curriculum (vedtatte), 3. the curriculum as perceived on authoritative levels, 4. the curriculum as perceived on a technical-professional level, 5. The operationalised (iverksatte) curriculum: by teachers and professionals and 6. The experienced curriculum (students' perception, their developed skills and knowledge. For further discussions of Goodlad, see Afdal (2006: 50–85).

taught as separate disciplines and other questions of relevance for curriculum organisation.

The *institutional level* would in England be the law, the Model Syllabuses (SCAA 1994) and the Non-Statutory National Framework for RE (QCA 2004) which replaced the Model Syllabuses, the local agreed syllabuses and the public examination syllabuses for RE (GCSE syllabuses). In Norway this would first and foremost be the law and the National Curriculum, but local work in schools to adjust the National Curriculum to local circumstances could also be seen as an aspect of the institutional level. In England, the local production of schemes of work could also be seen as related to the institutional level, as an element in between the institutional and the instructional level. In Norway, the parallel to this would have to be the textbooks (see chapter 6). The theme *curriculum policy* (chapter 4) is related to this level.

C. The *instructional level* is how teachers plan and deliver the curriculum to pupils, and this is in one way the same in England and Norway, but in another sense different because it relies heavily on regulations and expectations which come from the more remote levels. It is still on this level that the final decision is made for what is delivered in classrooms. Circumstances such as available resources and teaching skills would be decisive factors along with the teacher's education and what priority RE has in the general school agenda. The theme *curriculum practice: Teacher's perspective* (chapter 6) is related to this level.

D. The *experiential level* is the curriculum that is internalised and made personal: its effects on the individual learner. According to Goodlad, this is the most important of all the curricula, and 'the final test of all curriculum organization' (Goodlad & Su 1992: 239). Because of this, this model should not be seen as a top-down perspective, as the interest of the learner is at the core of this way of thinking.

In both England and Norway, the *experiential level* is the effects of RE teaching on the individual learner. How are aims from the institutional level reflected in pupils' accounts of what they have learned or what the purpose of multifaith RE is? How are they affected by debates on the societal level, or the views of their teachers? The theme *experienced practice: Pupil's perspective* (chapter 7) is related to this level.

2.11 Summary and Conclusion

In what I have explored of relevant literature, I have found some basic principles for comparative work in RE and I have tried to put the essence of these into this suggested template for comparative studies in RE. The main aim would be ensuring a synthesis of the idea of the three dimensions (supranational, national and subnational processes) and a version of Goodlad's ideas of levels of curriculum. This combination provides a framework for capturing different levels in each national situation within the wider international context (see model chapter 8).

My taxonomy for selecting themes is based on a combination of Goodlad & Su's (1992) different 'levels' of curriculum and the view that supranational factors have an impact on national developments (Haakedal 1983, Osmer & Schweitzer

2003, Dale 2006, Karlsen 2006). I adapt both sets of insights to my own purposes. The book is structured through a set of selected themes, which are covered in the following chapters. These are: *academic debate (chapter 3), legal and policy developments (chapter 4), and curriculum practice: teacher's perspective (chapter 6) and pupil's perspective (chapter 7).*

I will apply this methodology through textual and empirical examples. The societal and institutional levels (chapters 3 and 4) are explored through theory and documentary studies; while empirical studies are part of the material for the chapters where the instructional and experiential levels are discussed (chapter 5, 6, 7). The themes move from the general to the particular and from historical and theoretical issues to political and practical issues in religious education.

Instead of trying to compare whole systems, I select specific themes for comparison. Generic issues emerging from these different 'levels' of comparison provide some key points of similarity and difference which are seen in an international context (see chapter 8). The fact that this is an explicit comparison involving two countries inevitably makes it supranational. This necessitates supranational perspectives in explanations especially for similarities but also for differences though differences are often linked to the national dimension. I hope that this attempt to work through this new suggested methodology for comparative studies will assist others who wish to work in the field of comparative religious education.

In conclusion, I must add that there is of course much literature that opened up on various relevant topics that I have not had the opportunity to pursue fully. There is no doubt that further valuable insights for comparative work in RE could be found in exploring comparative studies in related fields more, and possibly especially in exploring literature on policy-borrowing and the effect of supranational regimes on national educational policy in general. However, the matrix outlined above remains consistent with literature I have read from comparative education, religious education, comparative religion and other sources.

In chapter 3 I will begin to explore the levels of curriculum, starting with the societal level. I will also carry out a comparative analysis of some themes within English and Norwegian academic debates.

3. Societal Level: Themes within Academic Debates about Religious Education in England and Norway

3.1 Introduction

This chapter explores the theme *academic debates* in religious education in England and Norway in order to investigate the societal level of curriculum (Goodlad & Su 1992). The main focus will be on the national dimension but the supranational dimension will also be considered. The subnational dimension is here only represented where research which explores local contexts are referenced. National characteristics forming part of a *national style* (Schiffauer *et al.* 2004, see chapter 2) are seen as factors explaining differences, while supranational processes are seen as a main source of explaining parallels and convergences.

Research and academic debates regarding RE has had school practice[36] in RE as a main concern, but academic debates have also dealt with matters which primarily relate to the societal level of curriculum. Since the beginning of school legislation, in England 1870 and Norway 1739, Christian Instruction has been reduced from being the most central aim of schooling to now being one of several equally important subjects taught (Copley 1997, Haraldsø 1989). This has not happened without a great deal of controversy and debate, and today the change towards cultural and religious plurality in society is a main issue in the societal debates about religion and school. Using the concepts developed in this thesis, these debates are seen as informal international processes (see chapter 2) that are connected to the question of how and why religion should be taught in school. This is of concern for educators and scholars in the field of RE, but also for other actors.

On the societal level of curriculum (Goodlad & Su 1992), stakeholders include pupils, parents and parents' representatives, school leaders, teachers and teacher organisations, politicians and political parties, and not least the representatives of different religious and non-religious interest groups. The interrelations between these are complex and difficult to grasp, not to mention compare between countries, and in this chapter I will restrict the comparative perspective on the societal level of curriculum to aspects of the academic debate.

My key research question is:

What are main similarities and differences in the academic debates regarding RE in England and Norway, and how do we account for these?

In order to address this question I have chosen to focus on two specific topics for comparison:

1) *the role of academic disciplines in the development of multifaith approaches to religious education in England and Norway;*
2) *analysis of two 'power texts' that are characteristic examples of academic debate in England and Norway.*

---

36 In the structure of this thesis practice is represented by the instructional (chapter 6) and experiential levels (chapter 7) of curriculum (Goodlad & Su 1992, see chapter 2).

Towards the end of this chapter I will also discuss briefly the supranational dimension in academic debates on RE in England and Norway today by addressing some issues related to internationalisation of research.

3.2 The contribution of 'secular' religious studies to the development of multifaith approaches to RE in England and Norway

In order to address the role of academic disciplines in England and Norway I will look at how the traditions of RE research have developed. It is already clear that, in England, the development of a multifaith world religions approach was initiated by RE professionals in the 1960s (Jackson & O'Grady 2007: 193; Copley 1997; Hayward 2009), while in Norway a similar multifaith approach was initiated politically in 1997 and was then followed by research (Skeie 2004: 319).

This section will address some reasons for this difference and particularly explore one specific factor; namely, the different roles of 'secular'[37] religious studies vis a vis theology as academic disciplines in the two countries against a backdrop of other differences; in the national dimension, in school ideologies/ politics as well as differences in the research traditions.

In both England and Norway changes in RE responding to secularisation in each society preceded later changes which more explicitly addressed the new plurality. The teaching of religion in state schools – in effect Christianity – was in process of change both in England and in Norway towards a less confessional/ denominational approach (England: less confessional, Norway: less denominational)[38]. Then the plurality resulting from immigration since the 1950s and 1960s presented its challenge to RE.

The development towards a more child-focused, pedagogically-based, *Christian* RE, where Loukes (1961)[39] and Winsnes (1988)[40] respectively were key fig-

---

37 The use of the term 'secular' raises some critical questions. One may remark that the term 'secular' is connected to specific historical conditions emerging from a development in some Christian cultures and that 'secular' religious studies grew out of a certain kind of liberal theology. However, in this chapter the term 'secular' religious studies are used with reference to the academic study of religion as opposed to religious thinking about religion (Jensen & Rothstein 2000: 8, Smart 1968).

38 In England, it was non-denominational since 1870 but in law it had a confessional element until 1988, whilst in Norway it was denominational to the church of Norway until 1997, but had been in principle non-confessional since 1969, see chapter 1 for how these concepts are understood differently.

39 Loukes pioneered empirical research in the field of RE, and following him and others a research tradition emerged (Francis 2004: 279). Loukes' research revealed that Religious Instruction in schools was unpopular among teenagers as well as ineffective. Loukes (1961) suggested a more pedagogically-based teaching of religion, i.e. Christianity in schools in England. Two Swedish researchers who follow in his tradition are Erikson 1999 and Hartman 1986 who both explore children's life views and ways of thinking regarding religious questions or other questions regarding life views (Jackson 2004b: 23).

40 In Norway, Winsnes (1988) pioneered empirical research in Norwegian RE based on the ambition of making RE more relevant to children and young people in Norway. He was partly inspired by research in Sweden (Hartmann) which in turn had been inspired by Loukes,

ures, is an important background for the debate about RE in the context of plurality. Children's educational needs were increasingly seen as learning about *religions* and *life views* in the plural, and learning how to deal with the presence of this plurality in their lives. Even if this general trend could be traced in both countries, it did not have the same consequences at the academic level.

In *England*, Ninian Smart established The Department of Religious Studies at Lancaster University[41] in 1965. Smart initiated a major research and curriculum development project that promoted a phenomenological, undogmatic approach to RE in schools (Smart 1968). Especially influential was The School Council Working Paper 36 (Schools Council 1971, see also O'Grady 2005: 228). 'Smart's project was to create a multidisciplinary, open setting for the study of religion conceived as a global human phenomenon' (Jackson & O'Grady 2007: 193).

Further, the Shap Working Party on World Religions in Education was set up in 1969 as an organisation committed to 'promoting excellence in the study of religion at all levels and in all types of education'.[42] At the same time, the situation in some city schools was that religious plurality was increasingly overt, and this was reported for example by teacher trainers (Cole 1972). These initiatives were important for the development of the first local agreed syllabuses that reflected Britain as a religiously plural society (Birmingham 1975; Hampshire 1978). This development was recognised nationally in the 1988 Education Act. In other words, the change towards a multifaith approach to RE in England had a 'bottom-up' character and scholars from 'secular' religious studies were involved from early on.

In *Norway*, prior to 1997 scholars from the discipline of history of religions/ science of religion had shown little interest in school RE (Østberg 1998b: 239)[43]. Even if several scholars from 'secular' religious studies in Norwegian universities did publish some books expanding the availability of knowledge about the different religions since 1997,[44] the difference compared to England is particularly clear

---

Goldman and others in England. In order to get away from the limitations of a confessional and theologically dominated RE, Winsnes suggested a more pedagogically-based religious education, i.e. teaching of Christianity where a pedagogical aim was to aid pupils' reflections on life questions (Skeie 2007: 235). Winsnes argued that Religious Education in schools should be based more on pedagogy than on theology (Winsnes 1984: 7, Haakedal 1995: 10-11). One reason for this had also to do with his basic children-orientated perspective.

41 http://www.lancs.ac.uk/fass/religstudies/ (Accessed 11.08.2009). Eric Sharpe was also a member of staff in the department for religious studies at Lancaster University.

42 Shap was set up by professors in comparative religious studies - Smart, Hilliard and Parrinder - in 1969 after a conference at the Shap Wells Hotel on 'Comparative Religion in Education'. It was set up as a working party, implying that their aim was to do something, and besides the above mentioned professors it also included from the beginning seven lecturers in education and nine teachers. This collaboration between people from different levels of education is a hallmark of Shap (Hayward 2009). Shap aims both at religious studies in universities and colleges and religious education in schools. See http://www.shapworkingparty.org.uk/mission.html (Accessed 01.05.2008). Shap also has a European 'stickling'- the European Association for World Religions in Education was created in the 1980s: http://www.eawre.org/

43 Some researchers did produce some material for upper secondary schools as these schools have had more of a religious studies approach than the 'grunnskolen' (primary and lower secondary school, for example Groth *et al.* (1985)).

44 Rian (1999) from the University of Trondheim addresses world religions in education from a religious studies point of view and refers (again) to Smart's dimensions in religion as a pedagogical tool. Rian both gives an historic overview of the place of world religions in Norwegian curricula since 1960s, discusses principles for teaching world religions in relation to

when looking at the role of Shap. By the autumn of 1970 Shap had produced over twenty books about 'world religions' as aid for teachers (Hayward 2009: 4). A similar, if not equal, interest from 'secular religious studies' in educational issues hardly came before 2000 in Norway. Still, there are some nuances in this picture that should be considered. Since more has been written about the English history of RE research than the Norwegian (Copley 1989, Grimmitt 2000, Jackson 1990, 2004a, 2004b, Alberts 2007, Hayward 2009), I will go into more detail in the Norwegian case.

In the early 1980s, the University of Trondheim decided that the teaching of academic subjects that correlated with school subjects should include educational perspectives. The reason for this pedagogical interest in this university lies in its history of partly emerging from the former 'Norges Lærerhøgskole' (The Norwegian Higher Teacher Training College)[45] which was established in 1922 as the country's main teacher education institution.[46]

In the 1980s, courses focusing on religion and pedagogical issues were offered to teachers, and a tradition for a more school-oriented university study of Christianity developed there as something slightly different from the theological studies of Christianity. Materials from these courses were published in a range of books, for example Rian & Kværne (1983) *History of religions and teaching religion.*[47] In this publication, Rian quotes Smart's ideas of religious dimensions, which were later widely used in various RE publications in Norway.[48]

Trondheim was also the place where Ole Gunnar Winsnes delivered his doctoral thesis (1988) and later became professor in RE. Winsnes was influenced, for example, by the American sociologist T. Luckmann. His research was marked by

---

aims for RE in the Norwegian state school, including some principles for how to compare religions (p. 40), and basic knowledge about religions. The main bulk of the book (pp 71-184) is on classic topics in religious studies and is basically of a phenomenological nature. Rasmussen & Thomassen (1999) was a collection of sources and background materials which was needed in relation to the new KRL subject. This publication was initiated by professionals from religious studies in Bergen and theology at the University of Oslo. They offered a high quality presentation of source material from Christianity, Islam, Judaism, Hinduism and Buddhism: and Humanism. Several texts were translated for the first time into the Norwegian language, from Arabic, Latin, Sanskrit, and Hebrew. Jacobsen (ed. 2001) addressed multireligious Norway: Experts contributed to knowledge about Buddhism, Hinduism, Islam, Judaism and Christianity in a Norwegian context. These are, as far as I know, the main contributions from university-based religious studies in the time following the introduction of the subject of KRL.

45 My suggestion for the English translation of the name of the institution.
46 With its present organisation and name, the Norwegian University of Science and Technology, NTNU (Norges Teknisk Vitenskapelige Universitet) dates back to a reform in 1996, but it was first established as Norway's third university in 1968 after a merger of 'Norges Lærerhøgskole', and 'Norges Tekniske Høgskole' (NTH) and a museum and a library connected to 'Det kongelige Videnskabers Selskap' (The Royal Science Association). http://www.ntnu.no/omntnu/NTNUs_historie, (Accessed 12.08.2009), NOU 1995: 28, see http://www.regjeringen.no/nb/dep/kd/dok/nouer/1995/nou-1995-28/5/1/3.html?id=338358 (Accessed 12.08.2009), or for further details see Kirkhusmo (1983).
47 Original title: Religionshistorie og religionsundervisning: Noen fagdidaktiske synspunkter.
48 These courses were often aiming at upper secondary school teachers, as in upper secondary there was more of a religious studies approach prior to the 1997 reform, which concerned primary and lower secondary: for details regarding differences in the organisation of age groups in English and Norwegian schools, see chapter 5.

having a strong religion-society focus, and this can be said to be at the core of the Winsnes tradition.[49] This tradition may, in other words, just as well be described as a social science perspective than a pedagogical perspective; and there is also a hermeneutical dimension in it which was influential in part of theology at the time.

In other words, the Winsnes tradition also built on theological traditions, even if it also suggested a new direction. Geir Skeie, who was supervised by Winsnes, and did his doctoral studies at the University of Trondheim (1998), could be said to continue the Winsnes tradition, focusing on pedagogical issues and making use of theories and methods from the social sciences.[50] Researchers who have since been doing empirical work in RE in Norway have often used methodology from social sciences (see Skeie 2004, 2007).[51]

Also, the first Norwegian research network focusing on culture, religion and identity in a multicultural context (NEKRIF)[52] had its first meetings in Trondheim. It was initiated in 1993, and here a new generation of RE scholars started to emerge, exemplified by the founders of the network – Sissel Østberg, coming from 'secular' religious studies, and Geir Skeie with a theology background (and at the time a PhD student at the University of Trondheim).

The background for NEKRIF was a felt need for research in relation to 'focus on religion in relation to the multicultural challenges educational institutions are now facing' in Norway (Skeie 1993). This is very similar to reasons given by several of the English researchers who initiated/ participated in RE research projects from the mid 1980s (Grimmitt 2000), and reaching back many years before that, especially through the activities of Shap.

NEKRIF was an initiative aiming at assembling educational researchers working with questions related to pedagogy of religion or migration (Skeie 1993), and this seemed at the time to be a marginal issue in academic circles.[53] From an extensive national list of institutions and scholars invited, only ten persons responded (Skeie 1993). Internationally, the group was well orientated, and in 1993 Monica

---

49   Winsnes became the director of research at the Oslo-based 'Stiftelsen Kirkeforskning' (Church Research Foundation), a church-related sociology of religion institute. See http://www.kifo.no/ (Accessed 16.08.2009).

50   Skeie claimed RE in state schools needs to be justified within the cultural context of plural society. Skeie (1998) argues that RE should be sensitive to cultural factors, and discusses especially plurality as an important factor.

51   Later empirical work is, for example Lied (2004), Afdal (2006), Haakedal (2004), Skoglund (2008). In addition to my own study (Bråten 2010), there is also von der Lippe (2011) who, as part of a larger EU – project (REDCo), examines 14-16 year olds' relationship to religion and religious education in a multicultural society; Anker (2011), who explores pupils' construction of respect and disrespect in a multicultural school; Iversen (2012) who in his book based on his Warwick-based PhD is looking at how teachers and curricula represent national identity, especially 'Norwegianness' in religious education; Nicolaisen (2013) who is looking at Hindu children in Norwegian schools, and Jørgensen (2013) who, in her PhD study, is investigating one of the basic skills: writing, in relation to the RLE subject. She is analysing secondary school pupils' texts with regard to independent critical thinking, empathic engagement and courage.

52   'Nettverk for forskning på kultur, religion og identitet I en flerkulturell kontekst'.

53   This was prior to the Norwegian Research Council'_s initiative to fund research into migration (the IMER, see below).

Taylor[54] from the National Foundation of Educational Research[55] and Robert Jackson from the University of Warwick in England participated in the first NEKRIF seminar in Trondheim.

At this point in time, Jackson was participating in the *first RE research project* to have received a research council grant[56] in England. This was the Ethnography and Religious Education Project which included a curriculum project, the Warwick RE project, as one of its components.[57] The English participants expressed at the time that participation in NEKRIF answered a need on their part to expand their networks (Skeie 1993).

The next NEKRIF seminar, entitled *Religious Education in Pluralistic Societies,* was held at the University of Warwick in February 1994. One day of the seminar was used for academic exchange and two were used for visits to various local religious groups in the Birmingham/ Coventry area (Skeie 1994).[58] This was the first of many such visits to England by Norwegians interested in RE.[59] Up until today, these visits have typically contained a mixture of academic discussion and visits to faith communities. This 'genre' can be understood in light of one of Shap's activities from the mid-1970s through to the mid-1980s, namely providing in-service courses 'which provided teachers with the opportunity to follow interests in the field of religion at their own level, as well as considering the implications for their study for the classroom' (Hayward 2009: 6).[60]

The NEKRIF network was invited to a larger seminar in Kristiansand in November 1994, resulting in a publication: *Religious and Pedagogical Ideals* (Leganger-Krogstad & Haakedal 1995)[61] and NEKRIF initiated one more seminar in Stavanger in March 1996.[62] However, after 1997 (when KRL was introduced), there were no further activities in NEKRIF. Instead, a KRL network emerged and continued some of the same debates. But this was not a research network as such, so for many years there has not been a research network for RE in Norway. Ten years later, in 2008, Skeie together with Lied initiated a new national research net-

---

54 According to Gatherer (2005: 125) she is regarded as one of the most distinguished leaders in moral educational research.
55 The National Foundation for Educational Research (NFER) was founded in 1946 and has since then, amongst other things, founded research that underpins 'the drive towards excellence in education'; see http://www.nfer.ac.uk/about-nfer/ (Accessed 24.08.09). It is registered as a charity (no. 313392).
56 The grant was from the Economic and Social Research Council; see http://www.esrcsocietytoday.ac.uk/ESRCInfoCentre/about/ (Accessed 24.08.09).
57 See http://www2.warwick.ac.uk/fac/soc/wie/research/wreru/research/completed/ (Accessed 24.08.09).
58 Sissel Østberg became a part-time PhD student at Warwick, replicating in Oslo the type of ethnographic research carried out by Jackson and Nesbitt in Warwick (Jackson & Nesbitt 1993, Østberg 1998, Østberg 2003).
59 One example is Breidlied and Nicolaisen course 22. – 25th April 2008: to Redbridge in northeast London. Breidlied and Nicolaisen participated in this first trip to Warwick in 1993. See www.krlnett.no, (Accessed 16.06.08.).
60 This also included perspectives on Christianity in World Perspective.
61 Norwegian: religiøse og pedagogiske idealer.
62 'Religiosity and dissemination of tradition as a field of research: theoretical and methodological challenges': Norwegian: Religiøsitet og tradisjonsformidling som forksningsfelt; teoretiske og metodiske utfordringer'. Again, Robert Jackson participated.

work in Norway, named NoReFo.[63] In this network, *pedagogy of religion* is defined broadly including both Church and School perspectives and suggestions are that members should at least have PhDs in the field. By this time, the academic scene in Norwegian RE was quite different from the time of NEKRIF.

When the subject of KRL was established in 1997 as a political initiative, it was unrelated to the emerging, but still marginal research into the plural challenge for RE. None of the NEKRIF researchers played any role in the process, and they were even critical of the curriculum of 1997 for being too Christianity-based and for having no general right of exemption.[64]

Because of the strong tradition of the centrality of Christianity in the subject, when KRL was introduced, politically, in 1997, there was little foundation in the schools and the education system to receive and apply the new multifaith approach (Skeie 2004, 2007). Few teachers were qualified to teach such a subject. There was an obvious lack of knowledge especially about the non-Christian religions, and also a lack of comprehension of the idea of this attempted inclusive multifaith RE subject.[65]

In Norway, this resulted in measures from the state education authorities after the new subject was established, to meet the challenges. This is in contrast to the English context where the lack of appropriate resources and lack of teachers who had an understanding of religions was a central motive for the founding of Shap in 1969 (Hayward 2009: 2). Shap's production of resources and its other activities, for example the conferences for teachers put on in the north and south of England, had been ongoing for a period of 20 years when the shift towards multifaith approaches was sanctioned nationally in 1988.

In contrast to the 'bottom up' character of the development in England, in Norway the shift to a multifaith approach to school RE had a 'top down' character, even if in Norway the increasing religious plurality in some cities and some schools was also an important motivation for the change.

The explanation for this is found in the difference that, in England, there is a decentralised system for producing RE syllabuses locally (Jackson & O'Grady 2007: 184)[66] whilst, in Norway, there is a long tradition of having a National Curriculum in all subjects, RE including (see for example Haraldsø 1989).[67] Further,

---

63   Norsk religionspedagogisk forskningsforum: Norwegian forum for research on pedagogy of religion. The initial meeting was held on but 04.12.2007. Participants in the first meeting were Elisabeth Haakedal, Erling Birkedal, Geir Afdal, Geir Skeie, Heid Leganger-Krogstad, Jon Magne Vestøl, Njål Skrunes, Peder Gravem, Sverre Mogstad, Sidsel Lied and Berndt Krupka. They discussed the idea of such a forum and who it should be for. The next meeting was held in Oslo 10.10.2008, where a board was elected: Skeie, Lied, Afdal, Leganger-Krogstad. Following this there has to date been two more meetings, in Hamar 24.04.2009 and in Oslo 08-09.12.2009.
64   This is personal information obtained from both Geir Skeie and a member of the political 'Pettersen committee' which suggested the KRL, Ola Moe (see NOU 1995: 9). According to Moe they were not aware of this existing research interest in this topic.
65   See Gravem 2004 which will be discussed below.
66   Prior to 1988, England had a decentralised educational system and, after 1988, when England got its first National Curriculum, RE remained in a special position as statutory but outside the National Curriculum (though still being part of the 'basic curriculum').
67   Norway's centralisation is a strong feature of the unitary school tradition. From 1939 there was a national curriculum for all (Haraldsø 1989: 100), but in practical terms the content of

when it comes to the very different roles of 'secular' religious studies, the quite theological, though increasingly pedagogical, tradition of the school subject of Christian Knowledge, and the school law preamble which made Christian nurture the central object of schooling (see chapter 4 for more on this), may have kept scholars from 'secular' religious studies away from engaging with RE in schools.[68]

It was perhaps convenient to leave 'grunnskole' (primary and lower secondary school) RE to the theologians/ scholars of pedagogy of teaching Christianity, while the 'secular' religious studies had more of a responsibility for upper secondary school RE.[69] Only when multifaith RE was established politically and centrally were scholars from religious studies in the universities called upon to contribute with knowledge of religions *other than* the Christian. Compared to the English scene, however, there has been less distinct influence from 'secular' religious studies to the development of *pedagogy* for RE.[70]

3.3 The institutional basis for RE research

Moving from the research field towards the institutional basis for research, there is also a difference between England and Norway. Whilst in England RE research is mainly done in university departments of education, in Norway it was until 1997 mainly an interest in some theological institutions, in particular the most church-oriented one. In many ways this resembles the German situation more than the English (see for example Knauth 2007, Alberts 2007).[71] Especially since 1997, RE research in Norway has also increasingly been done in other institutions.[72] This

---

school curricula have basically been the same everywhere ever since Pontoppidan's catechism (1737) (Haraldsø 1989: 28). This claim can be justified by the widespread use of certain textbooks (for example 'Jensens lesebok' see Haraldsø 1989: 55).
68 This preamble was changed in 2008, see details in chapter 4.
69 See chapter 5 for details on the differences in organising of schools in England and Norway.
70 In Norway, 'Pedagogy' is a large independent field of research and practice which deals in theories of teaching and learning (Haakedal 1995). In the English language, this field, to the extent that they are parallel, is called *Education* or *Educational Science (or teaching and learning)*. The term 'didactics' (Nor: 'didaktikk') is used in both the English and Norwegian languages in connection with Pedagogy/ Educational Science, but has different meanings in the two contexts. Whilst in English, 'didactic' is somehow negatively loaded, referring to archaic methods of teaching, as used by Cooling to describe uninspiring RE, in Grimmitt (2000: 154) for example. In the Norwegian language, it is a fairly neutral concept referring to theories of how to teach a specific subject, for instance the didactics of RE. The meaning of 'didactics of RE' would be overlapping in meaning with the term pedagogy of religion. Sometimes 'didactics' also refers to 'methods of teaching' (general didactics): which is something different from theories of teaching and learning/ pedagogy. This is seemingly more similar to how these concepts are used in the German language, according to Alberts (2007: 63-74). In both England and Norway, however, there is a dispute over the meaning of concepts (see for example Haakedal 1986, 1995, Jackson 2004b).
71 There are two theological faculties in Norway, The Faculty of Theology within the University of Oslo, http://www.tf.uio.no/english/ (Accessed 19.03.09), and the Norwegian School of Theology ('Det teologiske menighetsfakultet'), http://www.mf.no/index.cfm?id=179065 (Accessed 19.03.09), which is also situated in Oslo.
72 In Norway there has been a change in policy towards rights as well as obligation for people working in the University Colleges to do research. In England, not all units which offer teacher training do research, as they depend on getting external funding for it. The systems or

includes some departments of education in universities and most prominently the teacher training colleges.

Historically, it has been in the teacher training institutions that the interest for doing RE-related research has been strongest, but since doctoral programmes are still rare in these institutions, the main research projects have often been PhDs linked to the theological faculties, to other Norwegian university faculties, or universities abroad (see Lied 2006). Between 1997 and 2012, nineteen people in Norway have been awarded PhDs which can be said to be within the field of pedagogy of RE as defined by NoReFo (see Lied 2006).[73] Most of them, but not all, are relevant for multifaith RE, and Østberg (1998a), Andreassen (2008a), Bråten (2010), von der Lippe (2011), Anker (2011) and Jørgensen (2013) (ongoing) have a religious studies background.

The Norwegian School of Theology[74] has been particularly active in establishing itself as a strong actor in the RE scene. To a certain degree its traditionally strong position as a main research institution has been challenged since 1997, but it has continued to be central and is, for example, still the only institution offering a separate PhD programme in pedagogy of religion (RE).[75]

An interesting question in light of the differences between England and Norway discussed above (disciplinary basis of research, relationship between research and

---

funding are also different. In England, funds mainly come from sources outside the universities such as charities and funding agencies. For example, Shap was initially supported by The Spalding Trust which, since the early twentieth century, has given out grants 'for the study of the great religions', see http://www.spaldingtrust.org.uk/ (Accessed 29.08.09). The Ethnographic study of Hindu children at the University of Warwick was supported by the The Leverhulme Trust which, from 1925, has given out 'scholarships for the purpose of research and education'. Funds for research are also found in one of several research councils (Jackson 2004b), see for example http://www.rcuk.ac.uk/default.htm (Accessed 19.08.2009). In Norway, funding still often comes from the institutions or from The Norwegian Research Council. A main source of funds for research in Norway is The Research Council of Norway, but it is only lately that they fund educational research in a substantial way. It is both a funding agency and an advisory body on Norwegian Research policy. For instance, it encourages international research cooperation. Most of its funds come from the Ministry of Education and Research, i.e. the state, http://www.forskningsradet.no/en/Home+page/1177315753906 (Accessed 19.03.09.) At any one time, the Research Council of Norway has got a number of research programmes under to which it gives out its funds, one relevant example being the International Migration and Ethnical Relations program (IMER). It has encouraged and funded research into the life worlds of religious minorities in Norway since 1993, with a pause from 2002–2005, and revived for the period of 2005–2010. According to its websites it has funded projects in this area also when the programme officially was paused. Even if Norwegian institutions also now increasingly encourage its staff to find research funds from other sources, for example the EU, there are few non-governmental sources of funding in Norway.

73 These are Skeie (1998), Østberg (1998a), Birkedal (2001), Mogstad (2001), Sagberg (2001), Haakedal (2003), Lied (2004), Afdal (2004), Bø (2006), Flornes (2007), Andreassen (2008a), Skoglund (2008), Lerheim (2009), Bråten (2010), Eriksen (2010), von der Lippe (2011), Anker (2011), Hovdelien (2011), Skrefsrud (2012).

74 The Norwegian school of Theology is a private theological faculty. Even if private higher education institutions are quite rare in Norway, this is less so in the field of theology. It was established in 1908 as a conservative alternative to what by some was perceived as to liberal attitudes in the Faculty of Theology at the University of Oslo. Traditionally there has been some tension between these institutions even if they are less pronounced in later years.

75 Other educational institutions offer programs within which a PhD in pedagogy of religion can be obtained. For instance Hamar University College is now offering a PhD in Teacher Education, where specialising in pedagogy of religion is one of the options.

curriculum changes, and institutional structure), is how this may have influenced the focus of debates in the two countries.

One of these debates is related to the concept of religion. Michael Stausberg from The Department of Archaeology, History, Cultural Studies and Religion at the University of Bergen[76] has criticised the National Curriculum for RE in Norway (UD 2008)[77] for being based on an outdated understanding of 'religion', giving an essentialist understanding of each 'world religion' remote from children's own experience (Gripsrud 2008). This was still a problem, even if it has been discussed, for example, by Østberg (1998b)[78] and Skeie (2006a).[79] This has similarities with English debate about RE, but it had a different starting point.

The world religions approach that Smart and others promoted from the late 1960s was based on the phenomenology of religion. The phenomenological approach in English RE was later criticised for being remote from the experience of children and for not providing pupils with the opportunity of toiling with issues of competing truth claims (Jackson 1997: 10). In *Religious Education: An Interpretive Approach* Jackson (1997: 7-29) discussed the phenomenological approach both generally and as applied in English RE. He argued that Waardenburg's 'new style phenomenology' in part answers the critics of the phenomenology of religion, and that it 'begins to resemble hermeneutical approaches such as that exemplified in interpretive anthropology' (Jackson 1997: 27).

With respect to phenomenological approaches in school RE, Jackson (1997) argued that some criticisms of it '(…) are misplaced, being applicable only to poorly designed materials which misapply principles from phenomenology' (Jackson 1997: 27). Jackson (1997, 2004a, 2008b) offers what might count as an updated discussion on the concept of 'religion', as well as 'culture' and 'ethnicity', where inner contestability and plurality in traditions are recognised (see also Alberts 2007: 161), and this becomes the basis for his suggestions about pedagogy for multifaith RE in a plural context.

Because of the closeness to the religious studies tradition, developments in RE in England reflected trends in the study of religions – for example, in its focus on diversity within traditions (Hayward 2009: 6). This has only recently come into the Norwegian debate, focused in Andreessen (2008a, 2008b), for example.

3.4 Can we talk about 'traditions' for pedagogy of RE?

The field of RE has been conceptualised in different ways and researchers have operated with different preconceptions about the nature and aims of the subject

---

76 He expressed this criticism in the University's web news page (Gripsrud 2008), but he or others have not often raised this issue in Norway.
77 http://www.udir.no/grep/Lareplan/?laereplanid=707207 (Accessed 29.08.09).
78 Just after the introduction of multifaith RE in Norway in 1997, Østberg (1998b) discussed some points of critique of the phenomenological approach from the English tradition (with reference to Jackson (1997)) as relevant for Norwegian RE. At the same time she argues for enhancing the religious studies profile in Norwegian RE.
79 Skeie has a wider international outlook drawing on his increasing international experience in pedagogy of RE.

(Jackson 2004b: 20). This is sometimes related to having different academic traditions as a base for understanding RE. Part of the academic debates within each country is the question of different and sometimes competing ideas about the nature of the RE, and especially about what multifaith RE is. In a comparative perspective the variations are even greater as the two countries' complex histories have to be considered. The section above has exemplified how the understanding of what RE is, and developments in RE research, are related to the two countries' different school and research traditions.

In an attempt to summarise developments in Norwegian RE, Haakedal (1995) suggested that in Norway the pedagogical tradition for RE was first established at the Institute of Christian Upbringing (IKO) from the 1950s as principally Lutheran thinking in combination with the German tradition for 'buildung' (Haakedal 1995: 9).[80] Asheim, Norway's first professor in the pedagogy of religion, had this kind of background,[81] but had his professorship at the Norwegian school of Theology (from 1970). In 1995, however, Haakedal described two directions in the development in Norwegian RE and suggested a principal distinction between the theologically-based pedagogy of religion, the Asheim/ Mogstad tradition[82] (see for example Asheim 1977, Mogstad 1999) and a pedagogically-based pedagogy of religion, the Winsnes tradition (Winsnes 1988, Lied 2006, Skeie 2004, 2007). Perhaps this deserves the name the Winsnes-Skeie tradition, see above.

In English RE, theologically-based and pedagogically-based approaches are not described as two main traditions. In England, one may point to a religious studies tradition, and some approaches which reflect a theological tradition more, but perhaps it is more accurate to refer to an educational/ pedagogical tradition in which it seems that a range of distinct *pedagogies* 'compete' in one field, that of the *pedagogy of religious education* (Grimmitt 2000, Jackson 2004a).

For example, Grimmitt (2000: 24-25) suggests that there were nine different approaches to RE coming from different RE research projects. [83] Some of those

---

80   The German 'bildung' could be translated to 'formation' meaning 'cultured' or maybe civilised, or simply 'educated'. In Nordic languages one would translate it to 'danning'. Alberts (2007: 56-57) suggests that 'Bildung includes the acquisition of cultural knowledge as a basis of a further development of one's own personality' and that the German concepts of bildung and Erziehung 'are meaningfully integrated in the English concepts "Education"'. There is presently a new debate about 'danning' in Norwegian educational contexts.
81   Asheim had done a German PhD in 1961 which was the first PhD in pedagogy of religion in Norway entitled 'Glaube und Erziehung bei Luther: ein Beitrag zur Geschichte des Verhältnisses von Theologie und Pädagogik' (Lied 2006: 164).
82   Mogstad (2001) is a PhD in the tradition after Asheim, building on the theological Asheim tradition for RE. Mogstad (2001) is investigating the relationship between biblical texts and human experience making use of perspectives from German theologians Stock and Baudler. His research is relevant for religious nurture within a church context.
83   These are: 1. Liberal Christian Theological, Experiential, Implicit Models (for example Loukes (1961), Goldman (1964)), 2. A Phenomenological, Undogmatic, Explicit Model (for example Smart 1968, The School Council Lancaster Secondary RE project 1971, the Chichester project 1982), 3. Integrative Experiential and Phenomenological Models (for example Grimmitt 1973, The School Council Lancaster Primary RE project 1977, Hammond, Hey), 4. Human Development, Instructional, Learning About, Learning From Models (The Westhill Project, Grimmitt 1987, The religion in the service of the Child Primary RE project), 5. An Ethnographic, 'Interpretive', Multifaith Model (The Warwick RE project, for example Everington 1993, Jackson 1997), 6. A Revelation-Centred, Concept-Cracking, Trinitarian Chris-

approaches could be said to be mainly theologically-based while others more clearly are based in a religious studies approach (see also Alberts 2006). If there are tensions between background disciplines such as theology and religious studies, they are not very clearly communicated while, in the Norwegian case, this immediately became a very explicit question in RE after the political introduction of multifaith RE in 'grunnskole' (primary and lower secondary school).

For example, Thomassen (1998),[84] a professor at The Department of Archaeology, History, Cultural Studies and Religion at the University of Bergen, discussed the challenge posed by KRL in terms of needs for cooperation where there traditionally have been tensions between these disciplines. While acknowledging positive aspects of this increased cooperation, he also defends the maintenance of 'unquestionable differences' between theology and religious studies. Like Thomassen, Østberg (1998b) too thought it interesting that the new multifaith RE in schools was now challenging the scholarly disciplines, but adds more of a pedagogical perspective and calls for a new discipline which focuses on the children and on developing pedagogy for this new subject (Østberg 1998b: 240, 253).

Despite the fact that tensions between academic disciplines are more tuned down in English RE, such tensions can also be found for example in the different approaches as they are summed up by either Grimmitt (2000), Jackson (2004a) or Alberts (2007).[85] In England as well as Norway, research in RE could be said to have different disciplinary bases, and types of RE research could have been categorised according to a disciplinary focus as theological or having a study of religions approach and/ or a social science /anthropological approach, for example. Research in RE is, however, focused on pedagogical issues reflecting (mainly) an institutional base in departments of Education. As such, they can be seen as contributing to the *pedagogy of RE* as a separate and distinct research discipline.

Haakedal suggested (in 1995) that *pedagogy of religion* in Norway should not be theologically-based but rather an independent, interdisciplinary pedagogically-based academic discipline, and mentioned also religious studies as relevant to that. However, she was rather ahead of her time, because until very recently there has not been a religious studies tradition in Norwegian RE (see, for example, Lied 2006). However, since 1997, people with a religious studies background increasingly have been hired in teacher training institutions[86].

In 2008, the German religious studies scholar Wanda Alberts was hired for a new chair in the pedagogy of religion at the University in Bergen. This university

---

tian Realist Model (The Stapleford RE project, for example Cooling 1993), 7. A Literacy-Centred, Critical Realist Model (for example Wright) and 8. Constructivist Models of Learning and teaching in RE (The Children and World views project, for example Erricker & Erricker).

84 The title of the article was 'Theology and History of Religions – towards a new cross disciplinary identity'.

85 It is possible for example to interpret the recent disputes between Jackson (2008) and Wright (2008) (see also Jackson 2004a) as one where arguments are mainly drawn from different academic traditions.

86 Although when I and others with a religious studies background were applying for positions that became available in teacher training institutions after the introduction of KRL in 1997, some of those institutions mentioned only theology or studies in Christianity as relevant background.

now offers a study-of-religion approach course in pedagogy of religion.[87] In 2008 Andreessen delivered a thesis in pedagogy of RE which can be said to reflect an emerging religious studies tradition within Norwegian RE. He has worked at Tromsø University College Department for Teacher Education, and also in the above mentioned course in Bergen. Since 2008, Bråten (2010), von der Lippe (2011), and Anker (2011), all with a religious studies background, have also delivered PhD theses in the field of *pedagogy of religion*.

Coming back to the broader question of whether traditions for the pedagogy of RE can be identified, it must be noticed that the varieties within these traditions, if they are traditions, are great, and also that they are evolving. The comparative perspective brings in the *supranational dimension* which, on the one hand, adds to the complexities of the question of how the field is understood. On the other hand, it is also in the increasing international exchange, collaboration and networking (see below) that certain hallmarks of what might be described as an international tradition for the *pedagogy of RE* can be found. Included in the International Seminar of Religious Education and Values (ISREV), for example, are all kinds of teaching into, from and about religions (and life views and ethics/ values) in different countries. Seen as an international research discipline, *pedagogy of RE* would, in my opinion, be defined by research questions which originate in questions of relevance to educational practice in different contexts.

I think it is important that the *pedagogy of RE* needs to be connected to a tradition for educational research rather than the traditional university disciplines of theology or religious studies, or such like. An argument in support of this is that the school subjects are constructions that do not correlate directly to any of the established university disciplines. For example, Skeie (2006a: 94) notes how the 'real world diversity' of the school teaching practical context even presents an implicit critique of the scholarly traditions.

Another reason is that there are many common themes, for example about learning or motivation etc., across school subjects that are the concern of pedagogical researchers. Also, issues of social concern, such as community cohesion, have an impact on a variety of subjects in schools. I see this as especially important for the further development of RLE[88] into a subject which is also perceived as inclusive by those who are currently critical to it. It may also be seen as important for English RE, but this is perhaps more already the case there.

In my view, a basic criterion for an *inclusive* multifaith RE is that it needs to be pedagogically based in educational research. Christian theology and the theologies of the other religions, and 'secular' religious studies (and other disciplines such as philosophy, anthropology etc.) will continue to play a role, which can be seen as constructive to the extent to which they provide relevant information (or theoretical concepts and tools or even debates, such as the question of what religion is) for the study of the interface between religion and teaching of religion in various contexts. I think that today there is sufficient research in the area of the teaching about/ from/ into religion (and life views and ethics) in Norway as well as in England, as well as

---

87   http://www.uib.no/ahkr/utdanning/religionsvitenskap/laererutdanning-i-religionsvitenskap (Accessed 24.08.09).
88   The name was changed from KRL to RLE in 2008, see chapter 1 and 4.

in a broader supranational context, to say that *pedagogy of RE* can be seen as an established separate field of research.

3.5 The reading of two 'power texts' by looking for characteristics of academic debate in England and Norway

Following up a broader analysis of academic and disciplinary features of the English and Norwegian research of RE, this section analyses two rather recent texts, one from each country, in order to dig deeper into the similarities and differences between the RE research traditions in the two countries. The texts have been chosen as being 'power texts' in a 'Foucauldian sense'.[89] Foucault has a radical critique of modern society as based on power and inequality.[90] Power is seen as rooted in institutions and manifests itself in texts.

Interpreting the religious education research scene from this perspective, Jackson (2004a) and Gravem (2004) are 'power texts'. They can be seen as dominating the discourses in the field, not in the sense that they are not controversial, but rather in the sense that controversies often tend to refer to these texts. Their ambitions are reflected even in the titles, where Jackson says that he wants to *rethink* Religious Education and Plurality, while Gravem says that he wants to present *a more precise interpretation* of the subject of KRL (in the 1997 National Curriculum) than in his opinion exists. Because they are 'power texts' – in the concepts from Schiffauer *et al.* (2004) – they illustrate aspects of *the national styles* (see chapter 2) in the academic debates about RE.

The English publication Rethinking Religion and Plurality: issues in diversity and pedagogy (Jackson 2004) and the Norwegian publication KRL – a subject for all? The KRL subject as answering to challenges in a multicultural school context (Gravem 2004)[91] have in common that they both identify what they see as the main positions in the debates about English and Norwegian RE at about the same point in time. However, they do this on a quite different basis. Gravem and Jackson refer to different traditions[92] when they each are attempting to identify the main positions in the societal debates about RE in their country. In this way the texts are not 'speaking to' each other, and Gravem and Jackson so far have had no contact in

---

89 The establishments of 'order of things' are (seemingly) empirical and hesitant, and Foucault looks for explanations for established 'orders' in western culture. Based on such (established) 'orders' which are seen as ontologically true, general theories of 'the order of things' are constructed. Foucault's theories become Meta theory as also the establishment of scientific traditions are seen as dependant on these basic (but empirical and not ontological) 'orders'. (Foucault 1966)
90 According to Eliassen (1996) seen in Foucault's authorship from 1971, for instance in Madness and Civilisation (see also Taylor 2007: 600).
91 Thesis from 2002, published as a book in 2004. Original Norwegian title: *KRL - et fag for alle? KRL-faget som svar på utfordringer I en flerkulturell skolekontekst*. This is Gravem's second doctorate (which is slightly different in profiles from PhDs). When he was hired as a professor in KRL at the Norwegian school of theology, he was also granted professorship in systematic theology.
92 This can refer to the different traditions for RE in England and Norway (see above) but also that they refer to different academic disciplines within those national traditions.

academic terms. This also increases the asymmetry between the texts, and this brings out more distinct differences, which is an intended purpose of choosing these two here.

The two scholars base their main arguments in different academic traditions and different research experiences. To some degree they can be said to represent opposite (or different) positions in the debates, as the debates about (multifaith) RE in England and Norway are in many cases parallel or even converging. Gravem (2004) evaluates certain positions in the debate against a 'more precise' interpretation of 'the text' referring to the 1997 KRL curriculum (KUF 1996) and its contested meaning. As an experienced interpreter of theological texts, Gravem uses his skills to discuss the degree to which some interpretations are in line with 'the basic text' or not, and whether other interpretations are better.

This type of text-interpretation has a certain resonance in the research tradition for RE in Norway as Haraldsø (1989), Skottene (1994), Skrunes (1995) and Bø (2006) all have done historical studies of curricular texts and also of the role of Christianity in the development of the Norwegian unitary school tradition. Jackson's perspectives also draw on the traditions for RE research in England with reference, for example, to Loukes (1961), Smart (1968) and others, but his perspectives also reflect his background in social sciences and empirical ethnographic research. There is less focus on curriculum analysis in Jackson's text and in one sense the curriculum is the background and research in the foreground. However, Gravem analyses the curriculum, but through this he also evaluates and comments on research perspectives.

Both the different national traditions and the different academic traditions can be seen as Foucauldian 'orders' (discourses). If I perceived them as belonging to different orders, however, one could claim that there is a lack of common ground for comparing these two texts. Only if one sees these two as within the same 'order' or field (of pedagogy of RE) does it become logical to compare them (see above).

However, it could also be expected that that which is based in one tradition (academic/ national) would be challenged by the other as arguments could be seen as based in different discourses. Had I chosen to compare scholars with more similar positions like, for example, Jackson and Winsnes/ Skeie, or Gravem and Hull or Wright, this might have brought out more similarities between the English and Norwegian academic debates about RE. When Jackson (2004a) and Gravem (2004) are chosen for comparative reading this is to bring attention to differences that could help me identify what may be seen as specific to these national styles of academic debate about RE in England and Norway.

The fact that the institutions that they represent – in Norway a Theological faculty, and in England an Institute of Education at a university – are main institutions for research and pedagogy of RE in their national context, is in itself an indication of differences in national styles (see above). Gravem works at the Norwegian School of Theology, which has a long tradition for being interested in the field of pedagogy of religion in Norway.[93] As shown above, the Norwegian School of Theology has in a most systematic way established formal competence and both organised courses for school RE teachers and facilitated higher studies and degrees in pedagogy of religion (RE).

Three of Norway's current four professors in the field (Mogstad, Gravem and Afdal) have their chairs in the Norwegian School of Theology.[94] This is part of the explanation for why Gravem's thesis is seen as a major text in the Norwegian context. Jackson, working in England, established the Warwick Religions and Education Research Unit (WRERU) on the formation of the Institute of Education at the University of Warwick in 1994, building in part on the existing tradition for ethnographic research (for example on Hindu Children in Britain) in the former Arts Education Department. Since then, this research unit has established itself as a main actor in RE research in England[95] with, moreover, increasingly international engagements.[96] The Institute currently has three professors in religions and education (Robert Jackson, Eleanor Nesbitt, Leslie Francis), and the institute also offers masters and PhD courses in religious education.

Comparing these two texts brings attention to how having a binding National Curriculum (Norway) as opposed to having the system of locally agreed syllabuses (England) influences the academic debates differently. One of the things Gravem (2004) demonstrates is how central the National Curriculum is to the Norwegian discourse and this emphasis is an important element in the Norwegian tradition, even though research and academic debate about RE in schools in Norway is also much more than that (Skeie 2004, 2007). I think it is justified to claim that much societal and academic debate in Norway relates to discussing the content of the National Curriculum and interpreting it in the context of the unitary school ideology (Haraldsø (1989), Skottene (1994), Skrunes (1995) and Bø (2006)).

This does not have an immediate parallel in the English debates. In England, there is neither a National Curriculum for RE nor a unitary school ideology. In this respect the contexts of English and Norwegian RE are very different (see chapter 5).[97] Nevertheless, discussions of legal issues, for example the change in law in 1988 (which sanctioned multifaith local agreed RE syllabuses) is also present in English debates. For example, Hayward (2009: 8) notes that 'from the time of the

---

93 Its interest in school issues had links to the establishment of a school focus study in Christianity at the University of Trondheim. This included also a network of Christian teachers with a background from The Norwegian School of Theology.

94 Sverre Dag Mongstad, Peder Gravem, Geir Afdal. The fourth professor (Skrunes) is based in a Christian teacher training institution; Norsk Lærerakademi (NLA): 'The Norwegian Teacher Academy' in Bergen. http://www.nla.no/ (Accessed 25.03.09).

95 Through, for instance, receiving the first Research council grant for studies in Religious Education in England in 1990 for the Ethnography and Religious Education project, see http://www2.warwick.ac.uk/fac/soc/wie/research/wreru/research/completed (Accessed 24.08.09).

96 Especially though its engagement in the REDCo project, see chapter 2, see http://www2.warwick.ac.uk/fac/soc/wie/research/wreru/ (Accessed 16.08.09).

97 There is variety of types of schools even within the state system in England, while this is not the case in Norway. The four main types of state schools are: Community schools, Voluntary Controlled schools, Voluntary Aided Schools and Foundation schools and in addition a number of independent schools, see http://www.inca.org.uk/england-system-mainstream.html. The support of schools with a religious character within the state system is disputed in England, see Jackson (2004a: 39-57).

consultation on the National Curriculum through to current discussions of the revised secondary curriculum, the non-statutory national framework for RE, QCA schemes of work and the proposed national strategy have similarly been the focus of discussions and response by members of the Shap Working Party. Another example, which lies further back in history, is Hull's (1989) The Act Unpacked which is about analysing what the 1988 Education Reform Act meant for RE and collective worship (see chapter 4). However, the strong focus on the National Curriculum in the Norwegian debate brings attention to how the English academic debates relate to the context of the decentralised system for producing RE syllabuses. Despite tendencies in Norway towards decentralisation and in England towards centralisation, they are still far apart on this point (see chapter 4 & 6).[98]

Both Jackson (2004a) and Gravem (2004) include political as well as academic perspectives. Drawing on their own as well as others' research, they argue what kind of RE is best suited to meeting the religious plurality in the English and Norwegian school systems (school ideologies). Both Jackson (2004a) and Gravem (2004) evaluate what they see as the main positions in the debates about RE with plurality as the sociocultural backdrop. Their views of plurality are, however, different and this becomes especially evident as Jackson (2004a) and Gravem (2004) both relate to Geir Skeie's theories of plurality (Skeie 1995, 1998). But while Gravem raises the question of how useful it is to distinguish between traditional and modern plurality in relation to his project (Gravem 2004: 210)[99], Jackson integrates these concepts in his discussion of plurality (Jackson 2004a, for example in pages 1, 8, 12, 92, 113, 126). Jackson sees a mix of traditional and modern plurality as the context for religious education in the twenty-first century (Jackson 2004a: 20).[100] This is the basis for discussing the developments in RE in England, from Christian Instruction as a binding force in society through a divorce of RE and moral education and citizenship education, to being able in RE to explore this plurality (Jackson 2004a: 20-21).

The main problem being discussed in Jackson (2004a) is different approaches to RE in the light of plurality seen as a mix of modern and traditional plurality. Jackson (2004a) summarises the debate about RE in England and Wales through a discussion of six different approaches to RE in (state) schools in relation to their relevance in a plural context RE. These are:

1. *'Religion as cultural heritage' which denies that society is plural and argues that Christian indoctrination is a valid form of RE in the state school;*

---

98 There are movements back and forth between tendencies to centralise and decentralise in each country, but with the constant that in Norway there has been a central National Curriculum for RE while in England there has been a decentralised system of producing the syllabuses locally (further details in chapter 4). The National Curriculum in Norway has, however, emphasised local adjustments in the curriculum in varying degree, and in England the introduction of Model Syllabuses and the Non-statutory National framework may be seen to represent centralising tendencies.
99 Which is interpreting the text of The National Curriculum for RE in the context of the Norwegian plural society.
100 This could also be seen as many types of modernities coexisting (as do Taylor 2004, see chapter 7 and 8).

2. *'State funding for religious schools'* which allows schools with religious profiles to take care of religious nurture in plural societies[101]:
3. *'Postmodernist approaches to religious education'* which wants pupils to explore religion through personal narratives:
4. *'Religious Education as religious literacy'* which wants to present the different religions as distinct systems and help pupils identify with a particular religion (a position which could bee seen as having some similarities to Gravem's view):
5. *'Interpretive approaches to religious education'* which try to keep the debate open and involve pupils in participating in interpretation through reflexive studies of source materials:
6. *'Dialogical approaches to religious education'* which aims to increase pupils' understanding of religion through interaction (Jackson 2004a: 2-3).

The main argument is that interpretive, dialogical and religious literacy approaches to RE are better suited for the plural context than the others. The arguments for this are based on an understanding of the plural nature of society which takes account of a distinction between traditional and modern plurality and sees plurality as purely descriptive as opposed to seeing pluralism as normative (Jackson 2004a: 8, with reference to Skeie 1995). There is an understanding of modernity and postmodernity/ late modernity and globalisation as the context of RE (Jackson 2004a: 9-10). There is also a focus on the inner diversity and contestability of cultural and religious traditions (Jackson 2004a: 2), reflecting the tradition of the ethnographic research done in WRERU at the University of Warwick, and the Interpretive Approach which was developed there (Jackson 1997).

Important perspectives relevant to an inclusive pedagogy of RE include the critique of 'orientalism' (Said 1978). This critique is about recognising the complexities of the inner diversity in 'traditions' (Jackson 2004a: 81). Furthermore, the critique of early multiculturalism is also relevant as this points out that RE sometimes reifies stereotypes through presenting religions as distinct and homogeneous systems. Considering power relations within different cultural groups (Jackson 2004a: 128) is also considered important to an inclusive RE. An important point in this *rethinking* of the pedagogy of RE is a view of ethnicity, culture and religion not as bounded entities, but as flexible phenomena 'in a state of flux and rapid change' (Jackson 2004a: 15) and with fuzzy edges and inner contestability. These points reflect ideas from the social sciences, especially social anthropology. This is resembles traits of the Winsnes/ Skeie tradition in the Norwegian scene. Jackson's perspectives are rooted in the tradition of ethnographic research at the University of Warwick where the identity formation of young people from different backgrounds has been researched and is seen as an ongoing process influenced by many different kinds of religious and non-religious sources.[102]

The idea of religion perceived as part of a cultural heritage is seen as problematic (Jackson 2004a:13, 22-38). Prior to the 1988 Reform Act some argued for a continuation of a predominantly Christian RE and even for the need to strengthen

---

101 Similar to the Dutch model of pillarisation, see for example in Avest, Bakker, Bertram-Troost & Miedema 2007.
102 This makes the Interpretive Approach developed in Warwick child-oriented Jackson (2004a: 19-20), Jackson & Nesbitt (1993), Østberg (1998), Ipgrave (2002).

this in the face of the increased religious plurality in English society. Some argued against sanctioning a multifaith type of RE as developed for example in the Birmingham (1975) syllabus.

In this line of argument, a special British brand of Christianity would be closely linked to British cultural heritage (Jackson 2004a: 22). This lobby influenced how the wording of the law was formulated both with regard to RE and in relation to collective worship (see chapter 4). This association of morality with one particular religious tradition ignores the moral concerns of other religions and of humanistic traditions within British society, Jackson argues. That tensions such as these are strongly felt also on the Norwegian side becomes evident in Gravem (2004), but he takes a different stance towards this issue.

Gravem's (2004) *KRL – a subject for all? The KRL subject as the answer to challenges in a multicultural unitary school*[103] is an attempt to make 'a more precise interpretation' of the subject according to the 1997 National Curriculum than, in his opinion, existed at the time of writing, applying a method he calls 'systematic reconstruction' (Gravem 2004: 5). It is also an analysis of the different understandings of the subject of KRL as expressed in the discussions following its introduction in 1997, so it can also be seen as an attempt to sum up the debate about KRL so far. Gravem evaluates what he sees as the main positions in this debate against his 'more precise' interpretation of the text (the 1997 National Curriculum for RE). It is the only published book to date which summarises and discusses the societal/academic debate related to RE in Norway.[104].

Gravem's agenda is to argue against those who, from various positions, have criticised KRL and to defend the view that, more precisely interpreted, the subject should be understood as a coherent and justified solution to the challenges a multicultural society raises for Norwegian RE. This debate can be seen as the first reaction in Norwegian society to the idea of multifaith RE, and, as such, it may have more similarities to the reactions in England after the Birmingham (1975) syllabus. This also triggered public and political debate where, on the one side, Christian organisations argued that RE should be about Christian nurture and, on the other, was humanists who wanted to be included on equal terms (Haakedal 1983: 46-47). Hull (1978), who had been one of the main engineers behind the document, defended it.

Under the heading 'The contested subject'[105] Gravem claims there have been three main perspectives in the debate about KRL:

1. *KRL has got an insufficiently clear Christian education rooting and profile.*
2. *KRL has a Christian education profile which is too distinctive.*
3. *Because of political compromises, KRL has strong inner tensions and contradictory demands which makes it impossible to put into practice* (Gravem 2004: 148).

---

103 Norwegian: 'KRL – et fag for alle? KRL faget som svar på utfordringer I en flerkulturell enhetsskole'.
104 But several articles and book chapters attempt the same, for example Haakedal 1995, 2001, Skeie 2004, 2006a, 2006b, 2007, Lied 2006.
105 Norwegian: 'Det omstridte faget'.

Those holding the first position as described by Gravem use the preamble of the school law[106] to argue that KRL still had to be seen as confessional. It was Christian voices mainly coming from NLA university college[107] who argued this position (Gravem 2004: 149) as they wanted to continue to have a denominational/ confessional type of RE in the state school. Those who argue the second position, that KRL has too distinctive a Christian character, also referred to the school law preamble. They argued that the tradition of the Christian subject would continue to shape the parts about Christianity in KRL (in the 1997 National Curriculum) in a qualitatively different way compared to the new parts about 'other' religions, philosophy and life views.

There is also quantitatively more material on Christianity and only a limited right to opt out, and these factors together are seen as KRL (in the 1997 National Curriculum) being a form of indoctrination into state religion (Lutheran Christianity). It is especially the Norwegian Humanists Association, together with other minority groups, who have argued this position (Gravem 2004: 171-172).[108] The third position is argued by analytical scholars who have pointed out inner tensions and weaknesses in the 1997 National Curriculum for KRL, and raised the question of whether there are too many inconsistencies in it. The main arguments for this position were seen to come from Plesner (1998) and Skeie (1998) (Gravem 2004: 198ff).[109]

Gravem (2004: 390ff) concludes that the new RE that Norway adopted in 1997 must be understood as *a new type of subject* and not as denominational (or confessional) Christianity, as both the first two positions claim. Neither does he see it as a 'religious studies-based' subject. Gravem chooses to look for coherences between the different parts which others have seen as inconsistent and argues that KRL can be seen as consistent enough to defend.

Through employing Thor Ola Engen's theories of integrative socialisation (Gravem 2004: 249, 393-394) he claims that KRL (in the 1997 National Curriculum) can be seen as a solution to how to construct RE as a common subject for all (multifaith approach) in the *Norwegian* plural society, but also in the traditional Norwegian unitary school. An important aspect of his analysis is the relationship to the ongoing court cases, and especially the ruling of the Norwegian High court that KRL was not in violation of the human rights (more on this in chapter 4).

His opinion is that this subject reflects, firstly, that in *the Norwegian* plural context the main part of the population is Christian, and, secondly, that the curriculum includes other religions and life views in a percentage proportion similar to the size of the minority groups (Gravem 2004: 390). He sees it as fair to emphasise the spe-

---

106 Which until 2008 stated that aiding parents in Christian upbringing of their children is the overall purpose of education, but the addition that this is in cooperation with the children's home is stressed in a verdict in the Norwegian High Court (details in chapter 4).
107 NLA is short for 'Norsk lærerakademi' (Norwegian teacher college), and this is a private Christian educational institution, see http://www.nla.no/eng/new?lang=eng (Accessed 04.04.2013).
108 After losing in the High court in Norway, their complaint about this subject and the lack of right to be fully exempted was recognised in a verdict in Strasbourg in 2007 (see chapter 4).
109 Against this, more optimistically Lied (2004) later argues, based on empirical studies, that KRL can work in practice, despite perhaps being theoretically impossible, see also Thomassen (2006).

cific Norwegian Christian tradition more, because of its longstanding historical roots in the country, which is a 'religion as a cultural heritage' argument.[110] However, Gravem does emphasise the possibilities of local adjustment as a means of offering minority pupils RE which is better adjusted to their needs.

According to Gravem (2004: 391), central core values of importance for KRL are to respect the different religions truth claims and to accept group pluralism, which he takes to mean treating individuals as well as groups with different cultures, religions and life views equally. Another of these values is to support minority cultures as far as they do not violate the coherence of the shared community (Gravem 2004: 391). These values, on which the Norwegian school rests, are in Norwegian culture informed through the Christian and Humanist traditions, Gravem says that this makes it possible to claim that the Norwegian school rests on a consistent set of values while also being open to alternative values with which it is in a dialogue, because these values exclude forced conformity (Gravem 2004: 392).

Gravem's main perspective with respect to plurality is majority vs. minority, where he does grant the majority certain extra rights, though not the right to discriminate against minorities (see also Skeie 2006b: 24-25). The alternative would be to not grant the majority any privileges or not conceptualising society in terms of minorities and majority at all. Rather, the emphasis could be on how individuals may situate themselves differently towards such ideas of groups (Iversen 2012).

Skeie (1998, 2006b), for example, represents a different position in the Norwegian debate with his different understanding of plurality stemming from the social sciences (in the Winsnes tradition, see above). For example Skeie (2006b: 30) notes that 'As researcher, I suggest that presently our political responsibility should be towards *the individual child* (my italics) and the context the child lives in'.[111] However, Skeie and others with similar positions, such as Iversen (2012), become controversial in a Norwegian context, not because of the emphasis on the individual child as such, but because this challenges what may seem like a strong and dominating idea of seeing Christianity – and Humanism – as 'our cultural heritage' (see chapters 6 and 7). For those having a similar view as Skeie, however, Gravem's

---

110 Bø's (2006) thesis is a study in the Norwegian National Curricula as such (not just the RE curriculum) and their attempts to create unity (helhet: unity/ cohesion) in a differentiated society, and the role of religion in this enterprise. Bø discusses 'the longed for cohesion in the Norwegian school' implying the underlying unitary school ideology. Parson's theory of generalised values is central in his analysis (Bø: 116 ff, 176) – which I think resembles Bellah's concept of civil religion (see chapter 4). Bø (2006) does not discuss Gravem (2004) but they are both discussing possibilities of harmonising tensions in the 1997 National Curriculum in the context of the Norwegian unitary school ideology/ plural society. While Gravem goes much further in claiming such harmonisation is possible, Bø concludes that it is not possible to omit tensions in a complex society, and suggests a strategy of accepting that there have to be tensions in such a document (Bø 2006: 179).

Gravem has a much more explicit political agenda of defending KRL. Bø is less political and is also looking at a broader spectrum of tensions within the curriculum as a whole.

111 (...) We should work for curricula as well as teaching that gives the individual person access to knowledge that can support both different kinds of believing and not-believing, and give opportunity to exchange thoughts on views and values with others, (...) with the possibility of developing in new directions (Skeie 2006b: 30).

view of preserving values seen as Norwegian and linked to a certain tradition (Christian – and Humanistic – cultural heritage), may be seen as controversial.

The idea of a nation-specific heritage and the conscious political construction of this heritage, or national imaginary (Schiffauer et al. 2004), are at the core of the Norwegian unitary school tradition (Engen 2005).[112] It is linked to a conscious nation-building as a political project in post-colonialised Norway after its liberation from Denmark (1814) and finally Sweden (1905) (Engen 2005). Radical ideas of plurality, such as Skeie's, deconstruct this imaginary. Gravem, on the other hand, may be seen as arguing to preserve a consistent imaginary. This is, he says, for the political purpose of aiding social cohesion, and he sees KRL (in the 1997 National Curriculum) as a constructive compromise in the plural *Norwegian* society.

Although Gravem is inclusive, seen from a majority perspective, his view could still be seen as offensive from a minority perspective. This point has indeed often been made in the societal debate in Norway. For example, in a critical book published by the Norwegian Humanist Association just after KRL was introduced politically, the social anthropologist Thomas Hylland-Eriksen (1996: 157) characterised this kind of tolerance as the traditional Christian benevolent but patronising way, without allowing others to become equals to the state religion.[113]

It is important for Gravem that school education as such, including its RE, is not value-free, and in the English context this is a point Hull also underlined in his defence of the Birmingham (1975) syllabus (Haakedal 1983: 47). In this, Gravem's position also compares to Wright's position in the English debate (see for example Alberts 2007: 163).

It is the Norwegian Humanist Association which has represented the most persistent critique of KRL in Norway (including law suits, see above and chapter 4). I see the role of the critique of early multiculturalism and orientalism in England that Jackson discusses (2004a: 81, 127) as serving some of the same aims of problematizing minority perspectives. However, Jackson goes much further than Gravem in incorporating this critique into his suggestions for appropriate RE in the English plural context, thus taking a different approach to the question of how to deal with or even conceptualise minorities as well as the majority.

As noted above, there is a tendency to emphasise Christianity as part of Norwegian cultural heritage in a rather strong strand of historical studies in Norway. Here the argument has often been to preserve Christianity as part of our cultural heritage within the tradition of the unitary school (Skeie 2004: 323, Lied 2006: 170). I see Gravem's thesis as relating to this strand in the Norwegian tradition. This historical research interest does not have a parallel in England where theoretical contributions in the field of pedagogy of RE have been more interested in methods of teaching RE in schools, in an educational science tradition, more than in a theological/ historical tradition (see above). This does not mean, however, that the relationship between state and Church in England has not also formed both the school tradition

---

112 Both Schiffauer and Engen refer to Benedict Anderson's concept of imagined communities (Anderson 1991).
113 Paraphrased from this original Norwegian text: 'For tiden ser det imidlertid ut til at de ikke kristne religiøse minoritetene skal "tolereres" på den tradisjonelle kristne, velvillige nedlatende måten, men ikke at de skal få være likeverdige med statsreligionen.'

in general and RE specifically, in a certain way (for example Copley 1997, Jackson 2004a).

From the point of the first educational legislation, in England 1870, in Norway (then a part of Denmark) 1739, the English legislation reflected a 'traditional' (Christian) religious plurality, while the Norwegian legislation reflected a 'traditional' (Christian) religious unity. The English legislation, for example, allowed private schools to teach religion according to their own denominational faith, at the same time ensuring that religious education (Religious Instruction) in state schools was non-denominational (but with a confessional element).[114] In addition, there was also a general right for parents to withdraw their children from 'RI' from 1870 onwards in England (Copley 1997) while, in Norway, the right to withdraw was first granted in 1889 after longstanding battle over this (Haraldsø 1989).[115] In Norway there was no traditional religious plurality; in fact, Norway and its school system is traditionally religiously monocultural. It is not unreasonable therefore to describe the development in English RE as negotiated on the basis of *difference* (as essential to the English [British] National Imaginary) while developments in Norwegian RE are negotiated on the basis of *'sameness'* (as an essential idea in the Norwegian National Imaginary (see also Everington (2009) and Lund Johansen (2009), see chapter 6).

This can perhaps also be part of the explanation why the English school system as such is also more plural, allowing for different kinds of (religious) schools both within and outside the state system. This is also very much in contrast to the way the Norwegian unitary school – with its traditionally strong connection to the state religion (see chapter 4) and the nation-building project (Engen 2005). Today, for example, independent religious schools in England also include Muslim and Hindu schools, and since 1997 policy has changed towards including more faith-based schools in the state system as well. There are now some Muslim and Sikh schools and one Hindu (primary) school (Jackson & O'Grady 2007: 187-188). In Norway, some religious schools also exist outside the state system, but only very few, and these are all Christian schools (Skeie 2004).

In comparing these two 'power texts', I have brought out some essential differences between the academic debates in the two countries, and also suggested some reasons for them.[116] Essential controversies are brought out as they are discussed in

---

114 In England, religious schools existed before 1870 when Britain passed its first Education Act. The point of the legislation was to extend education to all, in other words to places where church schools did not provide schooling. Since then, schooling has been a shared project of the state and the Church of England. This is referred to as 'the dual system' (from 1902) (Copley 1997). The purpose of the first school law in Norway in 1739 was to ensure the nurture of children into the state religion (Lutheran Christianity). This remained the main aim of schooling till the mid-1800s, but since then RE in school has been part of an intrinsic education with a broader content (Haraldsø 1989), which is broadly similar to the English situation.
115 The law of dissenters in 1845 allowed other Christian denominations into the kingdom, and from 1851 it became legal for non-Christians to enter.
116 Although I acknowledge fully that explanation for differences in the two countries academic debates are more complex than I am able to illustrate here. For example, the two countries have different, even opposing position with regards to colonial times, where Norway in near past was colonised and therefore had a 'need' for nation building, while in England the past of being a colonial power would give a very different point of departure. Historic research has not been a strong strand in English RE, however the different pasts and differences in *use*

these texts, which can be seen as major texts in each context. For example, their different positions on the question of representing religion as cultural heritage highlight differences in what is dominating the discourses.

It becomes evident that, when Jackson *rethinks*, it is a different tradition that he rethinks: one where contemporary society and its growing plurality have been the centre of attention for RE for a long time, with a stronger studies-of-religions/ social science influence. Gravem can be seen as rooted in a theological tradition, or rather pedagogical Christian education tradition[117], which, until 1997, was dominant in Norway, and which has often been preoccupied with interpreting curricular texts in a historical context. With the 1997 reform, this tradition was severely challenged by plurality as the sociocultural backdrop, and this is the challenge which Gravem addresses in his book. Although his arguments explicitly concerns one particular text, the 1997 KRL curriculum, the issues he discusses continue to be relevant even after the changes to the National Curriculum that has occurred since then. Perhaps it is the case that others have since continued the debate on many of the issues that Gravem raises in this book, and thus contributed to negotiating those issues further.

However, Gravem and Jackson can both be seen as suggesting or pointing out that a change of paradigm is necessary, or has happened. Gravem concludes that KRL (in the 1997 curriculum) must be understood as a new type of RE in Norway, and thus defends the break from the traditions of the Christian school subject. Jackson, from his point of view, concludes that approaches to RE which take account of plurality (as a fact and not as a normative idea) are the ones which are suited for society in the present and the future.

Gravem has a narrower national view compared to Jackson. Even though Jackson also refers to the national context, he does, to a significantly greater degree than Gravem, also report international research, including Norwegian RE research. Gravem, from his point of view, refers back to history and tradition, reflecting the national dimension more in a *Norwegian style*, while Jackson's book, to a greater extent, also reflects a supranational dimension; in this he can be seen to negotiate the *English style* further in a supranational context.

3.6 The supranational dimension in academic debates on RE today

So far in this chapter I have emphasised some core differences, and looked for explanations for these, with the intention of illustrating how shared international challenges are shaped by the national traditions. I have also shown that there are many examples of contact between England and Norway, for example through NE-KRIF.[118] Many impulses have come from English RE into Norwegian RE and also

---

of historic research towards nation building as part of the academic debate about multifaith RE may explain why defending the representation of Christianity as part of a national cultural heritage is seen by some as more justifiable in the Norwegian context.

117 Gravem has a background in teacher training in Hamar, where Engen is based and where there is a certain focus on migration perspectives in pedagogy.

118 For example Winsnes (1988) had international references (including Smart 1968) and Rian (1983) introduced Smart's ideas on the dimensions in religions (see above). Further, at the

vice versa, as for example Jackson (2004a) refers Norwegian research. In this section I will address the supranational dimension directly, drawing attention to how this is shaping developments in each of the countries.

One important example of a supranational process is the *Christianising* of European countries, which, in spite of its common features, has taken different forms in each county. The same is true for the Reformation, the development of European Nation States (see Schiffauer et al. 2004), the European Enlightenment, secularisation, pluralisation and globalisation. In each case, there is also a question of what the term means; 'secularisation', for example (see chapter 2, see also, for example, Davie 2007, Taylor 2007). In this chapter, and in this thesis, the main focus is on pluralisation: what it means and how it has affected English and Norwegian RE. But all those other processes are also present as its context. Religion, the main subject matter in RE, is in itself international and, in addition, there is a general trend in academia that research and academic debates develop more and more as international fields in the face of globalisation.

> *Religion is a very evident factor in international relations and in processes of globalisation and no country can afford to see its educational provision in isolation (Jackson 2004b: 29).*

Both in Norway and in England, RE research has been heavily influenced by the supranational processes of pluralisation, as this chapter has shown. This is not special for the field of pedagogy of RE, but is in line with the general developments in academia including educational research, related both to *formal* and *informal international processes* (see chapter 2). RE research in England has made significant advances since the 1950s, especially through the inclusion of empirical methods, and has in later years developed further through increasing collaboration and international contacts (Jackson 2004b). There is a similar trend in Norway. Here, early theoretical research, which tended to focus on historical issues of relationship between Christianity, state and school, has become more complemented by empirical work and work focusing on practice and on issues of social context and contextuality (for example Leganger-Krogstad (2007), Haakedal (2004), Afdal (2006), Lied, (2004) Breidlied & Nicolaisen (2004)). In Norway, the increased international contact has also been important for the development of the subject.

The special history of the University in Stavanger is interesting in this respect as it used to be a University College which traditionally was a carrier of pedagogical interest in RE outside the theological institutions. It was granted full university status in 2005, and here Professor Geir Skeie has been the key figure in building a research centre for RE based in a Norwegian secular university. Especially important for this development has been the involvement in the international and comparative EU- funded REDCo research project (see chapter 2). But the hiring of the German scholar, Wanda Alberts, for a new position for RE in the Department

---

eve of the introduction of KRL, English scholars were invited to share their experiences at Norwegian conferences. For example, Robert Jackson and Judith Everington from the University of Warwick participated in two conferences prior to the introduction of KRL in 1996, and John Hull from the University of Birmingham was invited to talk about 'Gift to the Child' at one of the first national conferences on KRL in Gran in November 1997.

of Archaeology, History, Cultural Studies and Religion at the University of Bergen, indicates that international processes influence developments in the field of RE nationally.

International inter-exchange of ideas also happen through (increasingly) international channels of publications – for example, the British Journal of Religious Education (BJRE)[119] and Waxmann's book series 'Religious Diversity and Education in Europe' (main editors of the series are Robert Jackson, England, Geir Skeie, Norway, Cock Bakker, The Netherlands, Hans Günter Heimbroch and Wolfram Weisse, Germany)[120] – and also through international networks, seminars and research projects.

I think that the history of the International Seminar on Religious Education and Values (ISREV) deserves special mentioning.[121] In the ISREV context, religious education (and values) is seen to include both teaching in religious contexts, such as church schools or religious state schools (which are common in many countries) and multifaith RE or 'secular' RE. Both Norway and England have active delegations in this network. In recent years there has been a great deal of focus on issues of religious and cultural plurality. There are also other networks of various kinds[122], and the International Association for the History of Religion (IAHR) also has sessions on religious education now (Pye et al. 2006).

In an increasingly internationally developing 'educational market' (Karlsen 2006), PhDs in RE have also become internationalised. For example, Østberg (1998a) is a Norwegian researcher who did an English PhD in the Warwick tradition of ethnographic research, focusing on questions of identity for young Pakistani Muslims in Oslo. I myself and Lars Laird Iversen, both Norwegian, also have submitted PhD theses at Warwick. Kari Flornes from Bergen University College did a PhD at the University of Birmingham (Flornes (2007). Marie von der Lippes' thesis (2011) was part of the international REDCo project and, even if it focused on Norwegian youth, must be seen as part of an international context for research. These PhDs could be included in both English and Norwegian contexts.

Further, Alberts (2007) is a German scholar having compared English and Swedish RE in her thesis, having worked in The Department of Archaeology, History, Cultural Studies and Religion at the University of Bergen, Norway. Comparative studies (such as mine and Alberts') and international and comparative research projects (such as the EC REDCo Project) are characterised by having an interna-

---

119 Jackson has been Editor since 1996. This was formerly a national forum for RE called (up to 1978) Learning for Living, and was partly a publication channel for Shap (Hayward 2009), but it has been developed into an international peer-reviewed research journal.
120 http://www.Waxmann.com/index.php?id=21&L=&cHash=1&tx_p2Waxmann_pi1[reihe]= REI100189 (Accessed 07.01.2013).
121 See http://www.isrev.bham.ac.uk/ (Accessed 06.09.09).
122 Further international networking has gone on, for instance, at the Nordic Conference of Religious Education (NCRE), which also vocationally has had guests and participants from outside the Nordic countries, among them England. There is also a European Network for Religious Education through Contextual Approaches (ENRECA) which was initiated in 1999. It includes researchers from Northern European countries and focuses intercultural issues such as changing patterns of religious and secular plurality in a European context, aiming at policy-makers (Jackson 2004b: 26). Another example is the International Network for interreligious and intercultural Education which was initiated in 1994 and involves researchers from some Northern European countries and South Africa (Jackson 2004b: 26).

tional outlook. These international PhDs and research projects are, in my view, characteristic of the development in the field towards becoming more international with increased networking and cooperation across national borders.

3.7 Summary and conclusion

In this chapter, I have explored the societal level of curriculum comparatively by narrowing this down to a focus on aspects of the academic debate, looking for significant differences and reasons for these differences. I have focused, firstly, on the role of academic disciplines in the development of multifaith approaches to religious education in England and Norway; where I had a special focus on the different roles of 'secular' religious studies in developing pedagogy for multifaith RE, and, secondly, on two books which I see as significant contributions to the academic debates in each national context.

I found that reasons for the different role of academic disciplines should be seen in relation to the different development of the tradition of religions studies, noting that in England religious studies was more closely connected to school RE than in Norway. Also, differences in the school systems are seen as an important source of explanation, especially because the less centralised and less unitary English tradition made it possible for initiatives from certain actors in religious studies to initiate important developments.

In Norway, religious studies has been relatively cut off from contact with school RE for many years, until the effect of the 1997 subject of KRL changed structures and dynamics in academia. The analysis of two 'power texts' showed that Jackson (2004a) and Gravem (2004) both attempt to summarise major debates about multifaith RE in England and Norway respectively at about the same point in time, but on a different basis. I showed the way in which their contributions reflect differences in the traditions of RE research in the two countries. In the last section I have given examples of how the academic study of *pedagogy of RE* today is increasingly international.

I can distinguish between two main sources of explanations for differences, both found in the national dimension (see chapter 2, 5, 8). One comes from inside the domain of RE, and this is the differences in how research traditions for RE have developed in the two countries. The other comes from outside the domain of RE as such, from differences in general school developments. One important factor forming this general school development in both cases has been the nation-specific traditional relationship between religion (Christianity), state and school. This can be seen in terms of traditional religious plurality (England) vs. traditional religious unity (Norway), having a national curriculum vs. the decentralised system for making local RE syllabuses and in the different role of 'secular' religious studies in the two countries. These are seen as major factors in explaining differences in the way that the field of *pedagogy of RE* has been conceptualised and developed.

In the next chapter (4), I will go on to explore the institutional level of curriculum (Goodlad & Su 1992, see chapter 2, 8), in relation to certain key law texts and curricular documents.

4. Institutional Level: Legal and Policy Developments in England and Norway

4.1 Introduction

This chapter explores the theme of *curricular policy*. This relates to the institutional level of curriculum (Goodlad & Su 1992, see chapter 2), which I have interpreted to mean in England the law, the Model Syllabuses (SCAA 1994) and the Non-Statutory National Framework for RE (QCA 2004) which replaced the Model Syllabuses, and local agreed syllabuses.[123] In Norway the institutional level would mainly be the law and the national curriculum for RE, but also local work in schools used to adjust the national curriculum. In England the local production of schemes of work could also be seen as part of the institutional level, or as a structural element in between the institutional and the instructional level. In Norway the parallel to this would have to be textbooks (see chapter 6).

In this chapter I have chosen to compare firstly laws regarding religion and school and, secondly, two representative curricular documents. Of the English documents I have chosen to look at the Non-Statutory National Framework (QCA 2004). In Norway the national curriculum for RE has changed frequently in recent years[124] and for this chapter I have chosen to look at the one from 2005: *The KRL book 2005: Knowledge of Christianity- religions- and philosophies of life: Curriculum for 1st – 10th grade: Curriculum-guidance and information* (UD 2005).[125]

My research questions will be covered in two main sections – on law and policy – and are as follows: What similarities and differences exist between English and Norwegian laws concerning religion and school? How do we account for these? What are the main similarities and differences in English and Norwegian policy as expressed in QCA 2004 and UD 2005? How do we account for these?

4.2 The Legal Framework

In this section I will compare laws regulating RE in state schools. I will examine what the law says about how religion and life views should be presented in state schools and laws regulating the right to opt out. Attention will also be given to laws which regard religion and schools in general, specified in England as laws regard-

---

123 Local agreed syllabuses are legally binding; the QCA 2004 is not and was originally directed at agreed syllabus conferences. However, it is now being used much more widely as a kind of position statement; see http://www.qcda.gov.uk/libraryAssets/media/9817_re_national_framework_04.pdf (Accessed 09.08.09).
124 1997, 2002, 2005 and 2008.
125 In original Norwegian language: 'KRL-boka 2005. Kristendoms-, religions- og livssynskunnskap, Læreplan for 1. – 10. årstrinn: Læreplanveiledning og informasjon.' In an English version of the Norwegian Education" Act it is translated "Christian Knowledge and Religious and Ethical Education, but I find that this translation has a different meaning than the much discussed Norwegian name for the subject. Lovdata: http://www.ub.uio.no/ujur/ulovdata/lov-19980717-061-eng.pdf (Accessed 05.02.09).

ing collective worship and in Norway as the school law preamble which until 2008 made Christian nurture the central object of schooling as such in Norway.[126]

4.3 Laws regulating RE in state schools

Laws relevant to RE have been made in England since the first Education Act of 1870. However, I will concentrate on legislation that relates to the present situation for RE in England, namely the 1988 Education Reform Act. In England it is stated in this Act of 1988 that all maintained schools should offer Religious Education. Every Local Educational Authority (LEA)/ Local Authority (LA) since 2007 is obliged to convene an agreed syllabus conference that must produce a local agreed syllabus (LAS) that shall be used in that area.[127] These syllabuses must be non-denominational and, according to the Education Act 1988, section 8.3, 'reflect the fact that the religious traditions in Great Britain are in the main Christian whilst taking account of the teachings and practices of the other principal religions represented in Great Britain[128].

It is interesting to note that the Act refers to Christian *traditions* in the plural (see chapter 3). It clearly gives Christianity priority over 'other' religions. Reasons for this have to do with the strong tradition of Christianity historically and still today in British society. There is no mention or reference in the text of the law to non-religious life views or a humanist tradition. Strictly speaking, the law excludes them, since the subject is *religious* education and, by legal precedent, humanism in English law is not regarded as a religion.[129] However, 'other' principal *religions* in Great Britain *should* also be taught – an innovation in the 1988 Act.

Guidance on the interpretation of the Education Reform Act of 1988, section 8.3, is found in Department for Education (DEF) Circular 1/94. Here the following is mentioned as aims for RE:

> *To develop pupils' knowledge, understanding and awareness of Christianity, as the predominant religion in Great Britain, and the other principal religions represented in the country; to encourage respect for those holding different beliefs; and to help promote pupils' spiritual, moral, cultural and mental development* (Copley 1997: 175).

The circular says 'to encourage *respect*' for those holding different beliefs, so this is an interpretation of what the law indicates when it says to 'take account of the fact' that there are other religions in Britain. It states that it is up to the agreed syllabus conferences to decide how many religions should be taught in depth at each

---

126 The laws statement that this should be in cooperation with the home has been emphasised.
127 The tradition of agreed syllabuses goes back much further. See, for example, Copley (1997) and Jackson and O'Grady (2007)
128 http://www.opsi.gov.uk/acts/acts1988/Ukpga_19880040_2htm (Accessed 25.10.2005).
129 The Birmingham 1975 syllabus, which was the first multifaith RE syllabus in England (see chapter 3) first included humanism on equal terms as religions, but when it was tried legally it was a juridical decision that humanism could only be included to inform knowledge about religion, and that RE meant the subject matter was *religion* (Haakedal 1983: 46).

key stage. When deciding the balance between Christianity and other religions, the conferences should consider both the national and local position of the religions, the age and background of the pupils, the wish of parents and governors, and to make decisions that minimise the number of parents who might withdraw their children. These 'other' religions were interpreted in the Model Syllabuses (SCAA[130] 1994a-d) to be Judaism, Islam, Hinduism, Buddhism and Sikhism, and these are the religions that tend to be included in most local agreed syllabuses.[131]

The law also requires that any LEA (LA) must have a Standing Advisory Council for Religious Education (SACRE). The SACRE has the right and duty to advise LEAs (LAs) regarding RE and to review the syllabuses regularly, at least every five years. Nothing specifically on RE has changed in law since the Education Act of 1988, but renewal is embedded in the system of the regular revision of local agreed syllabuses. RE continues to have a special status as statutory, though outside the national curriculum, but it might be said to have taken a step towards the same kinds of standardisation as the other curricular subjects with QCA 2005 (see below).

Norwegian RE is regulated by § 2-4 of the Norwegian Education Act. A law concerning the subject of KRL[132] was first included in connection with the introduction of multifaith RE in the education reform of 1997. This law was changed in 2002 when the KRL curriculum was being revised, and again in 2005, this time answering to critique of KRL given by the UN's Human Rights Committee. The latest change was carried out in 2008 following a verdict in the European Court of Human Rights in Strasbourg (see below).

In the 2002 document, § 2-4 from the 1997 law was unchanged except for the name of the subject, but only in such a way that the abbreviation KRL could be kept. The exact text of the law was quoted in the text of the curriculum, which was new in relation to the 1997 curriculum (see the exact wording of the law text in 1997 and 2002 in appendix 2). In 2005 the wording of the law was changed again:

'Teaching in the subject Knowledge of Christianity, Religions and Life views shall:

- *provide a thorough knowledge of the Bible and Christianity as cultural heritage*
- *provide a thorough knowledge of Evangelical-Lutheran faith and other Christian denominations*
- *provide knowledge of other world religions and philosophies of life*
- *provide knowledge of ethical and philosophical topics*
- *promote understanding and respect for Christian and humanist values*
- *promote understanding and respect and the ability to carry out a dialogue between people with different views concerning beliefs and philosophies of life*

---

130 The School Curriculum and Assessment Authority, later replaced by the Qualifications and Curriculum Authority (QCA).
131 They are also the religions identified by the Department for Children, Schools and Families (DCSF) for the research study of materials being used in RE conducted by the University of Warwick, http://www2.warwick.ac.uk/fac/soc/wie/research/centres/wreru/.
132 'Christianity with orientation about Religions and Life views' (KUF 1996), see chapter 1.

> *Knowledge of Christianity, Religions and Life views is an ordinary school subject that shall normally be attended by all pupils. Teaching in the subject should not involve preaching.*
> *Teachers of Knowledge of Christianity, Religions and Life views shall present Christianity, other religions and philosophies of life on the basis of their distinctive characteristics. Teaching of the different topics shall be founded on the same educational principles.*'[133]

The word 'thorough' was kept for the first bullet point after the changes in 2005. According to the UD 2005 (p. 26), this is not to be understood as a qualitative difference, but merely a quantitative difference which is justified by the relatively greater importance of the Christian tradition in Norway. The judgement in the European Court of Human Rights in Strasbourg in 2007 concerned the 1997 law and curriculum. Despite the changes in 2002 and 2005, the political leadership and central administration decided that the critique was of such a character that a further adjustment was needed.[134] A central symbolic act was to remove the special mention of Christianity in the name of the subject. After 10 years of KRL[135], it was now changed to Religion, Life views and Ethics (RLE).[136] The emphasis put on Christianity through the use of the words *thorough knowledge* as opposed to just *knowledge* of other religions and life views, was removed.

In the 1997 version of the Norwegian law the point that this subject should contribute to knowledge of different religions and life views, respect those holding different views and develop ability to dialogue, was already clear. The aims for RE in state schools changed quite dramatically in 1997: from the traditional aims of the teaching of Christianity to a multifaith type of RE. The rationale for the change was that school RE should reflect contemporary Norway as a multicultural and multireligious society (see for example NOU 1995: 9, Skeie 1998: 3, 2007: 223, Gravem 2004: 17ff, Lied 2004: 20). Through changes since, the emphasis on the multicultural context has been enhanced. From emphasising Christianity, and especially the Norwegian Lutheran tradition, more in the earlier versions, greater equal treatment of different religions and life views is stressed increasingly through these changes in the law. The point that the aim of this subject is to contribute to social cohesion through educating citizens of a plural society about each other's faiths – and even to give them the ability to take part in dialogue – has been emphasised and made clearer through the changes.

---

[133] http://www.lovdata.no/all/tl-19980717-061-002.html#2-4 (Accessed 11.12.07).
[134] http://www.regjeringen.no/upload/KD/Hoeringsdok/2007/200706054/Hoeringsnotat_om_religion_livssyn_etikk.pdf, (Accessed 11.12.07), p. 5.
[135] Although the name was changed in 2002, it was changed in such a way that the abbreviation could be kept, see chapter 1.
[136] In 2008 the name change from Knowledge of Christianity, religion and life views (KRL) to Knowledge of Religions, life views and ethics (RLE) was perceived by many teachers and general opinion as a real shift to a more neutral subject. Even the content was only modified and little changed.

4.4 Laws regulating the right to opt out

In England, according to the Education reform Act 1988 section 9.3, on parents' request a child has the right to be wholly or partly excused from RE. The right to opt out dates back to 1870 and the first Education Act in Great Britain's history (Copley 1997: 30). Some would argue that the opt out clause is an anachronism, but no one has yet suggested removing it (Copley 1997: 206-208). It does provide a safeguard against discrimination. This point is also recognised in the *Toledo Guiding Principles* (OSCE 2007: 70, see below).

Further, it is important to consider the many types of schools which exist in England. For example, parents could opt for a private school or a state maintained school with a religious character, such as a voluntary aided school.[137] Changing the right to withdraw would therefore not really be very meaningful within this system. It is a goal that most pupils shall attend RE, and even though there have historically been a few instances of mass withdrawals (Copley 1997: 207), this is not a major problem.

In English community schools, RE is not meant to contribute to any generic formation, not meant to give *all* pupils a common frame of reference in the same manner as in Norway. Even so, it is a goal that as many as possible participate and also that RE should contribute to Citizenship Education (Jackson 2003). The aim of promoting respect and tolerance then refers to those (in practice their parents) who choose to participate. In an English context the point that it should be the same for all is less important than protecting the individual's rights. This must be considered in the context of the English educational system being evolutionary, where every development builds on a historically evolving antecedent.

Prior to 1988, the right to opt out tacitly regarded what was then called Religious Instruction (RI) as having a Protestant emphasis, that was likely to be objected to by Catholics and Jews, for instance. After 1988, community schools (fully state-funded schools) got Religious Education (RE) with no nurturing goals, but the same right to withdraw was maintained. Its deep roots in the system seem to have given the opt out right a 'taken-for-granted-ness': which is interesting in this comparative context, since the opposite seems to be the case in Norway.

In Norway it is not possible to be excused (exempted) from the content of the teaching, i.e. from learning any of the content. The main argument is that school RE since 1997 is (formally) an ordinary school subject where the content is knowledge about religion. One can, however, still be partly excused from the subject, from *activities* that a pupil or her parents perceive as being practice of another religion or philosophy of life. This may apply to activities either inside or outside the classroom (see for example Kirke-, utdannings- og forskningsdepartementet (KUF) 1998).

---

137 At the time of writing, the four main types of state schools are: Community schools, Voluntary Controlled schools, Voluntary Aided Schools and Foundation schools and in addition a number of independent schools, see http://www.inca.org.uk/england-system-mainstream.html. The support of schools with a religious character within the state system is disputed in England; see for example Jackson (2004: 39-57).

4.5 The Norwegian law suits

The State of Norway was sued by a group of parents with the demand to be granted full rights to be exempted from KRL. The State of Norway was found not guilty at all levels of the Norwegian legal system, including a judgement in the Norwegian High Court (Norges Høyesterett 2001)[138]. The parent group went on to appeal to the UN Human Rights Committee and the Human Rights Court in Strasbourg. On the 3rd November 2004, the UN Human Rights Committee gave a judgement that KRL was in violation of the UN convention on Civil and Political Rights, Article 18.[139] This concerns parents' rights to provide for their children's religious and moral upbringing. This committee then went on to say that it would not be in violation of this convention had the teaching been done in a neutral and objective way, as intended in the law (Høstmælingen 2005).

However, the committee claimed that, even in theory, the right of exemption from certain parts of the subject laid an unreasonable burden on parents in terms of knowing what part of the teaching to ask their children to be exempted from. It also said they found the reference to the school law preamble 'formålsparagrafen', Section 1-2, which makes Christian nurture the central object of schooling, problematic (see appendix 2). In practice the committee found that the subject's educational and proselytizing parts were so intertwined that the arrangements for exemption were impractical (Høstmælingen 2005). Interestingly, it is not the curriculum itself which is explicitly criticised, but the practice of the subject, its association with the Christian object clause and the limited right to opt out. Still, the most immediate means to correct the situation was to launch a new curriculum for the subject.

Following this judgement, for a few months in spring/ summer 2005, there was a general right to opt out. However, when UD 2005 was launched ahead of its schedule as a response to the judgement by the UN Human Rights Committee, the general right to opt out was withdrawn. The limited right to withdrawal was reinserted (UD 2005: 52). In UD 2005 it is even more strongly emphasised that KRL is just another school subject, that no preaching is allowed, that it should be learning *about* religion, that schools should seek to avoid methods and activities in teaching that could be perceived by some as practising religion and that all teaching should be conducted in close cooperation with families. A reference to the preamble in the subject syllabus for KRL was removed, but it still applied to KRL (in the same manner as it did to all subjects).

The section concerning the right to limited exemption was made into a separate section of the law, Section 2-3a. The right to be excused from activities that may be perceived as religious now formally concerns school activities in general, and not activities in RE per se.

---

138 Norges Høyesterett 2001: Dom 22. august 2001 I sak nr. 2000/1533, sivil sak, anke, Humanetisk Forbund m.fl. mot Staten v/ Kirke-, utdannings og forskningsdepartementet. (Norwegian High Court 2001: Sentence 22nd August 2001 in case nr. 2000/1533, civil case, appeal, the Humanist Organisation and others versus the State by the Department for Church, education and research.

139 http://www.regjeringen.no/nb/dokumentarkiv/Regjeringen-Bondevik-II/ufd/233191/251920/Human-Rights-Committee-Communication-No-11552003.html?id=422478 (Accessed 27.01.09).

4.6 Religion in laws regarding schooling in general

In England, in the Education Reform Act 1988, there are two elements under the heading 'Religious education': the first is Collective Worship, section 6.1 ff., and the second is Religious Education, according to local agreed syllabuses (see above). Again, this follows historical precedent. In the 1944 Education Act, RE consisted of Religious Instruction (RI) and collective worship. The term RE became used from the late 60s to refer to the subject only, and came to mean teaching about, and perhaps also learning from, religions, but this was not a legal usage. 1988 was the first time that the term RE had been used in law more or less as it had been used in the profession. Collective Worship was now seen as a separate thing, but it was not removed despite a strong debate (Hull 1989: 15ff).

The part about Collective Worship states that any school is obliged to hold a daily act of worship, described as *collective* worship, that according to section 7.1 'shall be wholly or mainly of a broadly Christian character'. In section 7.2 it is explained that the act of worship is of 'a broadly Christian character (...) if it reflects the broad traditions of Christian belief without being distinctive of any particular Christian denomination'.

Hull (1989) has demonstrated how problematic it would be to know how to do this with enough sensibility of pupils' different backgrounds in a multifaith school and society. In a sense, it is an attempt to maintain a generalised non-denominational Christianity which can only be found in school, a school religion which has the characteristics of civil religion (Bellah 1970, Bellah & Hammond 1980, Davie 1994, 2007, see below). The right to opt out relates to both collective worship and education, meaning that you can opt out of one, but go to the other.

In Norway, section 1-2 of the Norwegian Education Act is the school law preamble, called 'formålsparagrafen': ('Christian object/purpose clause'). Until 2008 it stated the following about the object/ purpose of school education (as such):

> *The object of primary and lower secondary education shall be, in agreement and cooperation with the home, to help to give pupils a Christian and moral upbringing, to develop their mental and physical abilities, and to give them good general knowledge so that they may become useful and independent human beings at home and in society.* (See appendix 2 for the full text.)

This concerns education in Norway in general, and not RE particularly. Prior to the changes in the RE curriculum in 2005 there was a specific reference to this section. This reference was taken out of the text when it was revised in 2005 in order to answer to the statement from the UN's Human Rights Committee. I cannot see that this is a very significant change since it still does concern KRL (see also Høstmælingen 2005: 245).

It is especially the formulation 'to help give pupils a Christian and moral upbringing' which is controversial in relation to a school which is now multicultural, and in relation to the question of whether KRL can be called an inclusive school subject. The explanation given in UD 2005 (p. 26), is that this must be seen in relation to the first part of the sentence: 'in agreement and cooperation with the home'.

If the home does not give the school the mandate, the school shall not give the pupil a Christian upbringing. This interpretation was emphasised in the sentence in the Norwegian High Court which ruled that KRL was not in violation with Human Rights (Gravem 2004: 220, Norges Høyesterett (Norwegian High Court) 2001: 22-24).

Many considered this school law preamble to be an anachronism, out of touch with the general development in Norwegian education and the new KRL subject especially. The conservative Bondevik government (2002-2006) was unwilling to touch it, but the labour/ socialist Stoltenberg government (2006 – 2009) initiated a change. The Bolstad committee ('Bolstadutvalget') reviewed the preamble of the school law and suggested that it should be changed.

Their suggestion was printed in NOU 2007: 6 Formål for framtida: Formål for barnehagen og opplæringen: Purpose/ object for the future: purpose/ object of kindergarten and education (see the full text of their suggestion in appendix 2). In passing through parliament, the wording was changed in the direction of emphasising the cultural heritage more and keeping the traditional emphasis on the rights of parents. The emphasis in the suggestion from the Bolstad committee on the new plurality of society might be seen as somewhat weakened in the version that was finally passed in parliament. Still, it was a significant change from the former preamble (see the text as it was passed in the parliament in appendix 2).

Up until 2008, however, formally the overall purpose of education in Norway was to assist parents in giving their children a Christian and moral upbringing. Due to this school law preamble, the connection between state religion and state school has been quite explicit in Norway. The ordinary school subject KRL was bound by this in the same manner as other subjects, but it is difficult to imagine that this should not affect this particular subject more than mathematics, for instance. Also, the quantitative difference that 55% of the time was to be linked to Christianity, according to UD 2005, underlined the link between school and the traditional religion of the country.

4.7 Comparative discussion on legal issues

In both countries the right to receive religious education is determined by law. The basic principles for religious education in state schools are enshrined in the law which in both cases also states that religious education should reflect both Christianity and other religions. The Norwegian law is more detailed than the English regarding the content of the teaching. The English law gives LEAs/LAs the right and obligation to produce locally agreed syllabuses, while the Norwegian law refers to a central National Curriculum. The Norwegian law stresses the importance of the European humanist tradition whilst there is no reference to this in the English law.

The way RE is treated in law reflects the history of Church and state in both countries, as well as traditional cultural differences between Norway and England, differences in the makeup of civil religion, in the legal systems and in the school systems. In England, the law on this topic has remained relatively stable. The English law *specifically on RE* has not changed since 1988[140], even if there has been a significant amount of educational legislation since 1988, from both conservative and labour governments (see for example Jackson 2004a: 39ff, Copley 1997: 153ff). However, the system is flexible and systematic reviewing of curricula is a part of the system and regulated in the law, Section 14.3a. The details of the content of the teaching are to a great extent decided locally with the locally agreed syllabuses.

By contrast, in Norway the law has been changed frequently, and the content of RE syllabuses has to a great extent been decided nationally, even if UD 2005 represents a shift towards emphasising local adjustment of the National Curricula. The Norwegian law was changed in 1997, 2002, 2005 and in 2008. The basic principles are, however, the same as in 1997, although the law has been adjusted to make sure it is not in violation of Human Rights conventions. This has moved the aims of RE in Norwegian legislation more in the direction of emphasising its contribution to intercultural education.

The traditional aim of educating into the Christian religion had already been removed from the law in 1969 and, in 1997, teaching about other religions in addition to Christianity was dramatically strengthened. Nevertheless, developments since 1997 reflect a recurring need for strengthening the point that RE in state schools is not about proselytising. It could appear that this has still not been removed from how RE is perceived, or perhaps practised (see chapters 3, 6 and 7). In England, developments in the subject cannot be traced in changes to the law in a similar way. Changes like the ones traceable in the Norwegian law must be sought in non-statutory advice, such as that contained in the Model Syllabuses (SCAA 1994) and the Non-Statutory National Framework (QCA 2004), and in developments in interpretations of the law in local agreed syllabuses (which are statutory documents).

While, on the Norwegian scene, the changes reflect a conflict that has been ongoing both in the Norwegian jurisdiction and in international juridical institutions, there is less juridical conflict on the English side.[141] In a comparative perspective this might at first glance seem odd since the English law introducing a religiously pluralistic form of RE dates back to 1988. This can be explained historically and in relation to the evolution of the English educational system, and the 1988 Act builds very clearly on the 1944 Act (Jackson 2004a: 39ff).

Until 1988, no specific religion was mentioned in law: it was largely understood that Christianity was the one. However, since 1988 it became necessary to specify in more detail which religions applied to RE. Religions other than Christianity were first actually named in the non-statutory model syllabuses of 1994. However, in comparing actual documents it can be seen that the wording of the current English law is more similar to the 1997 version rather than later Norwegian legislation (§ 2-4). In both cases, Christianity is mentioned specifically and the other religions remain unspecified as 'others'.

---

140 Except what specifically relates to voluntary aided schools, where the 1996 Act made it possible to have a wider range of such schools see Jackson 2004a: 39ff.
141 There was a legal case in connection to the Birmingham 1975 syllabus, but it was never subject to any international legal judgement.

As a reason for the difference in conflict level I see, firstly, the difference in the right to withdraw. In England, such a right exists and has existed since the first education act in 1870 (Jackson 2004a: 39), while in Norway up until 1889 and again, since 1997, there has been no such right (Haraldsø 1989, Østberg 1998a: 26, Sandvik 1996: 39). The right partly to be exempted from certain activities, not from the content of learning, since 1997 concerns school activities in general, and not just RE. This point was already made clear in a 1998 circular in (KUF) 1998, and clearer when the rules of exemption were made into a separate paragraph in law[142] and was no longer a part of the law regulating RE (§ 2-4). One might say therefore that, in Norway, receiving RE is both a right and an obligation, while in England it is just a right.

There has been less government attention to this problem in England, despite the fact that there were organised withdrawals of Muslim children in some Northern towns, for example in Kirklees in the area of Yorkshire in Northern England and in Birmingham (see Hull 1998), while in the Norwegian context there has been a lot of 'noise' and strong uneasiness from some parties regarding the lack of the right to withdraw. Here, too, there has actually been only a small number of complaints.

In the Toledo Guiding Principles (OSCE 2007: 68-75) there are references to the case of Folgerø vs. Norway in the European court of Human Rights and a similar case concerning Turkish RE, Zenging vs. Turkey. In the Toledo Guiding Principles it is emphasised that the right to withdraw must be practical. They also stress the importance of the teaching being carried out in a neutral and objective way so as not to violate Human Rights, but remark that, in a strict sense, no teaching in any subject can be absolutely neutral. Even if it could be argued that, ideally, the opt out right should be abandoned, in practice it is important to keep it as a safety valve against violations of human rights.

Historical religious conflicts have forced England to have liberal legislation on this point. The Church of England is the *established* church, but other Christian traditions, such as Catholicism and the non-conformist churches, especially Methodism, have strong traditions in the country. In a sense, England has traditionally been religiously plural, and religious education in schools has reflected this. Even when it was Christian Instruction it was non-denominational, at least in theory, although it was perhaps a 'protestant' non-denominational RE reflecting an English type of civil religion (Bellah 1970, 1980, Davie 1994, 2007).[143]

---

142 Lov om grunnskolen og den vidaregåande opplæringa § 2-3a *Fritak frå aktivitetar I opplæringa.* http://www.lovdata.no/cgi-wift/wiftldles?doc=/usr/www/lovdata/all/tl-19980717-061-002.html&emne=lov*%20om*%20grunnskol*&& (Accessed 12.02.09).

143 The concept *civil religion* originates with Rousseau, but is developed by the American sociologist R. Bellah (for example 1970, 1980) to help understand the role of religion in American public life. Bellah is also influenced by Durkheim and Parsons and his concern is describing the non-institutional dimensions of religiosity (Davie 2007: 42, Davie 1994: 74). The concept 'civil religion' refers to features that bind Americans together, for example, while at the same time hold back from giving explicit privileges to a single church denomination, which would be against the American constitution. Davie (1994) distinguishes between features of civil religion originating explicitly from religion, and other features, such as the role of the Monarchy in Britain. Predominant among these features are, however, allusions to a

In Norway, there is a closer link between state and church. The Church of Norway was still a state church until 2012. The tradition of the Church of Norway has been very dominant in the Norwegian society since the Reformation. Only from 1845 did the law allow other *Christian* faiths in the kingdom, and eventually religious freedom developed (Haraldsø 1989, Sandvik 1996). However, it is still the case that no other religions or denominations have a *strong* tradition in the country. In Norway, religious freedom has in part come about through a fight by some to be non-religious, hence the emphasis on the humanist tradition (Østberg 1998a: 26). Davie (1994, 2007: 197) characterises civil religion in Britain as believing without belonging while religion in the Nordic countries as belonging without believing (Davie 2007: 141). In other words, historical contextual circumstances relating to the national dimension on Dale's (2006) scale makes for different characteristics of civil religion (see chapter 2).

Secondly, as a reason for more juridical conflict in Norway compared to England, I think the Norwegian history of there being two subjects is important. This relates to the nationally specific historical circumstances of Norway, and lacks a parallel on the English side. Prior to 1997, as an alternative to Christian Knowledge, one could opt for 'Knowledge of worldviews' (Østberg 1998a: 26). This alternative subject was initiated and developed by the Norwegian Humanist Association (HEF) and resulted from a long battle for freedom of (or from) religion in Norway (see for example Sandvik 1996). I think the sense of losing this subject might be a factor which helps to explain this conflict. Although it might seem fair to say that both the Christians and the secular Humanists lost their subject in favour of a common subject in 1997 (see chapter 3), the Norwegian Humanist Association has persistently claimed that the subject of KRL is discriminatory (see for example Hylland Eriksen 1996). After losing legal cases at all levels of the Norwegian system, two international legal institutions supported their claims. Despite the intention that KRL is meant to be an inclusive subject for different religious and non-religious people, the dominant role of Christianity is perceived as problematic.[144]

Thirdly, as a reason for less legal conflict in England compared to Norway, I see the presence of schools with a religious character within the state system in England (for example voluntary aided schools)[145] and in the independent sector as an important factor. In my view, this makes the non-confessional RE in English state schools easier to accept. One could always opt for a state or private school according to one's own religious preferences. This works in the case of Catholic education, but there is often much competition for places at Church of England schools, which operate usually as 'neighbourhood schools' and many parents cannot afford independent education. On the Norwegian side, no state schools have a religious character, private schools are mainly established based on religious

---

shared Judaeo-Christian heritage, emphasising commonalities rather than difference (Davie 2007: 154).

144 KRL/ RLE is still not perceived by some secular humanists as being sufficiently neutral for all to accept.

145 Still, however, religious schools within the state system are a contentious topic in England. There is now a pressure group, 'Accord', against state-funded religious schools, which includes many religious people and humanists: the driving force is the education officer of the British Humanist Association (http://www.humanism.org.uk/news/view/120).

grounds, but are rare (taking only about 2% of school children: Skeie 2007: 224) and only include Christian schools. Because of this, RE in Norwegian state schools could be seen as really meant to include *all*. Not granting a general opt out right, the Norwegian system therefore lacks the safety valve that the Toledo Guiding Principles recommend (OSCE 2007: 70) whilst England retains this safety valve.

The English tradition of collective worship and the Norwegian school law preamble 'Christian object/ purpose clause' are both elements that establish a link between the state school and the traditional religion of the country, or the nation-specific civil religion. In both countries civil religion could be described as dominated by a nation-specific brand of Christianity, expressed partly through the relationships between state and church. Both are generally seen as distinct from RE, but in both cases it could be argued that there is a connection. In the English case, the connection can be traced through the various Education Acts. In Norway, it was in KRL that the topic Christianity was taught explicitly. In addition to Christianity being the main object of teaching in the RE classes both in England and Norway, these parts of the law raise the question as to whether English and Norwegian state schools can be seen as belonging to either religious or secular spheres.

Habermas (2006) challenged the simple distinction between secular and religious spheres: as opposed to the formal public/ political sphere, the informal public/ political sphere is seen as an appropriate setting for communication between religious and non-religious people. The state school is considered such an informal public/ political sphere, and this makes school a category transcending the clear distinction between secular and religious, and consequently it can be seen as place for dialogue between religious and non-religious people (see also Jackson 2008a).

Both in English RE and Norwegian RE there are some tensions between – on the one hand – traditional religion or religion as cultural heritage (Jackson 2004a), or traditional religion as part of the *national imaginary* (Schiffauer et al. 2004), or civil religion (Bellah 1970, 1980, Davie 1994, 2007), or generalised values (Bø 2006: 116)[146] and – on the other hand – the plurality of society that multifaith RE is also meant to reflect (Skeie 1998, Jackson 2004a, Skeie 2006b). In both English and Norwegian RE there is a clear difference between Christian traditions and the sometimes unspecified 'other' religions and life views. We have seen this both in the academic discourse (see chapter 3) and in some policy documents.

There is a danger that those who belong to 'other' religions or have no religious beliefs are somehow 'others' which is not helpful for integration. The issue of what is the basis of shared values is not straightforward in a multicultural society. The development in both countries shows how the *national imaginaries* are negotiated to become more pluralistic: reflecting historical developments towards more multicultural and multireligious societies. But perhaps these are negotiated on the basis of 'sameness' in light of Norwegian history and the unitary school ideology, while it is negotiated on the basis of 'difference' in light of English history and absence of unitary school ideology (see chapter 3, 6).

---

146 Refers to Parsons (see chapter 4).

4.8 Introducing QCA 2004 and UD 2005

In addition to comparing legal issues (above), I have chosen to do an explicit comparison of two documents: The *Non-Statutory National Framework for Religious Education* was published in England (QCA 2004), and *The KRL book 2005: Knowledge of Christianity- religions- and philosophies of life: Curriculum for 1st – 10th grade: Curriculum-guidance and information* was published in Norway (UD 2005). In this section I will compare these two distinctive and influential documents. Both relate to specific issues in RE, but can also be seen as indicators of more general issues in the debates about RE.

In England, the *Non-Statutory National Framework for RE* (QCA 2004) follows in the tradition of the 1994 Model Syllabuses in that it offers advice to agreed syllabus conferences. However, its function is more than this. For some time there has been a debate over whether religious education should be a national curriculum subject like other school subjects. The 'national framework' has been used by the lobby supporting the idea of a national syllabus, and indeed has been used by teacher trainers and publishers as an indicator of current trends in the subject. It is thus a 'landmark' document. The English law did not change in connection to the non-statutory national framework (see above).

In Autumn 2004 and at the same time as the new non-statutory national framework for Religious Education was launched in England, a new revision of the Norwegian RE curriculum was being written. Normally all subjects' curricula are renewed simultaneously in connection with a reform. Since 1997, however, there have been three exemptions to this in relation to RE. Firstly, KRL was renewed after evaluation research following the implementation of KRL, and *KRL-boka*[147] Læringssenteret (LS) 2002 reflecting this evaluation replaced the KRL curriculum from 1997. Since it came as a separate subject revision, it was published as a separate document. Secondly, in 2005, *The KRL book 2005: Knowledge of Christianity- religions- and philosophies of life: Curriculum for 1st – 10th grade: Curriculum-guidance and information* (UD 2005) was published and implemented as part of the national curriculum: replacing the previous curriculum for KRL from 2002 (LS 2002). This was also published as a separate document.[148]

In 2005 the Ministry of Knowledge[149] was preparing a total revision of the entire National Curriculum, meaning new curricula for all school subjects with a new structure compared to earlier National Curricula.[150] The plan was to implement this

---

147 Knowledge of Christianity-, religions- and philosophy of Life: Curriculum for the 10 year long 'grunnskole' (elementary and lower secondary school, see chapter 5): Curriculum guidance, Circulars, Information to parents; Norwegian: KRL- boka: Kristendoms-, religions-, og livssynskunnskap: Læreplanveiledning: Rundskriv: Informasjon til foreldre.
148 The third exemption was the revision in 2008, following the verdict in the European Court of Human Rights in Strasbourg, when the name was changed to RLE: (see above, see also chapter 1). In this chapter I have chosen to do the comparison based on the UD 2005.
149 Norwegian: 'Kunnskapsdepartementet': Now named 'Utdannings- og forskningsdepartementet': Ministry of Education and Research (2009).
150 For the first time in Norway a curriculum document included *5 basic skills* ('grunnleggende ferdigheter') which should be obtained across the curriculum. Central to this reform was a change in Norwegian Educational policy from content-based curricula to aims formulated as *competence targets* ('kompetansemål'). The reform, named 'Knowledge Promotion' (Kunn-

reform in 2006. When, in the Autumn of 2004, a statement was made by the UN's Human Rights Committee that KRL was in violation of article 18, nr. 4 of the convention for civil and political rights (see above)[151], the work towards a new curriculum for KRL reflecting a response to this critique was speeded up. In the spring of 2005, UD 2005 was launched a year ahead of the rest of the reformed curriculum, and hastily implemented from the autumn of 2005. Having already this new structure that was to come with the 2006 reform 'Knowledge Promotion', KRL was for one year in the special position of being formally part of the 'old' national curriculum, but having the same structure as the new national curriculum, and could therefore also be seen as part of this. As a part of the Norwegian National Curriculum it was a legally binding document which textbook publishers, educators and teachers referred to regarding what RE in school should be like.

Illustration 1: Front page of The Non-Statutory National Framework for Religious Education (QCA 2004), and front page of The KRL book 2005: *Knowledge of Christianity- religions- and philosophies of life: Curriculum for 1st – 10th grade: Curriculum-guidance and information* (UD 2005).

4.9 QCA 2004

The official title of the English document is 'Religious Education: The Non-Statutory National Framework'. The name of the Government department respon-

---

skapsløftet) was meant to meet international challenges to the educational sector. Karlsen (2006: 27) characterises it as being part of a chain of reforms through which the Norwegian Educational system was adjusted to international trends and standards.

151 http://www.regjeringen.no/nb/dokumentarkiv/Regjeringen-Bondevik-II/ufd/233191/251920/Human-Rights-Committee-Communication-No-11552003.html?id=422478 (Accessed 27.01.09).

sible was the 'Department for Education and Skills'.[152] The slogan of the department is printed on the cover: 'creating opportunity, releasing potential, achieving excellence'. The religions of Christianity, Judaism, Islam, Hinduism, Buddhism and Sikhism are represented on the cover by their symbols. These are traditionally the religions which are included in the English context.[153] The publication has 50 pages, and the layout is in sky-blue (azure) and white.

Pages 6-7 are illustrative pages held in an opposite layout with white print on blue pages. They illustrate in an ideal way the intentions of RE according to this document. On top of page 6 there is a picture of pupils spelling the word 'peace' with their bodies. On page 7 there are two pictures, one of a group of ethnically diverse-looking pupils and the other of a jigsaw of seven pieces, one for each of the six religions together with their symbols, and a centrepiece with the text 'harmony linking all separate religions'. On these pages are also seven quotes from students showing in an exemplary way how RE ideally should work. For example Frances, aged 15, says:

> *In my RE lessons I have learned to become more broad-minded, to accept other people's beliefs and faiths and to not let race or religion come in the way of what you see in an individual. What I like about my RE lessons is that my opinion is heard and I can find out what my fellow students' opinions are.*

On the top of page 7 is a small text under the heading: 'The importance of religious education'. The main points here are that RE should provoke challenging questions about the ultimate meaning and purpose of life, issues of right and wrong, develop knowledge and understanding of Christianity and other religious traditions, challenge pupils to learn from the religions, and explore their own beliefs and questions of meaning, to develop their sense of identity and belonging, and develop respect for others and enable pupils to combat prejudice.

A relatively extensive section is called 'About Religious Education in the curriculum' (p. 8-18). This includes a number of structural elements which in effect also gives some information about the content of the subject. The main headings are:

- *The contribution of religious education' (p. 8): to support the values of the curriculum; truth, justice, respect for all and care for the environment, to support the aims of the curriculum like for instance to contribute to spiritual, moral, social and cultural development.*

---

152 In 2007 this was changed to the Department for Children, Schools and Families (DCSF), and changed again 2010 to 'Department for Education'.
153 The same religions were mentioned in the 1994 Model Syllabuses and arguably correspond to the main religions represented in Britain (although Zoroastrians/Parsis and Bahais might disagree). W. Owen Cole wrote an influential RE text called *Five Religions in the Twentieth Century*' which then had Buddhism – written by Peggy Morgan – added to it thus becoming *Six Religions in the Twentieth Century* (Cole 1985) which referred to the same six religions (Christianity plus – in alphabetical order – Buddhism, Islam, Hinduism, Judaism, Sikhism). This text may well have influenced the general perception as to which 'world religions' were the 'other principal religions represented in Britain' in addition to Christianity referred to, but not named, in the 1988 Education Reform Act.

- *'The structure of the national framework for religious education' (p. 10):* That it has the same structure as the standards for subjects in the National Curriculum, but has a different juridical status.
- *'Attitudes in religious education' (p. 13):* for instance aims to encourage students to develop positive attitudes towards learning, and towards other people's beliefs and values.
- *'Learning across the curriculum: the contribution of religious education' (p. 14):* addresses how RE should contribute to a number of general goals that exist in the National Curriculum, for instance to contribute to the development of certain 'key skills'.
- *'Religious education and general teaching requirements' (p. 17):* a set of general teaching requirements are specified with respect to RE.

'The non-statutory national framework for religious education' (pp. 19 – 32) is the main part of the document. The structure as described in the previous part is here filled with content, but it is still not very detailed. The content is described in terms of learning targets for each key stage 1-3, and also for the foundation stage (which is the stage of preschool) and ages 14-19 (part of which includes compulsory schooling). A separate section on 'Attainment targets for religious education' (p. 33-37) specifies what these should be for religious education. The last part is the 'Appendix: General teaching requirements' (pp. 38-50) which is attached to all national curricular subjects. How these are adapted to RE is specified in the main part of this document.

4.10 UD 2005

The title of the Norwegian document is 'The KRL book 2005: Knowledge of Christianity- religions- and philosophies of life: Curriculum for 1st – 10th grade: Curriculum-guidance and information.'[154] The name of the department responsible is the Ministry of Education and Research[155]. The cover is illustrated by a lithograph by the artist Bjørg Torhallsdottir called 'the golden egg'. It is an abstract picture so one cannot immediately see what it represents. The publication has 96 pages and the layout is in grey-blue and white.

There is a 'Foreword' explaining the relationship to 'The Knowledge Promotion 2006' and why the RE curriculum is published a year ahead (pp. 5-6). 'The Curriculum for Knowledge of Christianity-, Religions- and Philosophies of life for 1st – 10th grade' (pp. 9-19) is the main part. It has the new structure for curricula that was to be implemented through 'The Knowledge Promotion 2006' where content of teaching is described in terms of competence targets (kompetansemål). These have some similarities to attainment targets in the QCA National Frame-

---

154 In Norwegian: 'KRL-boka 2005. Kristendoms-, religions- og livssynskunnskap, Læreplan for 1.–10. årstrinn: Læreplanveiledning og informasjon.' In an English version of the Norwegian Education Act it is translated "Christian Knowledge and Religious and Ethical Education", but I find that this translation has a different meaning compared to the much-discussed Norwegian name for the subject.
155 This was changed to the Ministry of knowledge (Kunnskapsdepartementet) in 2006.

work. Basic skills are comparable but not identical to key skills in the QCA National Framework. The content is described in terms of competence targets after 3rd grade, 7th grade and 10th grade, which compares to the notion of 'key stages' in QCA 2004. UD 2006 is less detailed about content than previous Norwegian national curricula, also with regard to the RE curriculum.

The main headings are:

- 'The purpose of the subject' (p. 9): to contribute to generic formation, to the reproduction of common frames of references in Norwegian society.[156] It is stressed that KRL is an ordinary school subject in which dialogue and respect for others are central, and that no preaching of religion is allowed.
- 'Main areas of study' (p. 10) and 'Timeframe for the subject' (p. 11) reveal the main areas: Christianity (55%), other religions and life views (25%) and philosophy and ethics (20%).[157]
- 'Basic skills in the subject' (p. 11) are stated to be: oral expression, to read, to write, to count (numeracy) and to use digital tools (ICT). These are the same for all subjects and it is specified what it means to train these skills through KRL.
- 'Competence targets' (p. 13) are formulated aims for each stage that decide the content of the subject within the defined main areas of study.
- 'Assessment' (p. 19) refers to the final mark students will get at the end of year 10 and that they may in addition get an oral exam.[158]

A quite extensive part called 'Curricula guidance' (p. 21-42) is *about* the subject curricula, about problems and dilemmas for teacher education and development of competence. It contains elements like recommendations for methodology and progression. Much of what is found here I recognize as elements that were a part of the curriculum itself in earlier versions (KUF 1996, LS 2002). Local development of syllabuses based on the National Curriculum is emphasised more than before. This is said to be one of the major changes with this reform. The guidance to the curriculum is quite detailed, however, and gives the impression of being a sort of textbook on the curriculum. The main headlines are 'Introduction' (p. 23), 'About the Competence Reform' (p. 24), 'The Education Act' (p. 26), 'About the curriculum for KRL' (p. 28), 'The curriculum at work' (p. 32).

---

156 Generic formation (my translation/ interpretation) refers to the word 'allmenndanning', which is a central educational topic in Norway. The first part 'allmenn' refers to the general public, 'commoners' maybe, meaning 'for all'. The second part 'danning', may be known to some English people as the German 'bildung': translated from English as 'formation' meaning 'cultured' or maybe civilized, or simply 'educated'. Alberts (2007: 56-57) suggests that 'Bildung includes the acquisition of cultural knowledge as a basis of a further development of one's own personality' and that the German concepts of bildung and Erziehung 'are meaningfully integrated in the English concepts "Education"'. Schiffauer *et al.* (2004) use the concept civil enculturation which also seems overlapping in meaning with 'bildung' or generic formation: see chapter 2. There is presently an extensive debate about 'danning' in Norway, and a study group on the issue has been formed at the Faculty of Education in the University of Oslo.
157 Percentage indicating time to be used for each main part.
158 This follows the general system for assessment/ qualification in Norway. This is one area in which there is a major difference between the general school systems in England and Norway (see chapter 5), but it might be converging.

A separate section on 'KRL's history and current documents' (pp. 45-54) contains two circulars (F-02-05 and F-08-05) concerning the statement in the UN Human Rights Committee about KRL.[159] There is no additional subject history apart from what appears in these documents. The last part is 'Information about KRL to guardians (parents etc.) in 20 languages' (pp. 55-96). This section is meant to be of help for schools in their role of informing parents and others that KRL is not religious instruction but education about religion, considered to be an ordinary school subject.

4.11 Comparative remarks regarding layout and structure[160]

One immediate difference is that there appears to be six world religions in England and five in Norway, where Sikhism is not included. However, the Norwegian curriculum includes Humanism on the same terms as the religions. The simple explanation is that there are more Sikhs in England and a stronger secular humanist organisation, with a different and special history in Norway, combined with the fact that humanism, by legal precedent, is not regarded as a religion in English law.[161] The two documents are printed in different shades of blue. Both documents were published as separate documents, the Norwegian because it was published a year early in relation the total reform of which it was a part, and the English since RE is a 'compulsory' subject, but is not part of the National Curriculum – hence the perceived need for a non-statutory framework.

The English document has very clear, easily recognisable symbolism on its cover while the Norwegian authorities have chosen an artistic expression where symbolism is more esoteric. The English document includes pictures and quotes from pupils in its introductory paragraphs, which have no parallels in the Norwegian document. The QCA 2004 includes *attainment targets* for RE, in line with curriculum documents in other subjects in England since 1988, and the UD 2005 includes *competence targets*, a new policy in Norway introduced with the 2006 reform. In QCA 2004 certain *key skills* which are meant to be acquired through all school subjects are exemplified with regard to RE. In UD 2005 certain *basic skills* which are meant to be obtained through all subjects are exemplified with regard to RE. The nuances in meanings between *attainment targets* and *key skills* (England) and *competence targets* ('kompetansemål') and *basic skills* ('grunnleggende ferdigheter') (Norway) may well be a language question, and in a translation one might have chosen the existing English terms. However, as this is comparative work, I consider it important to maintain the precise differences in terminology used in the two countries.

---

159 http://www.regjeringen.no/nb/dokumentarkiv/Regjeringen-Bondevik-II/ufd/233191/251920/Human-Rights-Committee-Communication-No-11552003.html?id=422478 (Accessed 27.01.09).
160 I do not know if the ones responsible for the layouts have had any contact with those responsible for the content of the documents, but I am here comparing the finished documents.
161 QCA 2004 represents a shift to being more inclusive of non-religious beliefs in English RE.

Both documents include comments on recommended methods of teaching in additions to the actual curricula documents. They have the same length, ca. 50 pages, since pp. 55-96 of the Norwegian document consists of translations of information about KRL in 20 languages.

4.12 The place in the school curricula

In comparative work, one of the fundamental problems relates to translating terms and concepts (see chapter 2). It might be appropriate here to comment on the relationship between the concepts, syllabus, curriculum and framework. I have Goodlad's theory[162] of curriculum as the basis of my understanding of 'curriculum', but these concepts have a pattern of practical use in the languages which might cause misunderstandings. In England the concepts curriculum, syllabus and framework are sometimes used with overlapping meanings. The *curriculum* may mean the general activity of the school, a particular course of study or all courses of study. The concept *syllabus* means a concise description of a course of study. A framework is a suggested structure to support a subject, used especially in relation to RE because of the diverging status in relation to the National Curriculum. In Norwegian the concept *nasjonal læreplan* refers to centrally decided programmes of study for all subjects, correlating to the English *national curriculum*. The subject syllabuses are for instance called the '*læreplan for KRL*', which here will be translated as *the RE curriculum*.

RE in England has a special status as statutory but outside the National Curriculum. RE is a part of the basic curriculum. The basic curriculum refers to all school subjects. The basic curriculum consists of the National Curriculum and RE. This means that pupils who attend state schools (maintained) have an entitlement to RE. Reasons given for this right are their need to understand religion in order to understand contemporary society, and also that it should contribute to their personal development (QCA 2005: 5). When it comes to RE, the agreed syllabuses are designed by local committees. Schools design the specific curriculum on the basis of the agreed syllabus. This structural placement does give the signal that RE is different from other subjects; it is a subject with a special status in the formal structure, and perhaps also in people's minds.

This Non-Statutory National Framework for RE (QCA 2004) reflects a wished for national standard for RE, and QCA recommends that local authorities follow this advice. The document seems to many to be pushing opinion towards having a national syllabus. At the same time it is still emphasised that local curricula should reflect the needs of local communities (QCA 2004: 3). QCA 2004 is, in other words, one of several sources of advice and obligations that LEAs have to relate to in order to produce their locally agreed syllabuses. The most important obligations, however, are found in the law.

---

162 Or a version of it: as his theory develops, it would perhaps be better described as theories (Goodlad *et al.* 1979).

Norwegian RE is a central, integrated and integrative part of the Norwegian National Curriculum. The 2006 National Curriculum (UD 2006) is the first in Norwegian history where the RE curriculum does not appear as the first subject in the document. It is emphasised in Norwegian law and in several places in UD 2005 that KRL is an *ordinary* school subject where no form of preaching is to take place. It is a subject where pupils should learn *about* religions and life views. The aim of it is to learn *about* religions and, through dialogue and other means, to learn to respect different religions and values and Human Rights values. The three main reasons given for having RE are (UD 2005: 5):

- *the importance of Christianity in Norwegian and European tradition (Christianity as part of our cultural heritage),*
- *the humanist tradition's importance in Norwegian and European tradition and*
- *the importance of the plurality of religions and life views that characterises today's Norwegian society.*

Furthermore, it is a stated aim for the subject that it should contribute to generic formation ('Bildung')[163] and to pupils' personal development, and also give some common points of reference in a culture characterised by respect and insight into each other's particularities regarding religion and life views.

4.13 Comparative points

In both countries, state schools are obliged to offer RE which includes Christianity and other religions. In the case of Norway, secular life views also have to be covered. This is not a legal requirement in England, but happens increasingly, especially in secondary schools. In England, RE has a special status as statutory (as part of the 'basic curriculum') but outside the National Curriculum, while in Norway it is integrated in the National Curriculum, and it is emphasised that it is just another school subject. The need for this to be underlined may, however, indicate that it is not quite just another subject. The special status of RE in the English school system also makes it something other than *just* another subject.

The special histories of relations between school and religion, the fact that laws about general schooling make reference to traditional religion (Christianity), the special structural arrangements in England for producing RE syllabuses locally, the sometimes heated public debates about religion and schools, and the degree to which questions regarding RE in school are politicised can all be taken to indicate that RE in both countries is not quite an ordinary subject. In Norwegian RE there is a closer relationship between the political level and the institutional curriculum than in other subjects (Skeie 2004: 323). In these respects there is similarity between religious education in England and Norway. An important difference between UD 2005 and QCA 2004 is that the QCA 2004 is just a standard which authorities *recommend*. It is not meant to be a common frame of reference for all pu-

---

163 Generic formation (my translation/ interpretation) refers to the word 'allmenndanning', see above.

pils, like the Norwegian UD 2005. However, the law and non-statutory advice in England, taken together, make it clear that it is among the aims for RE that it should contribute to general educational aims and support the school's values.

Both QCA 2004 and UD 2005 reflect central guidance and obligations on the one hand and emphasise local curricular work on the other. Since QCA 2004 represents centralising tendencies in RE in England and UD 2005 represents decentralising tendencies in Norway, RE in England and Norway actually moved towards each other in this respect with these two documents. Nevertheless, local activity in England is much more extensive than in Norway since it includes producing the syllabuses locally and also because the practice of making the local agreed syllabuses is long established (see chapter 6).

4.14 Structure and content of RE in England and Norway exemplified through QCA 2004 and UD 2005

In England, for Key Stages 1, 2 and 3 (ages 5–14), the national framework (QCA 2004) has the same structure as subjects in the National Curriculum. All subjects have different attainment targets in relation to what 'knowledge skills and understanding' pupils should aim at (QCA 2004: 26). In RE, there are two attainment targets, relating to learning 'about religion' and learning 'from religion'. These terms originate in Michael Grimmitt's work (1987, 2000)[164], although the idea that RE should be both about knowledge and personal development has a longer history. However, 'learning about' and 'learning from religion(s)' has come to mean something different from the meaning intended by Grimmitt (Grimmitt 2000).

According to QCA 2004 (p. 11), in the section on RE in the curriculum:

Learning about religion includes enquiry into, and investigation of, the nature of religion, its beliefs, teachings and ways of life, sources, practices and forms of expression. It includes the skills of interpretation, analysis and explanation. Pupils learn to communicate their knowledge and understanding using specialist vocabulary. It also includes identifying and developing an understanding of ultimate questions and ethical issues. In the national framework, learning about religion covers pupils' knowledge and understanding of individual religions and how they relate to each other as well as the study of the nature and characteristics of religion.[165]

Learning from religion is concerned with developing pupils' reflection on and responce to their own and others' experiences in the light of their learning about re-

---

164 According to Grimmitt (2000: 15) the original concept of learning also from religion involved a pedagogical strategy in which pupils should evaluate their understanding of religion in personal terms and evaluate the understanding of self in religious terms. This is not unlike Jackson's (1997: 6, 47, 130-134) concept of edification.
165 According to QCA (2004: 34), in the part where the attainment targets are described in more detail and in relation to assessment, 'Learning *about* religion includes inquiry into, and investigation of, the nature of religion. It focuses on beliefs, teachings and sources and ways of life and form of expression. It includes skills of interpretation, analysis and explanation. Pupils learn to communicate their knowledge and understanding using specialist vocabulary. It includes identifying and developing an understanding of ultimate questions and ethical issues.'

> ligion. It develops pupils' skills of application, interpretation and evaluation of what they learn about religion. Pupils learn to communicate and develop their own ideas, particularly in relation to questions of identity and belonging, meaning, purpose and truth, and values and commitments.[166]

The choice of the term *religion* (singular) over *religions* (plural) in the first attainment target was a conscious one: reasons for this choice was

> (...) the concern that RE had been the study of separate religions where pupils did not get the opportunity to look across them for similarities and differences, connections and insights, etc, ie the study was too compartmentalised. Another was that the NSNF was concerned to promote more inter-religious dialogue so learning about religion was thought to be more appropriate for that. Yet another was that some people had felt that the thematic study of religion, so out of favour since the Model Syllabuses of 1994, needed some kind of way back into syllabus-making – as nobody wanted to use that terminology, making the first AT singular was found acceptable. It was also thought that the concept of religion itself, alongside belief, was more meaningful as a form of study to most pupils and teachers than the study of separate religions – I think this was partly because the second AT, being singular from the start, had helped this concept to become more widespread; religion (in its varying forms) is a constant yet changing and dynamic phenomenon of human life and society.[167]

In addition to the part about what *'knowledge, skills and understanding'* students are to get through RE, there are also three elements concerning the *'breadth of study'*: *'religions and beliefs'*, *'themes'* and *'experiences and opportunity'*. Concerning *'religions and beliefs'* ('religions' here in plural) the main points are that Christianity should be taught at every key stage; the other religions should all have been studied by the end of Key Stage 3. It is also recommended that religions other than the traditional six and secular philosophies such as humanism are taught 'where appropriate', but this issue is still controversial in England.[168]

---

166 According to QCA (2004: 34), in the part where the attainment targets are described in more detail and in relation to assessment, 'Learning *from* religion is concerned with developing pupils' reflection on, and response to, their own experiences and learning about religion. It develops pupils' skills of application, interpretation and evaluation of what they learn about religion, particularly questions of identity and belonging, meaning and purpose, truth values and commitments, and communicating their responses.'
167 This according to an email from John Keast, who was involved in drafting the QCA 2005, dated October 4th 2008, forwarded to me with permission by Professor R. Jackson.
168 The inclusion of secular humanism is a new phenomenon in the English context, see above. It had previously had a presence in some locally agreed syllabuses, but their inclusion was controversial (Copley1997). QCA 2004 represents a shift to being more inclusive of non-religious beliefs in English RE. At the moment, strictly speaking, the law excludes them, since the subject is *religious* education, and by legal precedent, humanism in English law is not a religion. Thus, QCA 2004 is pushing the debate in a particular direction. In 2008 an exam board wanted to include humanism as an option for GCSE exams, which is very important for what is actually studied in year 10 (see chapter 5 & 6). Since this would have meant that a pupil could have focused only on humanism, the Qualifications and Curriculum Authority turned the request down. The British Humanist Association reacted by taking legal action against the government's examinations agency, the Qualifications and Curriculum Authority's regulator Ofqual, arguing that this was against the principle of giving non-religious

Further, still under *'religions and beliefs'*, it is stated that how religions relate to each other should be studied, including interfaith dialogue which is also a new element. Attention should be paid to similarities and differences both between the religions and within them. RE should also contribute to community cohesion and the combat of prejudice and discrimination. Explicit reference to this is also new. The term *'Themes'* relates to the obligation of local agreed syllabus conferences to come up with themes for the subject and *'experiences and opportunity'* (see chapter 6) refers to students having an opportunity to have experiences to help their learning, like visits to holy places etc.

Regarding the structure for RE as expressed in QCA 2004, there are also a range of aims relating to learning across the curriculum (QCA 2004: 14ff): These are:

1. *'Promoting spiritual, moral, and cultural development'*[169]
2. *'Promoting citizenship'*
3. *'Promoting personal, social and health education' (PSHE)*[170]
4. *'Key skills'*[171]

In addition to this, there is a list of seven other aspects of the curriculum that are to be realised in a similar way through all subjects, including RE. Among them are thinking skills, financial capacity, and education for racial equality and community cohesion. The document is in other words very ambitious regarding what should ideally be accomplished through RE.

The English *key skills* are: communication, application of number, information technology, working with others, improving own learning and performance and problem-solving (QCA 2004: 15-16). It is specified in the subject syllabus how one can work on these skills in RE. For example, the key skills of information technology can be developed in RE:

> *(...) through using CD-ROMs and the internet selectively, researching information about religions and beliefs, teaching and practices, using email to analyse information with people of different beliefs and cultures, using spreadsheets and databases to handle the present data relevant to the study of religious education* (QCA 2004:16).

In Norway, *basic skills* (key skills) as introduced in the reform of 2006 (UD 2006: 39) are oral expression, to read, to write, to count, to use digital tools (ICT). These key skills are to be obtained through subjects. For example, to use digital tools is defined for KRL (UD 2005: 12):

---

beliefs equal status. (See http://www.guardian.co.uk/education/2008/sep/13/gcses.religion, Accessed 18.02.09)

169 This is related to the overall aims of the curriculum according to The Education Act, section 1.2 (a): 'promote(s) the spiritual, moral, cultural, mental and physical development of pupils (...)'.

170 Citizenship and PSHE are subjects which have their own curricula, but are mainly realized through the other subjects and general school activities.

171 These are generic skills to be obtained through the taught subjects.

> *To be able to use digital tools in KRL is a means to research religions and philosophies of life, to find different presentations and perspectives. An important skill is to use material that is available through digital tools, like pictures, texts, music and film in a way that unites creativity with critical evaluation of sources. Digital media give new possibilities for communication and dialogue about religion and life views. These media also gives opportunities for broad access to material concerning current ethical questions* (UD 2005: 12).

In UD 2005, the content of RE is described in terms of 'competence targets' (attainment targets) per stage. The stages are 1-4th grade, 5-7th grade, and 8-10th grade.[172] The competence targets are structured according to the three main areas of the subject; which are *'Christianity', 'Judaism, Islam, Hinduism, Buddhism and life views'*[173] and *'philosophy and ethics'* (UD 2005: 10). The competence targets for Christianity, the *other religions*[174] and *life views* and *philosophy and ethics* follow a pattern. For instance, the aims (targets) in relation to Judaism for 4th graders are formulated in three bullet points, the first referring to storytelling, the second to having conversations about certain topics such as prayer, and the third regarding Jewish art and aesthetics. The same kinds of aims, relating to storytelling, conversations about certain topics like prayer, art and aesthetics are specified in a similar way for the other religions as well. The pattern is the same regarding Christianity but here there are 7 bullet points and more details. The same pattern is applied to the topic 'life views', with stories from, conversation on certain topics and art and aesthetics from the humanistic tradition.[175] The topic philosophy and ethics has 7 bullet points and diverges to a degree from the main pattern.

While the number of bullet points representing competence targets after the 4th grade is 3 for some topics (other religions and life views) and 7 for others (Christianity and Philosophy and Ethics), the numbers are increased to 5 bullet points for the other religions and life views, and 10 for Christianity and 9 for philosophy and ethics after 7th grade. The pattern is that they concern conversations about certain topics, the ability to describe, present and explain certain issues (UD 2005: 14-16). After the 10th grade the bullet points are again more extensive both in number and content.

The bullet point is quite open and can be concretised in a number of ways. For instance, under Buddhism in the 10th grade, one of the bullet points is 'discussing some chosen texts from the Buddhist written tradition'. This allows endless opportunities for choice of text and how to proceed with the discussion. Thus, according to this national curriculum, very important decisions are formally left to the subnational level, to local schools or school districts who can adjust the curriculum. So

---

[172] This is new for UD 2005 and follows the structure of the rest of the 2006 national curriculum.
[173] This part used to in previous curricula (1997, 2002) go under the headline *'other religions'* but is here specified like this. In the targets for year 10, parallel to English key stage 3, 'additional religious plurality' ('annet religiøst mangfold') is added to the headline for these targets (UD 2005: 10).
[174] My generalisation.
[175] It should be noted how unfair it is to the concept of life views that it is reduced in the curriculum to one life view, namely that of (secular) humanism. In the aims after year 4 it is that exclusively, while in the aims after years 7 and 10 the concept is supposed to be discussed more widely, but still with a clear emphasis on (secular) humanism.

much responsibility being given to local curricular work is a new feature in the Norwegian context.

The content of English RE, according to QCA 2004, is described with reference to the structures mentioned above. I will here refer to Key Stage 2 for more detailed examples of how the content of RE is described in this document. Under one of the main headings, *'Knowledge, skills and understanding'* (QCA 2004: 26), points a-h specify what pupils should learn *about* religion and further points a-e specify what pupils should learn *from* religion during this stage. Examples of what pupils should learn *about* religion are 'b. describe the variety of practices and way of life in religions and understand how these stem from, and are closely connected with beliefs and teachings', 'g. use specialist vocabulary in communicating their knowledge and understanding', 'h. use and interpret information about religions from a range of sources'. Examples of what pupils should learn *from* religion are: 'a. reflect on what it means to belong to a faith community communicating their own and others responses', 'c. discuss their own and others views of religious truth and belief, express their own ideas', and 'e. reflect on sources of inspiration in their own and others' lives'.

Under the other main heading *'Breadth of study'* (QCA 2004: 27) it is stated that pupils should be taught knowledge, skills and understanding through the three main areas of study which are 'religions and beliefs', 'themes' and 'experiences and opportunities'. 'Religions and beliefs' as an area of study is specified like this: 'a. Christianity', 'b. at last two other principal religions', 'c. a religious community with a significant local presence, where appropriate', and 'd. a secular worldview, where appropriate'. This is identical for all key stages 1-3.

Examples from points e-m listed under 'themes' are: 'h. the journey of life and death: why some occasions are sacred to believers, and what people think about life after death', 'j. inspirational people: figures from whom believers find inspiration', 'm. belief in action in the world: how religions and beliefs responds to global issues of Human Rights, fairness, social justice and the importance of the environment'. Examples from points n-s listed under the heading 'Experiences and opportunities' are: 'n. encountering religion through visitors and visits to places of worship, and focusing on the impact and reality of religion on the local and global community', 'r. reflecting on their own and others' insights into life and its origin, purpose and meaning', 'r. express and communicate their own and others' insights through art and design, music, dance drama and ICT'.

The content of Norwegian RE is in UD 2005 described according to the structures mentioned above. I will here refer to more detailed examples of the content according to this document from the competence aims for the 7th grade, which would be parallel in age to Key Stage 2 in the English system. Examples of targets for 'Christianity' after year 7 (UD 2005: 14) are that pupils should be able to 'explain the Christian calendar (the Christian Era) and the rhythm of the Church Year, describe Christian festivals and central rituals', 'describe the church building and other Christian places of worship and reflect on their significance (meaning) and use, and use digital tools to seek information and make presentations'.

Examples of what competence aims pupils are to reach in the main area 'other religions and life views' after year 7 (equivalent to Key Stage 2) are, for example, in relation to Islam, to be able to 'explain the origin of the Islamic calendar (the Islamic Era), and describe Islamic festivals and central rituals', to 'describe the Mosque and reflect on its significance (meaning) and use, use digital tools to seek information and make presentations' (UD 2005: 15).

Examples of what competence aims pupils are to reach in the main area 'philosophy and ethics' after year 7 (equivalent to Key Stage 2) are to be able to: 'have conversation about current philosophical and ethical questions and discuss challenges related to the issues poor and rich, war and peace, nature and environment, ICT and society', and to 'participate in talks about ethnic minorities in Norway and reflect on attitudes towards multicultural society' (UD 2005: 16).

4.15 Comparative discussion regarding structure and content

Some structural similarities and parallels in QCA 2004 and UD 2005 are striking, especially since these similarities have come about *with* these two documents. In both cases the content is described in terms of targets to be reached, attainment targets/ competence targets, and in both cases these targets are related to key stages.[176] In both cases there are certain key and basic skills that are to be acquired through RE and other subjects. In both cases there are also a number of additional aims that are to be realised through the subjects. In England these are, for instance, economic skills and citizenship education, while in Norway they include the 'learning poster' (UD 2005: 25, UD 2006: 31) and aims stated in the general part of the curriculum, including generic formation ('bildung') (see a above).

The general part of the curriculum is a 'survival' from the 1997 reform (KUF 1996: 15- 50). The learning poster is a new feature with the 2006 reform in Norway. It is a one-page list of 11 points describing ideals to be realised across the curriculum and includes, for instance, 'giving all pupils equal opportunities to develop their abilities and talents individually and in cooperation with others' (the poster's first point) and to 'stimulate pupils in their personal development and *identity* (my italics), in their development of ethical, social and cultural competence and ability to understand and participate in democracy'. The latter has, in my view, clear connotations to the idea of citizenship education as understood in England.

In the case of England, these cross-curricular themes are identical to those found in the structure of the National Curriculum as developed in relation to the reform in 1988. These have, however, been developing and, for instance, citizenship education was introduced as a distinct subject area in 2002 (see Jackson 2003: 149). In Norway, the elements of the learning posters are an innovation with the 'competence reform 2006', but the idea that some aims are general and cross-curricular are of earlier origin, reflected for instance in the changing school law preamble (Haraldsø 1989).

In the Norwegian context this change to the content being described in terms of targets to be reached – (attainment targets) competence targets per key stage – must be understood in relation to the adjustment to European processes of standardisa-

---

[176] Although the term key stage is not used in the Norwegian document.

tion of education (Karlsen 2006). In asking my fellow English PhD students if this was also the case regarding the English curriculum, one answer was 'I'd be surprised if it was European – this was the height of Thatcherism'[177]. It was a working party that created this framework prior to the national curriculum coming into effect in 1988[178].

One motivation for the reform was economical, another was to strengthen the quality of education. This type of reorganisation of the public sector, known as New Public Management, has spread internationally (Johnstad, Klausen og Mønnesland 2003, Karlsen 2006). According to a source in the Norwegian committee that produced the 2005 curriculum,[179] they did not base the new syllabus on QCA 2004, although they knew about it and looked at it for inspiration. The mandate they were given to include these structures was not linked to the English curriculum explicitly.[180]

In both QCA 2004 and UD 2005, religious education includes both the Christian tradition and other religions and philosophies of life/ secular world views, even if the latter has a much stronger representation in the Norwegian document and is a new and disputed feature of English RE. Dialogue, personal/ identity development and working on respecting others are central perspectives in both. The multicultural society is in both cases the perspective of the subject, and aims include contributing to integration/ citizenship education.

There is, at the same time, both in QCA 2004 and UD 2005, a tension between traditional culture and religion, religion as cultural heritage and the 'new' idea of society as multicultural. In the terminology of Schiffauer et al. (2004),[181] the question would be what the relationship is between a traditional *national imaginary* where values from the Christian religion are generalised (Bø 2006), and forming a central part of the civil religion (Bellah 1970, 1980, Davie 1994, 2007), and a *new national imaginary* where the plural society is reflected. How is the new sense of plurality challenging the idea of 'the English' or 'the Norwegian', so that civil religion in its traditional form is challenged, and so that it challenges the way the community is imagined?

---

177 Email from Nigel Fancourt, 07.10.05.
178 Email from Bill Gent, 05.10.05.
179 Email from Heid Leganger Krogstad, 03.03.05.
180 It is possible that the basic ideas for this kind of curriculum were developed under the influence of the Thatcher government's educational policies in England, and that these structures, through Britain's central membership in the EU and other international institutions, have influenced the way educational policies in general have developed in Europe, including in Norway. This issue is discussed at a general level by Karlsen (2006).
181 A concept related to Anderson's (1991) concept of 'Imagined communities' and Taylor's (2004) 'Modern social imaginaries', see chapters 2 and 5.

4.16 Concluding discussion

Despite important differences, aims as formulated in the laws of the two countries reveal a basically similar approach to RE. New aims which address religious plurality are a shared feature. In both countries, aims for RE are to learn about (and from) Christianity and other religions in a way that is meant to promote tolerance and respect for others holding different beliefs or belonging to another religion (see for example NOU 1995: 9, Hull 1988). These aims reflect a plurality in society and a wish to educate to combat tension and promote social cohesion among citizens of a culturally and religiously plural society. These kinds of aim are strengthened in Norway through the changes in the law and the national curriculum since 1997 and, in England since 1988 through the non-statutory guidelines (QCA 2005), for instance.

The similarities in structure which appear in QCA 2004 and UD 2005, especially with the introduction of attainment targets and skills in the Norwegian curriculum, are related to *formal supranational processes*. Without pinpointing what actually led to this similarity, it is likely that this comes from general educational policy developed in international organisations in which both England and Norway participate.

It is an interesting perspective, I think, to see the long-established English right to opt out in relation to the traditional (mainly Christian and Jewish in 1944) religious plurality in Great Britain. However, the Norwegian fight for the right to opt out should be seen in relation to the strong and dominating role of the Norwegian State Church in Norwegian history – and the traditional fight for religious freedom (see for example Sandvik 1996). As such, English school history is more plural and less concerned with constructing a national imaginary while, in the young nation of Norway (from 1814), there has been a consciously political construction of fellowship through common school education for all, in which the State Church and the teaching of Christianity in School have played a central part (Haraldsø 1989, Engen 2003, 2005, Engen et al. 2006, Bø 2006, see chapter 3).

Now one strives for the common, Norwegian-ness, the Norwegian national imaginary, to be defined as more plural, while 'England' or the national imaginary of England (especially when it is seen as a part of the Great Britain) is initially more plural, perhaps looking for its commonness, the social cohesion. However, both are challenged by the new sense of plurality which has come about due to immigration since the 1950s/ 60s and perhaps, also, by a growing sense of globalisation (see chapter 2 and 8).

QCA 2004 and UD 2005 each have a different legal status. UD 2005 is a compulsory curriculum for *all* children growing up in Norway, with a limited right to opt out. This reflects the unitary school tradition in Norway. QCA 2004 is a non-statutory framework, although it undoubtedly has been influential, aimed primarily at agreed syllabus conferences, and encouraging a standard for most state schools, without being prescriptive for RE for all types of schools. The four main types of state schools since the 1998 School Standards and Framework Act are Community schools, Voluntary Controlled schools, Voluntary Aided Schools and Foundation schools (see for example Jackson 2004a: 42).[182] In all these types of school, the National Curriculum (since 1988) is followed and they work in partnership with local authorities (LAs). With regards to RE, however, *community schools* have to follow the local agreed syllabus for RE whilst the others may have a 'religious character' (although normally voluntary controlled schools follow the local agreed syllabus) (Jackson 2004a: 42). As Jackson points out, 'All schools with a religious character can have collective worship that is distinctive of the religious body concerned, but only voluntary aided schools can have 'denominational' religious education' (Jackson 2004a: 42). In addition, 7% of school children attend independent schools, which themselves are of different types, including some that are religious foundations.[183] This whole system is very different from the Norwegian unitary school tradition. Furthermore, in the English system there is also the additional safeguard for individuals' rights which the right to 'withdraw' or opt out of religious education provides.

The main differences between English and Norwegian RE have to do with the different contexts including different legal traditions, different school traditions and systems, differences in civil religion etc., elements which must all be seen as part of the national dimension.

Of differences there is, for instance, the fact that in England Sikhism is included in non-statutory guidance and in many agreed syllabuses, as one of the 'other' religions whereas, in Norway, the inclusion of secular world views/ philosophies of life is much stronger. This especially applies to the humanist tradition which, in the Norwegian case, clearly is made part of the national imaginary.[184] In England, secular world views have only been included in some local agreed syllabuses. In QCA (2004) it is included with the reservation 'where appropriate' – even though the law includes only 'religions' (see above). It might seem strange, therefore, that the British Humanist Association actively participates in religious education processes (often having a representative or an observer on agreed syllabus conferences, for example), while the Norwegian Humanist Association has expressed strong unwillingness to be included, arguing, for instance, that they do not wish to be perceived as a religion. It was parents with a secular humanist world view who took legal action against the state for discrimination, for example (see above), while in England there is now a case of the British Humanist Association taking legal action for not being included in an RE examination syllabus (see above).[185] The different contexts conceptualised here as *the national dimension* (see chapter 2) explain the different approaches to RE by the British and Norwegian Humanist Associations.

With regard to the English concepts of learning *about* and *from* religion, I take the view that these are parallel to the Norwegian aims of giving pupils both knowledge and personal experiences in their meeting with religions and worldviews. This is, for instance, formulated in the 2002 version of the national

---

182 Though under the present coalition government (2013), there has been a growth in schools, particularly academies, free from local authority control.
183 http://www.inca.org.uk/england-system-mainstream.html (Accessed 18.02.09).
184 Included, for instance, in the new school law preamble from 2008, see appendix 2.
185 http://www.guardian.co.uk/education/2008/sep/13/gcses.religion (Accessed 18.02.09).

curriculum for RE (LS 2002: 14: this will be discussed further in chapter 6) and is implied in the central background document NOU 1995: 09: *Identity and Dialogue*. By way of contrast to both England and Norway, the personal/ learning from side is entirely absent in the French approach to the study of religion in state schools (Willaime 2007). In UD 2005, the 'learning from' or 'experiential' elements have been toned down as a reaction to the critique that the subject has not been made sufficiently objective. The *learning about* aspect is now more prominent, so it can be argued that Norway, on the institutional level of curriculum, is to some degree moving towards a French kind of approach.

However, the idea that RE teaching should stimulate pupils' development is still a part of the equation in Norway. In the part of the text (UD 2005) called 'The curriculum at work', it is stated that 'The adaptation of knowledge, attitudes and values which are acquired through the subject as such, shall support the pupils in their work to form their own opinions and find their own position' (UD 2005: 32).[186] Aiding identity development is also one of the eleven points in the learning poster ('læringsplakaten') (see above). Any explicit reference to the concepts of 'identity' and identity formation, which were so prominent for example in NOU 1995: 9, have been removed from the RE curriculum text. Despite this, the 'learning from' aspect is, in my view, still present. It is present, for instance, through the reference to the school's role in *generic formation*:

> *'Through dealing with questions of ethics, values and central cultural knowledge and through the emphasis on dialogue and multicultural understanding, KRL stands out as one of the most important subjects in contributing to generic formation'* (UD 2005: 32).[187]

I see the similarities in content and ideology in relation to a number of supranational processes (the first dimension, see chapter 2). For example, *the informal supranational process* is reflected in the fact that immigration of people from various parts of the world has led to more multicultural societies. Immigrants have brought with them cultural and religious specifics that have not traditionally been a part of English or Norwegian culture; this is a similar and relatively recent feature in both countries. However, both countries must also be seen in a wider international context. Thus, England's role in the Commonwealth as well as its EU membership is an important difference since Norway is not a part of those international unions. In both countries there has been a shift in official policies from 'other' cultures and religions being imagined as exotic and distant (for example Said 1978) to being perceived in a more socially integrated way, where imagined limits between 'us' and these 'others' are being negotiated in school RE, among other (public) places[188].

Pluralisation is another of these *informal supranational processes*, and here I refer both to the result of immigration as discussed above and the alleged development from modernity to post-modernity, with perhaps the coexistence of traditional

---

186 My translation.
187 My translation.
188 At the time of writing – February 2009 – there are, for instance, serious public debates in Norway regarding whether Muslim police women should be allowed to wear hijab, including reference to England where this has been allowed.

and modern plurality (Skeie 1995). It could be argued that, in many ways, English and Norwegian cultures have always been plural (Skeie 1995), and that the real qualitative change is not the increase in the number of ethnic or religious groups, but the challenge that plurality presents to everyone individually, with all the options of individual choice that are opened up. At the same time, we are still influenced by our sense of belonging to social and/ or religious groups, as, for instance, Jackson's (1997: 136) ideas of membership groups illustrates. Perhaps this forms people's view of reality in so many different ways that it is appropriate to claim that many different kinds of modernities coexist. In the words of Charles Taylor (2004: 1-2), 'Western modernity on this view is inseparable from certain kinds of social imaginary, and the differences between today's multiple modernities need to be understood in terms of divergent social imaginaries involved.'[189]

Globalisation (see chapter 2), is the development of the world 'as one place' having to do, for instance, with modes of communication and the development of global ethics through human rights thinking. The development of international law is, in the case of RE in Norway, one point where *formal process* in the supranational dimension affects national policy making processes explicit, through the legal cases described above. There are differences in the way each country reacts to and relates to those same processes, reflecting their specific history and tradition. A puzzling question is, however, if QCA 2004 and UD 2005 are more similar in ideology and content than religious education in other countries, why is this so when England and Norway are different in so many respects?

In my view, there are strong similarities in content in relation to *informal supranational processes* (see chapter 2). Some informal sociological trends that affect all European countries (and beyond), like secularisation, pluralisation and globalisation, are addressed in similar ways in RE curricula in Norway and England. But, I believe that the main reasons in each case for why they react to this challenge in the way that they do is to be found in the *formal and informal national processes*. In Norway I would suggest that the unitary school tradition (Østberg 1998b) is a major explanatory factor accounting for why KRL was introduced in 1997. In England I would suggest the traditional plurality, the traditions of the evolving school system and the locally agreed syllabuses in RE are main factors for explaining why a multifaith type of RE emerged (see for example Jackson & McGrady 2007). Following this line of argument, it would seem that the specific similarities between English and Norwegian RE are incidental.

Norwegian RE must be understood in light of the Norwegian school system and its history and English RE too must be seen in relation to the English school system and its history. Major differences relate to the different school systems and their different histories and ideologies. This becomes especially clear in relation to ideas of 'the Norwegian' and 'the English' in relation to their *national imaginaries*. A question is, of course, to what extent these are seen as respective cultures with internally consistent ethics and cultural features and how much each is regarded as a plural society. The opposing rules for withdrawal, for example, I see as an indication that plurality is imagined differently in the English national imaginary than the Norwegian.

---

189 See also chapter 7.

4.17 Summary and Conclusion

The aim of this chapter has been to do a comparative analysis of RE policy in England and Norway through comparing legal issues and then focusing on two central curricular documents, QCA 2005 and UD 2004. I have looked at the place of RE in the curricula and the status and position of these two examples. I covered legal issues first, which I consider to be a part of the institutional level of curriculum (Goodlad & Su 1992), and which are important also for interpreting QCA 2004 and UD 2005 as expressions of RE policy. Last, but not least, I have looked at the structure and content of English and Norwegian RE on the institutional level of curriculum as it is expressed in QCA 2005 and UD 2004. In the final comparative discussion of these points, I have also looked at how elements from the supranational and national dimension affect each other.

From my discussion a number of questions emerge – the relationship between *supranational and national processes* of both a *formal and informal* character, for instance, and also what are the implications of those in English and Norwegian RE. The comparative perspective is helping to illuminate what developments in Norway are particularly 'Norwegian' in the sense that they are linked to Norwegian history and tradition, or the idea of it; the Norwegian *national imaginary*. Likewise, I have considered what is particularly 'English' and what has to do with supranational informal and formal processes. It is an important finding that things that are easily taken for granted from an insider point of view are put into perspective through comparison or viewing the issues in an international context. Another is that the traditional relationship between state and school is decisive for how multifaith RE in each case has been formed. It becomes clear how KRL can be understood differently when Norwegian history and traditions are the focus compared with the different focus of Norwegian participation in European and international society.

In a 'close-up' one-on-one comparison with the English situation, it becomes clearer how the development is a balance of the national 'style', the national dimension and participation in international processes (the supranational dimension). Both documents (QCA 2004 and UD 2005) can be considered as representing the institutional level of the curriculum (Goodlad & Su 1992) and, as such, reflect the main ideas of what religious education in state school in present day English/ Norwegian society is, or should be. Influences on the professionals and policy-makers who have formed these documents both stem from the national and supranational dimensions, and the societal level of curriculum.

In the following chapter 5, I will approach the levels of practise, the instructional (teachers) and experiential (pupils) levels, by describing and contextualising the empirical data which I collected in England and Norway. Following this, in chapters 6 and 7, I will explore how ideas discussed at the societal level and ideals formulated at the institutional level of curriculum are interpreted and executed through teachers' interpretations in their teaching (instructional level, chapter 6) and perceived in practice by pupils (experiential level, chapter 7).

5. Religious Education in Practice: Introduction to Case Studies from England and Norway

5.1 Introduction

This chapter introduces the empirical part of this book in which I explore the theme *curriculum practice*, and provides contextual material which helps to explain the differences experienced within the English and Norwegian systems. The fieldwork was a study of six related cases in state school RE, year 10 (14–15 year olds). Three of these cases were situated within English schools and three in Norwegian schools. The fieldwork was conducted in England between October and December 2004, and in Norway between January and April 2005.

The fieldwork was limited to day visits to each school allowing a systematic observation of one RE lesson, an interview with the class teacher and a group interview with four pupils from that class. Geographically, the fieldwork was restricted to an area in central England and one in central Norway. Both regions include rural areas where ethnic minorities are scarce, and more central areas of varying degrees of ethnic plurality. The schools chosen in my study represent a variation from heavily multicultural to almost monocultural in terms of pupil population.

This thesis is structured by the methodology as outlined in chapter 2. In chapter 3 I explored the societal level of curriculum and, in chapter 4, I explored the institutional level. More empirical studies are needed to better inform the theoretical and pedagogical discourses, and the politics on the institutional level could also be improved with better knowledge of practice. Contributing to knowledge of practice is one reason to include an empirical element, but the main reason for its inclusion here is as a means of exploring my suggested methodology for comparative study.

In order to explore the two remaining levels – the instructional level and experiential level (Goodlad & Su 1992) – it is necessary to use empirical data. I could have used existing studies, but decided to take the opportunity to make use of the material from my own fieldwork from 2004/ 2005. The questions asked in the interviews evolved around aims and descriptions of content of RE at the institutional level, which reflect the societal level (see appendix 1). My own fieldwork will be the main source of information regarding the levels of practice, but I also refer to other data. This chapter (5) was tailored to fit the aim of linking the field data to the other levels of curricula as defined here and, hence, also to the other chapters. For this chapter the research question is 'How does the empirical research fit into the overall methodology as outlined in chapter 2?'

5.2 Representation and national imaginaries

It is essential to acknowledge that there will be much variation within each education system when it comes to how RE is experienced in practice. My case study material does not attempt to answer questions regarding variations between schools or regions. I will reflect upon variation within the systems, but the material is very limited and can only be used to exemplify this. It includes three examples from each system and only demonstrates certain variations within the local areas in which the research was carried out.

The question of how representative these six cases are cannot be answered based on this qualitative study. Some indications can be found, however, when compared to other empirical research, for example the qualitative and quantitative research conducted by the EC REDCo Project (for example Dietz et al. 2009). The analytical tools from Schiffauer et al. (2004) will be used to illuminate connections between a non-representative sample and institutional levels and societal levels of curriculum within the national dimension.

The concepts used by Schiffauer et al. (2004) are employed to connect non-representative sample material and characteristics of each country's educational system. They argue that any one school within a nation state would be a representative example of the nation's specific *civil enculturation*.

> *Civil enculturation is 'the process by which an individual acquires the mental representations (...) and patterns of behaviour required to function as a member of (civil) culture, (...) taking place as a part of the process of education'* (Schiffauer et al. (2004: 2).

Civil enculturation involves pupils' socialisation as members of the *civil culture*, which includes *civil society, civic culture* and norms of civility[190] and a *social imaginary*. The *social imaginary* is 'the dominant national self-representation of a nation state', also called *'national imaginary'*. It refers to a symbolic imagery to which citizens of a nation state tie their identities, which I have mentioned also in previous chapters (see chapter 2). This may, for instance, be a certain view of history, but one that must not be mistaken for what 'really' happened. Norms of *civility* will be historically particular and include the knowledge of how to treat others depending on the situation. *Civility* describes the preferred method of interaction in the public sphere (Schiffauer et al. 2004: 4-8).

Others with interesting similar concepts are Jeffery Alexander (2006) who writes about *The civil sphere* and Charles Taylor (2004) who writes about *Modern Social Imaginaries*.[191] Both Taylor (2004) and Schiffauer et al. (2004) refer to anthropologist Benedict Anderson's [1983] (1991) concept of *imagined communities*. Also Engen (2005) which is the main reference on the relationship between a conscious (post colonial) construct of 'Norwegianness' and the unitary school ideology, refers to Anderson's idea of *imagined communities* (see chapter 3).

---

190 *Civil society* is a public space filled with networks and organisations such as churches, sport clubs, trade unions etc. Understanding how *civil society* works is one crucial ingredient in understanding any nation state's *civil culture*. *Civic culture* refers to conventions regarding expected behaviour vis a vis powers in the public sphere, including state bureaucracies (Schiffauer et al 2004: 4 - 8).

191 'Western modernity (...) is inseparable from certain kinds of social imaginary, and the difference between today's multiple modernities need to be understood in terms of divergent social imaginaries involved.' (Taylor 2004: 1-2)

When I reviewed Schiffauer et al. (2004) (Bråten 2006), a question I raised was why the relevant limits/ distinctions were seen to be the *national* limits. Might not imaginaries sometimes also be constructed as supranational? With all the international formal and informal processes that take place, the answer in my view clearly has to be yes. One very potent example would be international terrorism, which could be understood as *an international imaginary*. We see also, even in Schiffauer et al. (2004), that the students form patterns across national limits, for example in terms of being part of an international youth culture, as much as they are part of the *national imaginaries*. In my methodology, therefore, I consider both national and *international imaginaries* to be relevant for the interpretation of examples of practices.

I will argue that the comparative perspective does reveal differences in styles in the English and Norwegian samples, which can be said to reflect different *styles of civility*, or different *national imaginaries*. For example, one of the most immediate differences which can be observed is the school uniform worn by English pupils. Uniforms used to have a very negative press in England and disappeared from many schools in the 70s and 80s only to be brought back again, often due to pressure from parents, in the late 90s. So, in many schools they are a fairly new thing, being seen as a way of encouraging a sense of belonging and positive school ethos.

When I told the group of pupils in English School 1 (ES1-P) there were no school uniforms in Norwegian schools, their response seemed to be one of envy. Opposition to wearing of school uniforms could be observed in this school by the dynamics of pupils deliberately not tucking their shirts in and teachers constantly nagging them about it. Deviating from my interview schedule I asked:

O: So, when you're the grown ups, are you going to change this?
Boy 1: Yes.
O: Or are you going to follow the tradition?
Girl 1: Giggles. Oh, well. I mean um there's one school over at ...
Girl 2: the Trinity School ...
Girl 1: yeah,
Girl 2: no, no they have to wear school uniforms now ...
Girl 1: Oh. Well, they used to not have uniforms at all. And we played them in [...] and sorts of thing and stuff, and they didn't look like a team! And, just looked like seven people who stood around going to watch it rather than play it.
Girl 2: They were wearing trousers, skirts and shorts and ... we all were wearing a nice t-shirt and a black skirt and looked so much more organized.
Boy 1: Well, I'd have to agree with you.
Group giggles.

Despite the youthful opposition they display here, they are well on the way to being socialised into favouring the idea of the uniform, and this could clearly be seen as an example of *social enculturation* reflecting an English imaginary going on in this school.

Applying these concepts of *social enculturation, civil culture, civil society, civic culture, norms of civility* and, especially perhaps, *national imaginary*, the comparative perspective does highlight differences in styles of teaching RE in the English and Norwegian schools. It informs the discussion of the two educational systems and findings in other English and Norwegian educational research (see chapters 6 & 7). These concepts are important tools for discussing all my material but have a special function in the empirical part with respect to interpreting non-representative field data in the light of their representing a certain *national imaginary*.

5.3 Different styles of civility in the school systems

The comparative perspective reveals different styles of civility in the two educational systems as such. I stated in chapter 2 that both general educational policy and specific RE policy are seen as relevant to the national dimension. I see two of the main sources of explanation for the difference between English and Norwegian RE as:

1. *within the domain of RE, for example in the different scholarly traditions for RE research, and*
2. *outside the domain of RE, especially in the different school systems (see also chapter 1 and 3).*

The different school systems reflect a national history of education including the traditional relationships between church, state and school. This is why the school systems as such are relevant here: they are the main sources of explanation for difference between English and Norwegian RE, reflecting different *national styles* of civility. I have not, however, described the systems in full detail, nor have I covered every school type.[192] I have focused on some factors that I see as particularly potent in bringing out the different styles of civility in the two systems.

The basic structures of the educational systems in England and Norway are similar in some aspects; for instance, the length of compulsory education in both cases is 10 years. The coverage of the curriculum, in terms of traditional school subjects, is similar, and since 1988 both systems have had National Curricula. We have seen in chapter 4 that the way curricula are organised is converging as a result of international educational policy.[193] We have also seen that aims in RE aims are converging in most European countries, responding to challenges which are supranational[194] (see chapter 2).[195] However, it is the case that differences between the educational systems in England and Norway and the ways in which RE fits into them seem more obvious than similarities in many important areas, reflecting national traditions. In other words, different national styles can be detected.

The one element which most clearly brings out differences between civil cultures is the question of inspection. The Office for Standards in Education, Chil-

---

192 How religious education fits into the two systems is written about by Jackson and O'Grady, in the case of England (Jackson & O'Grady 2007), and by Skeie in the case of Norway (Skeie 2007).
193 With regard, for example, to including key or basic skills.
194 Secularisation, pluralisation and globalisation.
195 With reference to Willaime 2007, for instance.

dren's Service and Skills (Ofsted)[196] is an important and integrated part of the English school system. School inspections are required by law and the purpose is to provide impartial information to parents and others so that schools can be compared. The function of Ofsted inspections is also to ensure good standards across the manifold English school system. At the time of writing (2009), schools in the state system were inspected every sixth year, and a full report was published openly on the internet. Reports set out what the school does well and where there is room for improvement.[197] Inspected units receive grades ranking from Outstanding and Good, to Satisfactory or Inadequate. All inspected units which receive the grade 'outstanding' appeared on a list published on the Ofsted homepage.[198]

The 'outstanding' providers were listed by regions, and one example from the West Midlands is Bartley Green School, a Specialist Technology and Sports College.[199] The report includes a letter to pupils explaining the findings, telling them, for instance, that they 'are confident, well-adjusted, reflective and caring'. But the letter also points out the two concrete areas in which the inspection revealed further improvement was needed: to 'raise standards and accelerate progress in science, (…) and increase the numbers gaining the higher A-C grades in the subject.'[200] This is not one of the schools in my sample as they will remain anonymous, but two of these schools are given the overall grade 3: Satisfactory: the second lowest grade, while the third, the inner city school (see below), is given grade 2: Good. The identification of explicit areas for improvement and for external observers to describe the school and its pupils in the way demonstrated above would be inconsistent with the Norwegian style of civility.

It is difficult in a Norwegian context to explain (understand) what inspection means in the English sense, and to provide explanations for its non-existence for an English audience is equally difficult.[201] As defined by Schiffauer et al. (2004: 4-8), *civic culture* refers to conventions regarding expected behaviour vis a vis powers in the public sphere, including state bureaucracies. Ofsted[202] could be regarded as a state bureaucracy. In my interpretation, the state bureaucracy in Norway, which covers some of the same functions with regards to the purpose of helping schools to

---

196 http://www.ofsted.gov.uk/ (Accessed 20.04.09)
197 In 2009, Ofsted also inspected Local Authority Children Services, Teacher Training institutions and independent schools.
198 Ofsted has a new framework which was introduced in January 2012; see http://www.ofsted.gov.uk/schools, http://www.ofsted.gov.uk/resources/framework-for-school-inspection (Accessed 16.01.2013.) The grade "satisfactory" has been changed to "requires improvement".
199 http://www.ofsted.gov.uk/oxedu_providers/full/(urn)/103491 (Accessed 20.04.09).
200 http://www.ofsted.gov.uk/oxedu_reports/display/(id)/94066 (Accessed 20.04.09).
201 In a Norwegian – English dictionary of education on the Norwegian Directorate of Education and Training website: http://www.utdanningsdirektoratet.no/upload/ordbok_no_eng.pdf (accessed 24.04.09) there is no entry on the Norwegian word 'inspeksjon' (inspection). In searching the English word 'inspection' it was found in an explanation of a concept 'insynsrett' (right to inspect). This is different to an Ofsted inspection.
202 http://www.ofsted.gov.uk/ (Accessed 20.04.09).

develop,[203] is the Norwegian Directorate for Education and Training (Utdanningsdirektoratet: UDir)[204], especially via its site the School Portal (skoleporten).[205]

The main responsibility for quality development (improvement) in schools lies with the school owners, which in Norway is the communes, but the Directorate of Education and Training also has a responsibility for aiding the development (improvements) in schools through various functions.

One area of responsibility under the Directorate is *analysis and assessment*. This has several departments, some of these were, at the time of writing (2009), the Department of Documentation, the Department of Pupil and Teacher Assessment, project National Tests, and project School Gate ('skoleporten'). The statistics provided by The Directorate of Education and Training are the most important source of information about schools in Norway.[206] That is to say, in Norway there are statistics and research resembling some of Ofsted's work, but within a different framework, and with the important difference that Norwegian schools provide the information themselves; it is not provided by inspectors. There is no parallel to the practice of making graded reports of individual schools. The closest thing to inspection in the sense of someone external coming into school to evaluate them on the Norwegian side is something called 'tilsyn' (supervision) which is not about school achievements at all but only about whether school activities are legal.[207]

There seem to be differences regarding attitudes to what can and should be measured, as well as fundamental differences in attitudes to ranking schools. Norwegian schools are not ranked on the basis of inspections. On Ofsted's website (accessed 20.04.09) it was stated that 'Teachers welcome inspections and observation in schools: An independent survey of teachers' views of Ofsted inspections of schools have found that almost 90% of teachers think that inspections help their

---

203 In England, Ofsted aims at helping schools to *improve* while in Norway the terminology used is school *development*, but I interpret these terms as parallel.
204 http://www.utdanningsdirektoratet.no/Artikler/Norwegian-Directorate-for-Education-and-Training/ (Accessed 21.04.09).
205 http://skoleporten.utdanningsdirektoratet.no/english/Sider/WhatisSkoleporten.aspx (Accessed 20.04.09)
206 http://udir.no/templates/udir/TM_Artikkel.aspx?id=2132
207 The Directorate of Education can give various tasks to the 'fylkesmann' (County Governor). The 'fylkesmann' is the stately representative in a county ('fylke'). One of the tasks delegated to the 'fylkesmann' is 'tilsyn' (supervision): a kind of inspection that is about checking whether schools are following the laws and the National Curriculum. The National Curriculum has the status of a government regulation ('forskrift': legal document). The Department can 'supervise' ('ha tilsyn med') various sides of the educational system and the schools: in 2006, for instance, it was the system for self-evaluation in schools that was checked out. The reports from the 'tilsyn' (supervision) are made publicly available on the internet. This type of inspection is, however, not about assessing how the school or its pupils or staff perform, like Ofsted reports: it just checks whether the activities are legal. The communes – smaller units than the 'fylke' (counties) – are the school owners. The communes, through their 'rådmann' (Communal Advisor), also have a responsibility for 'tilsyn' (inspection), but a recent investigation has shown severe deficiencies in the system in this area (2007).
A main source of information on these issues, besides internet sites of the Directorate of Education http://www.utdanningsdirektoratet.no/Tema/In-English/, Trøndelag Fylkeskommune http://www.stfk.no/Om_fylkeskommunen/Kort_om_fylkeskommunen/Sor-Trondelag_County_Council/ and Trondheim Kommune http://www.trondheim.kommune.no/content.ap?thisId=1117631041 , is Ola Moe: former director of schools in Sør-Trøndelag County, now a colleague in teacher education in Trondheim.

schools set new priorities for the future'. I do not know the full context of this statement, nor their reasons for asking this in a survey or announcing it in such a prominent place on their webpage, but I would suggest that this reflects a process of social enculturation which involves accepting external inspection, in a system where there is a long tradition for this.[208]

On the Norwegian side I find that the only information about individual schools is the results of (controversial) national tests in Norwegian language, maths and English language.[209] Additional information about the schools exists, but is based on voluntarily participation in surveys. In a qualitative analysis of six schools commissioned by the Directorate of Education and Training, researchers[210] investigated how information collected in voluntary surveys[211] is used by schools. One of their concerns is how to raise response rates, and they even suggest that responding to these surveys should be compulsory. I will not go further into this topic here, but just point out that the difference with regard to attitudes to external inspection or display of information about the schools is markedly different in the two countries. In the Norwegian system, schools and teachers are less willing to accept external evaluation of their work. Even if these issues are negotiated in both systems, changing with shifting policies, I see this as an important indicator of the different styles of civilities in the two systems.

Diversity vs. uniformity is another fundamental difference and which must be seen in connection to the differences with regard to inspection. The English school system is more diverse in terms of different types of schools than the Norwegian. This is true for state schools, but even more so if one includes the private school sectors. Independent schools outside of the state system have a much stronger profile in the English system, and they are much more independent than in Norway.

In England, private independent schools get most of their funding from fees paid by parents[212] while, in Norway, they are 85% state-funded, and are not al-

---

208 Her Majesty's Inspectorate was established in 1840, 30 years before the first education act (1870). It was said to be more about affording 'assistance' and 'encouragement' than with 'exercising control' (Evans 1975: 21). There is insufficient space here to go into the founding and development of Ofsted since 1992, but since then inspection has become a significant feature of the English educational system. Ofsted's remit was recently renewed, its website stating that 'The new Ofsted – the Office for Standards in Education, Children's Services and Skills' – came into being on 1 April 2007. It brings together the wide experience of four formerly separate inspectorates. It will inspect and regulate care for children and young people, and inspect education and training for learners of all ages. We want to raise aspirations and contribute to the long term achievement of ambitious standards and better life chances for service users. Their educational, economic and social well-being will in turn promote England's national successes. (http://www.ofsted.gov.uk/Ofsted-home/About-us, accessed 24.04.09).
209 http://skoleporten.utdanningsdirektoratet.no/default.aspx (Accessed 24.04.09).
210 http://www.utdanningsdirektoratet.no/upload/Rapporter/2009/brukerundersokelser_caseundersokelse_08.pdf (Accessed 24.04.2009). (The researchers are Skaar and Stakkelend from 'Oxford research': 'Oxford research' is the name of a Scandinavian based company which conducts research for political and strategic actors to provide a better base for decisions, according to page 2 of the report. See their webpage: http://www.oxford.no/ (accessed 24.04.2009)).
211 ['Elevundersøkelsen' (pupils' survey), 'Foreldreundersøkelsen' (parents' survey), and 'lærerundersøkelsen' (teachers' survey)]: http://www.utdanningsdirektoratet.no/Tema/Brukerundersokelser/ (Accessed 14.04.2009).
212 http://www.inca.org.uk/england.html (Accessed 18.04.2009).

lowed to take fees exceeding the remaining 15% of costs.[213] In England, independent schools must be registered with the Department for Children, Schools and Families[214], but do not have to be state-approved, as must private schools in Norway. English schools, however, are subject to inspection.

In England, different types of schools are defined in relation to how they are funded,[215] while, in the Norwegian context, this would not be a meaningful way of distinguishing between types of schools since they are all state-funded (Skeie 2004).[216] Even the Norwegian independent schools (which are not really outside the state system)[217] are 85% state-funded. These differences reflect fundamental differences in the school systems as such, which can be accounted for by reference to different histories. They reflect different *civil cultures* and different *national imaginaries*. A state's dominating idea of its education definitely could be said to be part of the *national imaginary*.

Returning to state schools, diversity vs. uniformity is an even more obvious difference. For instance, there are some schools with a religious character within the English state school system (for example, voluntary aided schools); including schools based on religions other than Christianity (Jackson 2004a, Chapter 3). However, because of the history of the dual system[218], some Church of England schools operate as neighbourhood schools. By contrast, in Norway, there are no faith-based schools in the state system and, in the independent sector, there are only Christian faith-based schools, and no schools based on any other religions or life views.[219] Further, there are still in England some schools which are only for boys or girls: another variation which is not found in Norway. There are also differences in rules for admitting pupils, a variation that does not exist in relation to Norwegian state 'ungdomsskole' (lower secondary schools).[220]

---

213 http://lovdata.no/all/hl-20030704-084.html#map002 (Accessed 18.04.2009).
214 http://www.dcsf.gov.uk/ (Accessed 24.04.09). This became the Department for Education following the general election in 2010.
215 It needs to be made clear that certain types of state maintained schools receive some funding from other sources – for example voluntary aided schools are funded mainly by the state but partly by religious bodies (Jackson 2004b).
216 In Norway, a communal advisor, the 'rådmann' is responsible for the economy, meaning the distribution of state money to schools, for hiring staff, for maintenance of buildings and grounds and for purchasing of teaching resources like text books. The communes organise this differently, and sometimes responsibilities like hiring staff or setting up a budget are left to school head teachers.
217 By October 1st 2007, there were 292 private schools in Norway, of which 152 were 'grunnskoler': counting 13.939 pupils. http://www.regjeringen.no/en/dep/kd/press-contacts/Press-releases/2009/stortingsmelding-om-lareren.html?id=545074 (Accessed 18.04.2009). Private schools must follow state- approved curricula, like the National Curriculum, or a corresponding document specially designed by the school. This according to the law regulating private schools: http://lovdata.no/all/hl-20030704-084.html#map002 (Accessed 18.04.2009).
218 State partnership with the Church of England since 1902 to provide education everywhere, (Copley 1997): see chapter 4.
219 Except, perhaps, Rudolph Steiner schools, but I will not include a discussion of this here.
220 All the schools in my sample were state schools and none was selective in terms of intake. However, it is notable that, in England, different rules of admission exist while, in Norway, intakes to state schools are decided exclusively by the geographical borders of catchment areas.

The main difference reflecting different imaginaries in my view is that only one type of school is acceptable in the Norwegian unitary school tradition,[221] whereas there is an acceptance of various types of schools within the English system.[222] I see this in connection to the stronger centralising feature in the Norwegian system and the tradition for decentralisation in the school system in England (see chapters 3 & 4). Both countries have local authorities as a structural level between the individual schools and the central government, but the English system is still more characterised by a tradition for local governance of schools than Norway[223] (which will be exemplified in chapters 6 & 7). Applying the terminology of Schiffauer *et al.* (2004) one could say that in the English *national imaginary* variation of types of schools is seen as more acceptable than in the Norwegian. However, the *imagined unity* in the case of the Norwegian school system must not be confused with real unity. In some formal aspects, Norwegian schools would be more similar, but real differences between schools might be just as significant. Only empirical investigation could reveal what real differences between schools consists of.

Although the social enculturation in English schools would also in theory socialise pupils into a sense of 'Englishnness', this is to a lesser degree an explicit aim of schooling compared to Norway. In the English school system, strengthening of social cohesion is encouraged, but unity is not an explicit value in the same way as it is in the Norwegian imaginary (Telhaug 1994). One of the functions of inspection is to ensure a certain common standard, but not equality in all schools. In Norway, all children in theory have the same basic education, but there is little knowledge about what variations there are in practice, since public inspections are an alien idea in the Norwegian system. This is reflected in how teachers in my sample answered a question on how they see their schools compared to other schools (chapter 6).[224]

5.4 Characteristics of the schools

Above I have mentioned some areas where there are major differences in the school systems reflecting different *national imaginaries*. When I go on to describe the schools in the sample, it is possible to see how some characteristics stem from dif-

---

221 Telhaug (1994) describes the unitary school as four dimensional: 1. The resource dimension: that there should be equality in availability of resources (economically and other kinds of recourses, for example learning material and personnel), 2. The social dimension: The school should include all pupils within a geographic area to come together in heterogeneous groups, 3. The cultural dimension: pupils should acquire subject culture; in their subject learning shared traditions, values and knowledge should be emphasised as a common frame of reference. 4. The dimension of difference: Unitary school ideology includes respect for difference and plurality of backgrounds among its pupils. The education should be adjusted to their individual needs so that all receive education that they need regardless of different abilities. (My translation or rather paraphrasing of Oftedal Telhaug's account).
222 http://www.inca.org.uk/england-organisation-mainstream.html (Accessed 24.04.09).
223 The coalition government that came into power in 2010 is breaking down the system of schools being the responsibility of local authorities. Many community schools have now become 'academies' that have no link with their former local authorities.
224 There is not much research revealing what actually goes on in the schools, and what variation exists between schools.

ferences in the school systems, but also other societal factors, like how a sense of plurality and immigration history since the 1950s/ 1960s affects schools and their RE.[225] It is worth noting that Schiffauer et al. (2004) also claim that integration of immigrants takes on different *national styles* in schools as a result of nation-specific social enculturation. Does RE teaching and learning in English and Norwegian classrooms (that I observed) also take on different styles reflecting the different *national imaginaries*?

All the English schools in my sample are secondary schools with children aged 11-18, which means that they also provide sixth form education. This is usually the case with English secondary schools, but there are some examples of 11-16 schools. All the Norwegian schools were 'ungdomsskoler' (lower secondary schools) with pupils aged 12-15. Some Norwegian 'ungdomsskoler' (lower secondary schools) are part of comprehensive schools for children aged 6-15, even if these are not. In other words, when 'ungdomsskoler' (lower secondary schools) are linked with other schools it would be with primary schools, whereas, in England, it would be with upper secondary schools.

The English school categories of primary and secondary school include a wider age group (5-18) than the Norwegian 'grunnskole' (6-15). In Norway, young people of ages 15-18 are in a separate school category, 'Videregående' (upper secondary). At 16-18, English pupils would be in secondary school sixth forms, designated sixth form colleges or in other forms of further education. This difference is even reflected in the English and the Norwegian language: in English it is primary (aged 5-11) and secondary school (aged 12-18), with a differentiation between

---

225 England as a part of Great Britain, consisting of several nations shaped by internal migration and colonial history, has been plural (in a traditional sense), but it was mainly a Christian plurality (see chapter 3 and 4). However, due to labour shortage, people from old colonies, such as South Asia, East African countries (such as Uganda) and the Caribbean started to arrive for work in the 1950s. In the late 1960s, large numbers of people of South Asian origin from former African colonies came because of africanisation policies in these countries. These included Sikhs, Gujarati and Punjabi Hindus and Muslims. From the mid- 1960s new legislation led to more permanent settlements. Immigration continued in large numbers, and today British society is considered to be multicultural in a more radical way than it was traditionally (Jackson 1997: 92 (note 1)).

Norway has a less plural point of departure with its state religion and romanticised sense of 'Norwegianness' due to the conscious policy of constructing a national identity in the young nation (Engen 2005), even though reality might have been that local cultural variation was just as diverse as in England (Skeie 1995). In 1967, the first 10 Pakistani men came to Oslo for work, and more immigrants seeking work soon followed. From 1975 new legislation led to more permanent settlements. From 1975, as a consequence of new laws regarding right to family reunion on the one side and immigration stop on the other, their families joined them. This was the start of a more permanent settlement. Muslims, Hindus etc. began to organise communities in Norway, including establishing mosques, temples, and graveyards. Since then there has been a permanent flow of legal and illegal immigrants into the country, presently mainly refugees and asylum-seekers. Today, we speak of Norway as a multicultural society with relatively large groups of immigrants or immigrant descendants from a range of different countries (Jacobsen 2001). The largest religious group is Muslims, and the largest ethnic group was Pakistani, but is now Polish, with many Poles coming for work (Jacobsen 2005). Norwegian immigrants come from a variety of countries, for example Bosnia, Turkey, Iran, Somalia, Iraq, Morocco, Vietnam, Thailand, India, the Philippines, Vietnam, Sri Lanka, Chile, Poland, Russia and also from western countries. Apart from Muslims, there are also some Hindus, Buddhists, Catholics, and a few Sikhs (Jacobsen 2001).

lower and upper secondary, while in Norwegian it is 'grunnskole' (6-15) and 'videregående' (16-18) with a differentiation between 'barne' (children) and 'ungdomstrinn' (youth) in the 'grunnskole'. One could say that, in the structural sense, the Norwegian middle level is oriented more towards the lower levels while in England the middle level is more oriented towards the higher levels of schooling.

After 'ungdomsskolen' (lower secondary school) Norwegian pupils get a general certificate, a diploma documenting a wide generic education, while the English students take more specialised examinations known as the General Certificate of Secondary Education (GCSE) in certain subjects. [226] Later, English students can take Advanced levels (A-levels) in a few selected subjects. Very often one of these would be chosen for further study in higher education. In Norway, pupils get a school leaving certificate with marks in all subjects after year 10. This means the sum of their marks that they get on tests during the year will appear on this certificate. Examination subjects are selected in a lottery-like process and are not chosen by the students themselves (UD 2005: 19). If RE is selected, they may have an oral exam, in which case this will appear as a separate mark on their certificate.

In Norway, pupils do not really start to specialise before 'videregående' (upper secondary school) while, in England, specialisation begins at an earlier age in lower secondary school (usually at age 14, the beginning of Key Stage 4). Specialisation, the choice of focusing on certain selected subjects, has greater emphasis and occurs earlier within the English system. The relative importance of GCSEs in the English system, compared to what the Norwegian pupils may get if they are selected to have exams in RE, affects the material in my fieldwork, both in the lessons observed (see below) and in answers from English and Norwegian teachers and pupils (see chapters 6 and 7).

In England, government policy encourages schools to specialise and specialisation has been rewarded with extra funding. This affected all the English schools in the sample.[227] This adds to the plurality of types of schools in the English (state) system, and has no Norwegian parallel. This kind of specialisation and financial advantaging of schools would be contrary to the Norwegian ideology of school unity. Telhaug (1994) describes the unitary school as four dimensional, the first of these being 'the resource dimension': that there should be equality in availability of resources (economically and otherwise).

In one of the English schools (ES3), the pupils were divided into ability groups. This is a fairly common practice in English schools, but would be unacceptable in Norway. Norwegian school politics have in recent years propagated an inclusive pedagogy, where pupils ideally get individual attention in a mixed ability context.

---

226 Some students do 'short course'/ half GCSE option RE which often schools provide for students who don't choose the 'long course'/ full GCSE. Since RE is compulsory (unless the parents opt the child out), a half GCSE usually corresponds in teaching time to the time that would be taken for compulsory RE. In other words, the child can get a qualification for doing compulsory RE.
227 English school 1 had recently become a specialist sportscollege, English school 2 had recently become a technology college, and English school 3 had also specialised and become a technology college (further descriptions of the schools below).

This can be understood from a website of the 'Utdanningsdirektoratet'[228] which describes how Equity in Education is a central concept in Norwegian Education. This ideal is expressed clearly by Telhaug's (1994) second unitary school dimension: 'The social dimension: The school should include all pupils within a geographic area to come together in heterogeneous groups'.[229]

5.5 Location of the schools and characteristics of the school populations

When it comes to location, the English schools were spread across a rather large city in central England, while the Norwegian schools were located in and around a rather large city in central Norway. A shared feature was therefore not being capital cities but, nevertheless, having populations reflecting immigration since the 1950s and 1960s. The schools were selected to represent different types of local environments within those areas.

English school 3 (ES3) is a city centre school, while Norwegian school 3 (NS3) is a school on the outskirts of the city. They are grouped like this because these two schools are the ones with the largest proportion of pupils from ethnic minority backgrounds. In this English city, the ethnic minority groups are mainly gathered in the city centre while in this Norwegian city they are located mainly in a suburb.

About three quarters of the pupils in English school 3 were immigrants, refugees with English as an additional language or second or third generation descendants of immigrants. In the area surrounding Norwegian school 3 the population was also ethnically mixed. In addition, this school (NS3) had a special status as a 'reception school', which means that new immigrants came there for special courses before entering ordinary schooling. This added to the variety of various minority groups in this school and, because of this, many of the pupils were first generation immigrants. The area around this school (NS3) is otherwise characterised by the challenging economical and social backgrounds of those who are ethnically Norwegian, a feature which is most similar to the catchment area of English school 2 (ES2).

Today, both England and Norway have second or third generation descendents from immigrants who originate from the modern era of immigration (England from the 1950s and Norway from the 1960s). They might now be said to form groups of ethnic minorities, but there is an issue about how to describe them. Some individuals describe their identities as being influenced by different contexts. Thus, some writers speak of 'hyphenated' identities (for example Norwegian-Pakistani or British-Hindu).

In terms of children's sense of identity, Østberg (1998a) describes the Pakistani children she studied in Oslo as having an 'integrated plural identity'. Reflecting concepts of religion and cultures as dynamic and internally contested (Said 1978, Jackson 1997, 2004a), descendants of immigrants should not be considered as static

---

228 http://www.utdanningsdirektoratet.no/Brosjyrer/_english/Equity-in-Education-for-all-understanding-central-concepts/ (Accessed 26.04.09).
229 My translation.

members of certain cultural groups within the English or Norwegian society. Rather, all individuals in our societies shape *their* own identity by drawing on various sources including those related to their forebears' country of origin (Jackson & Nesbitt 1993, Jackson 1997, Østberg 1998a). In both countries, immigrants and asylum seekers still arrive, so it is fair to distinguish between those who themselves have recently migrated and those of families who are now well settled in society or, indeed, were born in England or Norway.[230]

English school 2 is located on the outskirts of the city while Norwegian school 2 (ES2) is the most central of the Norwegian schools. The pupils in English school 2 were mostly from a catchment area with a predominantly white population. Characteristics of this area are some government housing for people with economic and/or social problems but also some asylum seekers. A significant number of pupils have special needs. The pupils in this school are mostly indigenous English/ British, but some are visitors from abroad whose parents come to study or work in a nearby university. The pupils in Norwegian school 2 (NS2) were largely upper middle class in the sense that many belonged to families with high levels of education and earning power. In both of these schools, pupils were largely indigenous white with some examples of pupils or teachers with other backgrounds, but otherwise these schools were the ones where I was less successful in providing closely similar contexts. English school 1 (ES1) and Norwegian school 1 (NS1) are both located in rural areas with surrounding farmland. There are few ethnic minority pupils in those schools.

5.6 Do classroom activities reflect different national styles?

In this section I will analyse observations in the schools. As mentioned above, the uniforms worn by the English pupils represented one very notable difference from the Norwegian situation. With regard to appearance, the English pupils' particular hairstyles and the occasional untucked shirt were the only signs of their individual personalities, while the Norwegian pupils also had different style clothes. Because of this, it was easier to make assumptions about pupils, rightly or wrongly, based on their choice of clothes and styles.

The pupil population

In English school 3, there were nineteen pupils in the group and it was a medium to low ability group (see above). The girls in the group were ethnically mixed; and so were the boys, though none of them were white. Eight of the boys were Asian and three were black. One girl was wearing hijab, three girls were of Asian descent, one was black, one mixed race and three were white. In English school 2, there were eighteen pupils in the group; one girl was black, one Asian and the rest were white.

---

230 Regarding issues of plurality in society, see also chapter 2, 3 and 4.

In English school 1, there were about twenty pupils and they were all white and indigenous English.

In Norwegian school 3, there were two Muslim girls, one Bosnian and the other an Iraqi Kurd, and they sat together. Three Muslim boys, all of Arabic descent, also sat together. Some of the Muslim boys were possibly Serbs.[231] The pupils were all wearing different youth style clothes and one white boy had a Mohawk haircut. There were sixteen girls and eleven boys in the class in Norwegian school 2. It was a rather colourful group of pupils, but not in terms of being multicultural. As the lesson unfolded, it became clear that many of the pupils had good abilities, strong personalities and high self-esteem. In Norwegian school 1, the pupils were indigenous Norwegian except for two black boys who were UN quota refugees from Zimbabwe and Congo. In the second half of the double RE lesson that I observed, these two boys left to have lessons in Norwegian language.[232] The pupils demonstrated a great deal of independence in their work, and willingness to participate in discussions regarding the topics they had been studying.

Organisation of teaching rooms

A difference which clearly reflected national differences was the use and organisation of teaching rooms. In all the English schools, the rooms were the RE teachers' rooms, meaning that displays reflected that they were RE rooms, and the teachers kept their equipment and belongings there. The different classes came to the specialist teacher's room to receive their RE lessons. For instance, in English school 3 there was a poster with different pictures of Jesus from different cultures, another about Buddhism and a third about issues to do with weapons. On the back wall there was a poster showing the attainment targets for RE. In front, next to a whiteboard, was a small table with some religious artefacts and a collection of various religious symbols. On the wall next to it was a picture of Mecca.

In the Norwegian schools, the teacher came and went as the subjects shifted while the pupils stayed in the same place. In Norwegian school 2, the pupils had lockers in their room. On the walls were posters of pupils' work in various subjects – on the recent tsunami in Asia, for example. There were no visible signs of any RE work or RE teachings there although there is no reason why RE work should not have been displayed. This adds to the impression from structural differences that there is relatively more emphasis on subject specialisation in English schools while there is more emphasis on pupils' well-being ('trivsel') in Norwegian schools.

Even though there is, of course, a focus on class environment in England and on quality of teaching in Norway too, we have seen above that the structures sug-

---

231 I know their religion because they were asked about it in the lesson. The priest visiting in the lesson observed in Norwegian school 3 asked the pupils what their religions were, and about 1/3rd of the class raised their hands to confirm that they were Christians, and about eight confirmed that they were Muslims. No one said that they belonged to any other religion and they were not asked about whether they were humanist or 'nothing'.
232 They did not participate actively and it was obviously not seen as important that they were present in RE lessons. In the interviews they were not referred to, but, when I asked about them, the teacher said that they were refugees and Christian.

gest a stronger focus on (the quality of) the subjects in England (although measured in a very traditional way) since there is subject specialisation from an earlier age compared to Norway. By contrast, in Norway there seems to be more focus on the class milieu and on pupils' welfare and well-being ('trivsel') compared to the English scene. That subject achievements are inspected and published in England but not in Norway also supports this suggestion. This can be said to reflect different styles of civility.

Topics covered

When it comes to topics covered, there are a variety of GCSE religious education syllabuses from which English teachers select the one they want to follow with their pupils. Some have a strong religious studies or comparative religions base, while others focus more on Christianity with biblical options, and others are more philosophical and ethical in content. The teachers here had chosen a syllabus dealing with 'religious responses to life issues'. In Norway, the National Curriculum and its local adjustment decide the content of the teaching. These teachers were following the 2002 curriculum (LS 2002), but were using textbooks which had been made after the 1997 reform (KUF 1996) (see details on curricular history in chapter 4, and discussion on the use of textbooks in chapter 6). For example, the textbook used in Norwegian school 1 had a chapter which gave a presentation of all the religions and had a comparative phenomenological approach.

The main topics of the lessons were markedly different in the English and the Norwegian schools. In the English schools it was Christians' (and Muslims') attitudes towards poverty and wealth (ES3), sex in and out of marriage (ES2) and abortion (ES1). The topics related to a life theme type of RE (GCSE) syllabus. One could see these as ethical topics where certain views came across as right or wrong according to particular teachings.[233] In the Norwegian classrooms, I would say that the topics reflected a phenomenological approach: central issues in Christian belief in (NS3), 'humans and the holy' (NS2) and world religions (NS1).[234]

Although these are very specific examples, in the English case influenced by public examination syllabuses, I think they reflect differences in the national RE research and policy traditions, as well as some influence from one country to the other (see chapter 3). In England, a strand in the tradition of RE (following Goldman, Loukes et al. See for example Jackson & McGrady 2007) has been the use of 'life themes' while, in Norway, Rian and others at the University of Trondheim introduced ideas from phenomenology which were in part imported from phenomenology in English RE. An example of this is Ninian Smart's ideas of religious dimensions (Rian & Kværne 1983).

Interestingly, a similarity between the English and the Norwegian lessons observed was that, of the different possible topics from the curricula/ syllabuses, 'Christianity', or 'Christians' views', were the most represented. A second similari-

---

[233] This was clearly reflected in what English pupils said about why they had RE and what they learned (see chapter 7).
[234] Although the concept 'world religions' as such was not discussed.

ty is that Islam was mentioned, and in one school, (NS1) Judaism was also discussed. This reflect the institutional level of curriculum where, on the English side, *the local syllabus* (a statutory document reflecting the 1988 Act) requires RE to reflect Christianity and at least two other religions each year[235] while on the Norwegian side, it has to be 55% Christianity (see chapter 4).

Teaching methods and styles

Regarding teaching methods and styles, all the English lessons were quite strongly teacher-led, as all activities were initiated by the teachers (or visitors in a teaching role), and the classes were led from the front most of the time. For example, in English school 3 the main method of teaching was the teacher lecturing and writing on the blackboard, asking questions for the pupils to respond to.[236] The only pupil-to-pupil communication was whispering which the teacher attempted to stop. A contrast to this could, for instance, be found in Norwegian school 1 where the pupils sat in groups doing presentations to each other. After first having studied one of the world religions individually, they were now presenting their findings to each other in groups of five, each presenting a different religion.

The conversation in the second lesson in Norwegian school 1[237] started with the teacher asking the pupils' opinions on the way they had been working on this topic. All who spoke said they thought it had been a good way for them to learn. One argument for this was that it had been good to be able to learn from each other. In Norwegian school 2, the teacher did not exactly ask the pupils for their opinions, but they expressed them anyway, and she accepted that there would be negotiations between the teacher and the pupils regarding having a test or not, and about what topic they wanted to focus on next. In the second lesson in Norwegian school 1, there was a conversation/ discussion in class where there was also a lot of pupil-to-pupil communication, and where the teacher mainly had a facilitating role.[238]

In English school 1, the main activity was watching an episode of the soap opera East Enders from the 1980s, where a woman named Vicky was in a dilemma over whether to have an abortion or not.[239] The teacher prepared her pupils for writ-

---

235 The idea of dealing with Christianity and two other religions per year in an interpretation of the Act in this local agreed syllabus, coming from non-statutory guidance which a local agreed syllabus could incorporate or not.
236 An example of an argument against the statement 'none should be rich as long as there is poverty on earth' was that a lot of people think that, if you earned the money, you deserve to keep it. As examples of rich people, the teacher uses David and Victoria Beckham and Bill Gates. Some of the pupils did not know who Bill Gates was. The people starving in Sudan were used as an example of poor people. Compared to the Beckham's, the teacher and the people in this class were poor while, compared to those people in Sudan, they were all very rich.
237 Where I observed a double lesson.
238 The lessons were part of a larger scheme of work about five world religions. Their textbook was one important source of information, but they had also used internet sources and the library.
239 In the programme, she consulted various people who gave their different opinions. At one point she discovered there was something wrong with the baby. During the course of the episode she changed her view from wanting to keep the baby to having the abortion.

ing an essay on the topic by going through a set of six questions intended to help structure the essay. During the lesson, she occasionally stopped the video and underlined relevant points which related to these questions. She asked the pupils questions and thus involved them in dialogue, but in a highly structured way. The questions were leading and seemed to have a 'right' answer for the pupils to uncover.

A contrast to this could, for instance, be found in Norwegian school 2. Here, the method of teaching was initially less creative perhaps, consisting of repeating issues related to the theme 'humans and the holy', referring to the text book and writing on the blackboard.[240] However, the teacher (NS2-T) allowed for pupils to use their initiative in deciding the course of the lesson. When the teacher (NS2-T) reminded the pupils of having previously agreed that it is not always possible to describe 'the holy', one of the girls put her hand up and gave the comment that the holy is too 'large' in a way to relate to. This led to more pupils wanting to give their opinions[241] and discussion followed, very much on the basis of the pupils' interventions. From time to time, the teacher contributed viewpoints or summed up major points; in other words the teacher had a facilitating role.

Dialogue in the classroom

Dietz et al. (2009) report the main findings in the country-specific qualitative (Knauth et al. 2008) and quantitative (Valk et al. 2009) studies of the EU Framework 6 REDCo Project on religion, education, dialogue and conflict.[242] These studies looked into teenage perspectives on religion, interreligious dialogue and/or conflict in the eight European countries involved. One of their findings was that in Norway 'students see school as a place to learn about different religions and discuss religious and ethical issues' (Dietz et al. 2009: 12). One of the conclusions of the English researchers was that RE lessons in schools in England were the most likely place for students to engage in discussions (dialogue) between different religious viewpoints while, outside the RE class, students were more likely to discuss religion with those from similar backgrounds to themselves. In other words, if (inter-religious) dialogue is seen as an educational aim, the RE class is currently the safe space where this is most likely to take place.

In Norwegian school 2, many pupils were very eager to participate in the pupil-initiated discussion about 'humans and the holy', displaying quite an engagement. They often expressed opposite views to one another. The discussion showed the pupils' courage and willingness to express their own opinions but also to accept

---

240 It was the last of a series of lessons on this topic. In summing up the theme, the teacher talked about humans and the holy using examples from several religions.
241 Examples: 'When we are little we have our parents, but as we get to be grownups we still need parenting figures, so we make them, gods, as a replacement for parents.' 'Religion is however sometimes related to power, like class system, like the caste system, and then it is used to say that whatever bad happens to you, you deserve it.' 'Well, Christianity is not exactly perfect. For instance in the story of Adam and Eve, when they are tempted to eat the forbidden apple: the effect of eating the apple is that it gives them knowledge of right and wrong, so prior to this they could not have known the difference between right and wrong. So, how then could they have known that eating the apple was wrong?'
242 http://www.redco.uni-hamburg.de/web/3480/3481/index.html

other pupils' opinions. This observation supports the REDCo findings that pupils were quite accepting of different views (Dietz et al. 2009).

The REDCo research concludes that there is generally a high tolerance among religious students for religious plurality, though more on the ideological level than in practice. However, in this lesson in Norwegian school 2 there was good pupil-to-pupil dialogue where there was acceptance for different religious and non-religious views, even when very different points of views were put forward. For instance, one pupil argued that 'Before we had scientists I can see that humans had the need for religion, but why do we need religion now when we know everything?' and another said 'Humans need religion to explain why things are the way they are'. A boy who clearly came from a religious background still had the courage to argue his contrasting view: 'I believe that it was religion that came to humans and not the opposite. I believe that religions are based on something that happened, that they are based on something that is true. I don't think religion would occur without a reason'. There was acceptance of the right for both views to be held among the pupils in this class.

In Norwegian school 1, there was also dialogue in class, but this was not so much about their opinions as discussion of elements in their learning. They started summing up the topic, world religions, and covered Christianity and Judaism and were to proceed with the other religions in the next lesson. The conversation had many digressions where the pupils stopped and discussed issues more or less central to Christianity and Judaism respectively.

For example, at one point they talked of the Pope's health (John Paul II), since someone commented that they had heard on the news that he had had a heart attack. This led to a discussion about how new Popes were elected and also about what happened when the Pope was attacked in 1982. In connection with Judaism, at one point they were discussing circumcision, not just in Judaism but also in Islam. Some were very well informed and especially one girl who stood out as giving very sophisticated responses. The teacher clearly showed that he appreciated her contribution. There was a high degree of pupil involvement and pupil initiative in both lessons in this school (NS1).

Different styles?

The English lessons all seemed to be planned in detail beforehand and delivered in a very structured way.[243] I would say that in the Norwegian schools there was a different style, less formal and less teacher-led and lacking this 'starter, main and summing up' structure. For example, when the teacher approached the room in English school 1, the pupils lined up outside the classroom. The instruction for a

---

243 Since the 1990s, the language of 'delivery' has become very dominant in British talk about education. A lesson is 'delivered' etc. This implies something very pre-planned and structured. The very use of the term 'deliver' in relation to teaching is another sign of national difference. In the Norwegian context teaching would not be conceptualised as delivering something, but perhaps rather as organising or facilitating learning or perhaps as doing something together with the pupils. This is one of many differences in development in the languages: of how pedagogy/ teaching and learning is conceptualised. But this is also changing over time.

starter activity[244] was given in the hallway before they entered the classroom in a very orderly fashion. This was the clearest contrast to the teacher style I found in Norwegian school 1. Here (NS1), the pupils were mingling in their room as the teacher and I entered. No immediate order occurred, and the atmosphere was very relaxed. The teacher greeted them and told them to get on with their work, which they did. The presentation in groups had started the lesson before, and seemed to continue automatically when the teacher told them to proceed.

Norwegian school 1 stood out as having the most pupil-led activities with a teacher in a facilitating role. There were, however, also variations within the national samples. Of the Norwegian schools, school 3 (NS3) had the most teacher (visitor)-led[245] lesson while, in Norwegian school 2, the lesson was initially teacher-led, but the pupils were both allowed to negotiate future tests and the topics of future lessons, and to initiate discussion. In the English cases, the teaching was more formal, organised and rigid in its structure and had teachers in more formal roles. In the English schools, teachers were addressed by pupils with their surnames, 'Mrs Lakes'. (ES3-T), 'Miss Haley' (ES2-T) and 'Miss Fields' (ES1-T), while, in all the Norwegian schools, the pupils used the teachers' first names, 'Oline' (NS3-T), 'Ingunn' (ES2-T) and 'Jon' (NS1-T).[246] This added to a general impression of a more formal tone in the English schools and a more informal atmosphere in the Norwegian schools.

Visiting Christian believers

Two schools, one Norwegian (NS3) and one English (ES2), had visitors in class presenting insider Christian views. A priest from the local State Church congregation was visiting Norwegian school 3. She was a woman in her late 40s, wearing a red leather jacket, high-heeled red shoes and a red scarf and large earrings. Issues she talked about included God's nature and Jerusalem being a holy place for three religions.[247] She said she thought it was important to know what makes *us* different from other religions. This could be seen as her supporting the idea of learning about different religions, but she also made the distinction between *us* and *them* with her remark.

After a period of the visitor doing most of the talking, pupils were losing attention. This improved again when she attempted to involve the pupils with questions and especially when, towards the end of the lesson, she told a personal story of how

---

244 It consisted of patching together pieces of paper with information as a means of recalling the content of the last RE lesson.
245 The interview with the pupils indicated that the class was normally quite strongly teacher-led, as they complained that it was just 'Oline' talking all the time, see chapter 7.
246 Pseudonyms used here.
247 In more detail, topics she covered were Jerusalem being holy for three religions and for Christians because this was where Christ was crucified. She asked about the Trinity of the Christian God (and one of the Muslim girls answered). The priest further gave an explanation about God's nature – being human and divine at once – about Jesus being a bridge between God and humans, about conflict in the religion; the Reformation, Northern Ireland, ecumenical work, about Christian holidays and about prayer.

she got a strong calling from God despite initially being opposed to the ordination of women priests. This commanded everyone's attention.

English school 2 also had visitors, a group called 'Youth for Christ',[248] to present an insider Christian view on the topic 'sex in and out of marriage'. The moral was that it was best to wait until marriage. The group was leading the class from the front for the whole lesson, and they also followed this pattern of starter, main activity and summing up in the end.[249] Like the other English lessons I observed, it seemed very well planned and organised, which is interesting because they were visitors. They followed the same pattern of teaching as could be observed in other lessons.

Different *national imaginaries* could be seen to include certain basic ideas about schooling, especially about what constitutes good quality teaching. This could explain why dealing with the same supranational challenges to RE are done in different ways. Such supranational challenges could, for example, be dialogue in RE lessons, combating prejudice, learning about different religions and life views. I have no foundation to judge whether they represent a national tendency statistically. In Kevin O'Grady's work (2003), for example, there is more student initiative, but O'Grady was specifically experimenting with ways to include and motivate his students.

A factor to consider is also that my English examples reflect teaching for public examinations. Teaching might be less rigidly structured where exam pressures are not so dominant, but the culture of meeting attainment targets is still there. A reform in Norway from 2006 introduces similar kinds of targets (see chapter 4), so this is something that might now lead to more similarities in styles of teaching. However, in my samples from 2004 and 2005 there are differences that might be explained through looking at the other levels of curriculum.

Pupils' interest in the topics taught

Because of the different styles, reflected in factors like more acceptances of pupils' initiative in the Norwegian sample and a more rigid structure in the English sample, it was easier to observe pupils' interest and involvement in the topics taught in the Norwegian lessons. In Norwegian school 3, which was the most strongly teacher-led of the Norwegian schools, the pupils seemed interested in the topic of Christian

---

248 The class teacher had a student teacher on placement from a university, a Christian with a Pakistani background. He was responsible for the lesson I observed and had invited this group to present their view on this topic.

249 In the main activity they talked about what influenced people with regard to sexual behaviours, for example parents, friends and the media. The visitors compared God to a loving parent who did not want their children to play where it was not safe. The moral was that it was best to wait until marriage. They showed a video of an old moralist man who told a group of young people that it was best to have as little sex as possible. This was presented as an example of a stereotype and not representative of the view of Christians. God, they claimed, had created sex for people to enjoy but had also provided rules so that it would be safe. At one point, they asked if any of the pupils would fancy a chocolate, and a boy volunteered. Before offering the chocolate bar to him, a person from the group licked it. This put the pupil off wanting the chocolate and symbolized how sex was better if the persons involved were untouched by others.

beliefs at the beginning of the lesson, but they lost interest after a while, probably because the priest was doing most of the talking. In Norwegian school 2, pupils did not seem too engaged at the beginning, when the teacher led the class from the front, but their interest was triggered by the opportunity to be involved in discussion.

Most pupils in Norwegian school 1 were participating actively in the lessons that I observed, but the interest and degree of engagement seemed to vary, which the teacher judged as acceptable. For instance, when pupils were reading their texts to each other and some groups finished early, this resulted in their just sitting, looking abstracted, chatting or walking around. However, one group was so eager in their presentation that they stayed in during the break to finish. The pupils seemed to be allowed to progress according to their individual pace and interest. Quite a few of them (NS1) showed a strong interest in the discussions in the second lesson but some also seemed rather indifferent.

In English school 3 (NS3), the pupil group did not look very interested in the topic (poverty and wealth). Some were obviously not paying attention, but some engaged in answering the teacher's questions. At one point the teacher asked them to make a start on the essay they were to write. Despite the teaching being very clear, some of the pupils had not been able to follow her arguments. For example, one boy sitting in front asked what question they were supposed to answer, although this was written on the board at the beginning of the lesson and was still displayed there. When asked, some had difficulties in distinguishing between wealth and poverty.[250] However, some gave interesting answers and some of the chatting among the pupils was actually about the topic of the lesson. Of the English classes, this was the one with most 'chat': the teacher did try to stop them but was less rigid in her attempt than in the other lessons I observed.[251]

A group of 14 year-olds could be expected to be interested in the theme of the lesson in English school 2 – sex in and out of marriage – and I think they were. The pupils were invited to participate actively through the types of activities chosen, but in a quite structured way. The visitors introduced themselves through a starter activity. They gave some 'facts' about themselves and the pupils were asked to stand up if they believed a point to be true or remain seated if they thought it was false.[252]

Afterwards, they made the pupils stand up if they agreed to certain opinions: 'to stand up for their opinion', and they were asked to share that opinion. The pupils

---

250 It is tempting (but unpleasant) to say that a reason for this might have been that this was a so-called low ability group. If pupils are divided by ability, this is perhaps not ideal for pupils learning from each other.
251 Another issue related to different styles of discipline is that, in the English classrooms, 'chat' seemed less acceptable and was more or less effectively stopped by the teachers. However, this also varied somewhat between English and Norwegian classrooms respectively and, again, Norwegian school 3 stood out as the most disciplined. Small talk did occur in Norwegian school 3, but was silently stopped by the class teacher (not the visitor) who went and touched pupils' shoulders and gave them a 'look'. There are examples of a good deal of talk in some English classes, for example in O'Grady (2003) and also in examples in the REDCo qualitative study where having a chance to talk and express opinions was seen as a feature (Ipgrave & McKenna 2008).
252 One 'fact' presented was 'I am from Jamaica and married to an American woman'. The truth was that he was from Rwanda and married to an English woman.

were active and responsive although some seemed a little insecure, looking around to observe what their classmate meant before 'standing up' for an opinion, for instance. There were some giggles but some pupils looked quite serious. My impression was that this lesson made some sort of impact on many of them (see chapter 7).

In English school 1, it was not easy to observe signs of whether the pupils were interested or enjoyed the lesson regarding abortion, but some were quite active in responding. One girl at one point made the remark that she hoped they would not be watching any more soap operas, but I am not convinced that this meant she did not enjoy the lesson.

National styles and civil enculturation

I started this chapter with the question of whether classroom activities reflect different *national styles*? In summing up this part, I think that in many instances they are. This is not to disregard the great variation within the national samples, and surely more so had it been a larger sample. However, differences along national lines are, for instance, wearing of school uniforms, division into ability groups, the use of space in classrooms, the focus on subject vs. the well-being of pupils, ethical themes regarding different people's views vs. more phenomenological content about the religions as such, more teacher-led in the one case (England) and more emphasis on pupils' initiative in the other (Norway), and the use of teachers' surnames vs. first names. One could see this as supporting the view that a nation-specific civil enculturation can be traced in all schools[253].

5.8 Reflecting on the empirical studies in the methodology

With regard to my methodology, I see my case studies in relation to the wider context which is defined and limited by the combination of Goodlad's levels and the three dimensions of *subnational, national and supranational processes*. This is the function of the fieldwork here: to look at aspects of practice in relation to those 'more remote' levels (Goodlad & Su 1992: 239).

Goodlad sees the levels as more or less remote from that level which is most important, and 'the final test of all curriculum practice': the experiential level. This is how within my theoretical framework (see chapter 2), it becomes logical to consider the societal and institutional level as the context of the cases. Burawoy (1991) and Leganger-Krogstad (2007) represent other ways of making this logical: in extended case method (Burawoy 1991), a case must be considered in a wider context than just the immediate local topography of, in my case, the schools. Leganger-Krogstad (2007) includes globalisation as a contextual factor for RE today.

---

[253] *Civil enculturation* is 'the process by which an individual acquires the mental representations (...) and patterns of behaviour required to function as a member of (civil) culture, (...) taking place as a part of the process of education' (Schiffauer *et al.* (2004: 2)).

When it comes to the dimensions, the *sub-national dimension* is important in relation to the empirical example, as this would be the close context of the cases. The material discussed here in chapter 5 reflects the sub-national level but, since the sample is not representative, this is discussed in relation to the national dimension, especially the idea that different *national imaginaries* give schooling different national-specific *styles*. The national dimension is expanded through applying the concepts *civil culture, national imaginary and civil enculturation* from Schiffauer et al. (2004). Applying these concepts I can discuss how findings in the case study fit in with the imaginaries, taking account also of the other levels. I could say something about characteristics reflecting different styles of civility, like with the examples of the school uniform and inspection.

Even the *supranational dimension* can be seen as the wider context, as Leganger-Krogstad (2007) suggests. Teachers and pupils might have a direct participation in supranational processes, especially in RE where the topics often relate to world religions, life views or ethics (for example, in human rights), which are international phenomena.

Chapter 2 includes reflection on how a *supranational dimension* influences RE, and I think I have demonstrated how that influences both *the societal level* (chapter 3) and *institutional level* (chapter 4). However, in the empirical part I explore how the supranational dimension affects practice. Being an explicit comparison of English and Norwegian RE, however, this study is more than a discussion of how supranational processes affect each of the systems. Because of this, the national dimension will be important. With regards to this, the ideas of *national imaginaries* and *social enculturation* are useful.

The societal and institutional levels of curriculum which are discussed in chapters 3 and 4 are also considered the context of the empirical cases. Only through investigating what goes on in practice is it possible to discuss, for example, the institutional levels relevance for practice, or to what degree policy documents on the institutional level reflect the level of practice. The institutional level is where we find legally binding aims and a description of content for RE, so the relationship to practice is interesting, even from a legal point of view.

Afdal (2006) interviewed fifteen teachers (Afdal 2006: 25) in his study. He investigates how the concept of *tolerance* is understood in the intentional and perceived curriculum in Norwegian compulsory education. His basic conceptual framework comes from Goodlad's theories of levels of curriculum, but he uses a different definition of the levels from that which I use and sets out to interpret tolerance as a curricular value in three different curricula domains: perceived, formal and ideological.

Afdal (2006) argues for more communication between the levels, but tends to see them as separate systems (Afdal 2006: 332). He concludes that there is a lack of communication between the domains, and suggests two alternative explanations for this: one is failure of implementation of formal curricula (seen as normative) which he basically rejects for the second alternative: '(…) the multicultural classroom is not a place for teaching tolerance, but for finding out what tolerance is all about' (Afdal 2006: 350).

This I see as an argument for policy to be based on better knowledge and understanding of the levels of practice, which I support. Taking Afdal's (2006) point, there is also a question of how relevant those documents on the institutional level are for teachers and pupils in practice. This issue will be investigated in chapters 6 (teachers' perspectives) and 7 (pupils' perspectives).

5.9 Summary and Conclusion

In this chapter I have introduced the fieldwork and explained its purpose in the overall structure of the study. The main purpose of this chapter has been to contextualise the empirical part, and the analysis in chapters 6 and 7, and this is also done comparatively. I have pointed out several differences in the education systems which I interpret to represent the different *national styles* of civility in those systems. I have discussed examples of observations, pointing out elements that might be said to reflect the different *national styles*. This I see as a necessary contextualisation for the interpretation of the teachers' perspectives in chapter 6, and the pupils' perspectives in chapter 7, which in this book represents the instructional and experiential level of curriculum (Goodlad & Su 1992).

In this chapter (5), the sub-national dimension is present through the observations about and from the schools: the cases, and the local factors which influence those schools. At the same time, the national dimension has also been discussed, through applying Schiffauer and his co-researchers' (2004) concepts such as *social enculturation* and *national imaginary*. This provides a framework for my interpretation of a non-representative sample in the context of a comparative methodology. It makes it possible to consider differences in styles between English and Norwegian schools which reflect different *social enculturation* and different *national imaginaries*. However, I have also kept in mind the supranational dimension, and pointed out that some imaginaries might be of an international nature.

In the next chapter (6), I will explore the instructional level, which is represented here mainly through interviews with six teachers. Following that, in chapter 7, the experiential level will be discussed, and that is represented in this book mainly through interviews with six groups of students.

6. Instructional Level: Teachers' Perspectives

6.1 Introduction

In this chapter I explore the *instructional level* of the curriculum (Goodlad & Su 1992, see chapter 2, 8). In one way this is identical in England and Norway, but the differences lie in the ways in which this level relies on regulations and expectations which come from the more remote levels of curriculum (as described in chapters 3 and 4). These are 'more remote' in the sense that the most important level is the experiential: (Goodlad & Su 1992: 239).[254] Nevertheless, it is on the instructional level that the final decision is made about what is done in the classroom.

Teachers' perspectives are represented mainly through six semi-structured interviews which I conducted with the teachers of the lessons that I observed (see chapter 5). The interview schedules were designed to explore the relationship between the levels of curriculum (see appendix 1), and were related to central aims expressed at the institutional level of curriculum. The institutional level of curriculum was, in the English cases, represented by the Education Reform Act of 1988 and the local agreed syllabus (two different ones).[255] In the Norwegian cases the examples from the institutional level that the questions were based on were the law[256] and the National Curriculum for RE (LS 2002).

Based on these documents, it was possible to formulate *almost* identical questions for the English and the Norwegian interviews. In other words, regarding the aims for RE at the institutional level as specified above, there were strong similarities between England and Norway.[257] At the same time, I must note that differences in phraseology in those documents' descriptions of 'Christianity and other religions' were reflected in teachers' answers. Further, there were topics that I chose not to ask about[258] because I attempted to confine the interviews to issues where there seemed to be direct parallels at the institutional level. The schedules for the interviews had four main sections related to: general aims for RE; the content of the teaching; learning about and from religion; and, respect and personal growth. In analysing the material there was clear coherence between the two last sections.[259] For this part of the research, my key research questions were:

- *What are important similarities and differences between the instructional level in England and Norway as expressed by teachers in this sample material?*

---

254 The levels of the curriculum, according to Goodlad & Su (1992), are societal, institutional, instructional and experiential.
255 With pupils of this age group, the GCSE syllabuses, organised on a national basis, have a greater determining influence on what is taught in class than the local syllabi which tend to be sidelined at this level. This was, however, not considered when framing the questionnaires, but is taken into account in the analysis.
256 At this time reflecting the changes in 2002, see appendix 2.
257 See chapter 4 for more details about similarities and differences in the institutional level.
258 Philosophy, secular life-views such as secular humanism, and ethical issues.
259 Others investigating the role of the teacher have had an interest in looking at the importance of teachers' biographies in relation to their style of teaching (Everington & Sikes (2001), Haakedal (2004), van der Want et al. (2009)).

- *How do we account for these?*
- *How do we account for these with reference to the other levels (institutional and societal) of curriculum?*

6.2 The teachers and their contexts

The context of the teachers includes personal issues, such as their age, educational background,[260] teaching skills and religious affiliations. Further, it also includes subnational factors such as local geo-culture and school environment, and national factors including *national imaginaries* (Schiffauer et al. 2004, see chapter 5). Supranational processes could also be seen as part of their context (Leganger-Krogstad 2007), and international links may, for example, be their pupils' connections to other countries, or their own or their pupils' participation in supranational processes through media or travel (globalisation), or the fact that the major religions taught are international phenomena. Actually, *the local* and *the global* became two sides of the same coin when teachers drew on the experiences of the pupils in their classes. For example, Hajj is a yearly global event but, if anyone in the class has been to Mecca, or someone in their family is in Mecca, this event is both *local* and *global*.

Age-wise, all the English teachers and 'Ingunn' (NS2-T) were relatively young (between 25 and 35), while 'Jon' (NS1-T) and 'Oline' (NS3-T) were older (between 50 and 60). Haakedal (2004) investigated how the role of RE teachers in the compulsory Norwegian school was formed.[261] She found that teachers of different ages are 'influenced by their own time' and that older teachers tend to be more influenced by local geo-culture while a younger teacher typically would be more globally oriented.[262] Lund Johannessen (2009)[263] has recently conducted research which shows that Norwegian teachers seem to value 'sameness'. Meanwhile re-

---

260 For details, see appendix 3.
261 Including to what extent their philosophies of life influenced the forming process, and how much occupational freedom individual RE teachers had. It was a qualitative empirical study of general teachers who were also RE teachers, a common position in Norwegian schools. (See appendix 3). Haakedal (2004) interviewed primary school teachers in three different Norwegian counties. She based her analysis on quite extensive material from three sets of data, in 'REPILOT' she interviewed 17 teachers, in 'REBUS 1' she collected 100 texts and in 'REBUS 2' 14 teachers participated.
262 Haakedal (2002, 2004) presented a typology of teachers: which demonstrates that theories of culture generations as well as theory of life interpretations explain variations in how the role of RE teacher is formed. 1. The traditional religious elderly teacher; who systematically has additional assignments as an RE teacher specifically: 2. The self-conscious young Christian teacher; with personal initiatives in religious socialisation in school: 3. The tradition-conscious sceptic who loyally conducts his/ her role as RE and class teacher: 4. The self-conscious agnostic RE teacher, often aged 40/50, emphasising values education: 5. The privately religious younger teacher with occasional experience in teaching RE. See also Slanders' (2004) description of Haakedal's study.
263 A study in the REDCo project in a book about *Teachers Responding to Religious Diversity in Europe* (van der Want *et al.* 2009) which was based on qualitative interviews of six Norwegian teachers.

search on RE teachers in England (Everington and Sikes (2001)[264] and Everington (2009)[265] illustrate how English RE teachers view diversity positively. Promoting understanding of and a positive view of cultural difference were seen by English RE teachers as imperative in their teaching. This difference is echoed in the interviews which I conducted with Norwegian and English teachers and may refer to differences in the national imaginaries.

English secondary schools usually have a Faculty of Humanities and a Department of Religious Education, to which all the teachers in this sample refer.[266] This does not have a parallel in the Norwegian 'ungdomsskole' (lower secondary) schools, but there will be someone officially responsible for the subjects.[267] We have little knowledge of how much work is done in this capacity, and this is not something which the Norwegian teachers in the sample refer to. Many English secondary school heads of department will have some form of specialist qualification, but some do not. Only a few would have a master's degree in RE or religious studies, and a tiny number would have a doctorate.[268] In Norway, some teachers would have some sort of specialisation in RE, but most RE teachers would not. In Norway, many would be formally qualified for teaching RE without being subject specialists (see appendix 3).[269] It is notable that, in both countries, RE is in many cases taught by non-specialists.

6.3 Describing their school and its RE

There was a difference in English and Norwegian teachers' ability to describe their school and its RE. The Norwegian teachers had difficulties with describing their school in relation to other schools, and mostly referred to their personal experiences. The English teachers, however, immediately knew what criteria to describe their schools by and did not refer to their personal experience. All the English teachers also included comments on how their schools were improving. For example, 'Ruth' (ES3 – T) described her school as a 'state run inner-city school, with approximately

---

264 Who followed 'a cohort of students on a one-year post-graduate training course for secondary RE teachers through their course and into their first year of training' (Everington and Sikes 2001: 183). These English students/ teachers all had degrees, for example in theology, religious studies, and sociology, philosophy or women's studies. Like Haakedal, Everington and Sikes were also interested in the importance of the teachers' own life views, and what they see as aims for RE (more below).
265 A part of the REDCo research, in a book about *Teachers Responding to Religious Diversity in Europe* (van der Want *et al.* 2009).
266 Most English secondary schools are organised in Faculties and Departments, so in a school there will be, for instance, a Faculty of Humanities and a Faculty of Maths and Science. This is a kind of organisation we traditionally only find in Universities and University Colleges in Norway, but also now in 'Videregående' (Upper secondary). In the Faculty of Humanities in an English secondary school there will be a head of Department for Religious Education. In primary schools there is usually a designated co-ordinator (or 'subject leader') of RE, but these are usually non-specialists who may have had some in-service training in RE.
267 See Appendix 3.
268 Only very few people hold a PhD in pedagogy of religion in Norway, and all (who still work) work in higher education (see chapter 3).
269 This is the case with one of the teachers in this sample, 'Ingunn' (NS2-T).

1000 pupils from 11 to 18 years of age, which achieves well'. 'Vicky' (ES2-T) described her school as follows:

> *(...) it's a mixed comprehensive. We've got about 600 pupils on our role. A significant amount of our pupils have special education needs. We have an area within the school which caters for special needs children. And we're a growing school and an improving school. Our results are getting better. And we're attracting pupils from outside the (...) catchment area now (...).*

An example from the Norwegian teachers' responses is given by 'Jon' (NS1-T):

> *Wow. I have only worked in this school you know, I have worked here 25 years when this term is over. So, I can't say anything about this school in relation to other schools. My perceptions about the (Norwegian) school in general I have through the media, you know, TV, radio and newspapers and ... so it is difficult for me to say anything about that I think.* (NS1-T)

I was not able to get him to say anything about how the pupils were achieving either. Instead, he said he thought that they had a good school where most pupils learned a lot and were *thriving* (demonstrated well-being).[270] 'Oline' (NS3-T) answered in a similar way, but 'Ingunn' (NS2-T) described her school as having well-resourced pupils who usually had good exam results and a good reputation in the city. Perhaps a reason why she was more knowledgeable was related to her age. Haakedal (2004) suggests that older teachers tend to be more influenced by local geo-culture while a younger teacher would be more globally oriented. It may be that 'Ingunn' as a younger teacher was more aware of criteria for comparing schools from her knowledge of other countries' educational systems, for example.

One explanation for the different abilities to describe schools and their achievements is to be found in the different culture for inspections and for ranking schools in the two countries (see chapter 5). In the Norwegian context, it was not altogether unexpected that the Norwegian teachers had problems identifying criteria for describing their schools. They had little knowledge about real differences between schools within the unitary school system, because little research on this is done or communicated to them. The English teachers, however, knew exactly what criteria were normally used to describe schools, which could also be expected in view of the way Ofsted identifies explicit areas that need improving (see chapter 5).

The English teachers also volunteered information about what the school did to improve their RE. For example, 'Ruth' (ES3-T) explained that RE in her school is well respected among staff and pupils and is quite high on the school's agenda.[271]

---

270 'Trivsel' (thriving) is a frequently used concept in Norwegian context, and one of the things which may in fact be inspected. It refers to the degree to which pupils feel well in school.
271 Another example of the same was 'Vicky' (ES2-T) who said: '(...) my predecessor (as head of the RE department) was part-time for starts, so I don't think that did anything for the credibility of the subject. It wasn't a GCSE subject; it was a certificate of achievement subject. And it was sort of tacked on and there wasn't much subject specialism, because when the lady who was officially head of RE only was here part-time, when she wasn't delivering lessons, it was taught by a number on non-specialists around the school. (...) things like environment and teaching strategies and all the things that are making RE better now, weren't in

In the Norwegian case, the question about describing RE in their school was answered with reference to activities in RE lessons. In Norwegian school 1, I probed to see if the teacher might give similar answers to the English teachers. After having talked about sorts of activities they do in RE lessons, 'Jon' (NS1-T) asked if this was the kind of answer I was looking for:

> O: (...) in England they are preoccupied with issues such as whether a subject has got a low or a high profile, for example in relation to other subjects. For example, in this one school I visited, they talked about how they worked to improve the subject's status in that school, to get more recognition from the management and things like that.
> L: Mm. This is not a known approach to a subject here, I must say.

The question of a subject's status was not seen as meaningful in the Norwegian case, and I found it irrelevant to ask the same question again in the other Norwegian schools. There was no talk about school or subject improvements, nor were concrete areas for improvement identified or mentioned by the Norwegian teachers.

6.4 Aims of RE

All the teachers agreed with the aims of RE that I read to them, which is interesting in relation to the idea of social enculturation: that there is a socialisation into certain civil values or ideas through school activities.[272] The aims that I read to the teachers were, on the English side, that RE should be about Christianity and the other principal religions represented in Britain, that it should be non-denominational, promoting the spiritual, moral, cultural and mental development of pupils (see chapter 4). In Norway, the aims were that KRL should provide *thorough knowledge* of the Bible and Christianity as cultural heritage, and the evangelical Lutheran faith, give *knowledge* about other Christian denominations,[273] provide knowledge of other world religions, life views and ethical and philosophical questions, promote understanding and respect for Christian and Humanistic values and promote understanding, respect and dialogue between people with different opinions in questions regarding faith and life views.

All the English teachers identified promoting a positive attitude towards other people as especially important, which is consistent with the findings of Everington & Sikes (2001)[274] and Everington (2009: 32): 'All are concerned to promote an

---

   place then.' (ES2-T). (Short-course GCSE certificates compulsory RE, while full-course GCSE means they do more RE than they have to, and that RE is prioritised in this school.)
272 It was also the case with English and Norwegian teachers in a study in the REDCo project that they all agreed with the formal aims of the subjects (van der Want *et al.* 2009).
273 The difference between *thorough knowledge* and just *knowledge* was eliminated in the 2005 curricula and law change, see chapter 4.
274 They stress the need for RE teachers to reflect on their own world views, values and attitudes, the need to understand racism, and the need to have knowledge and understanding of the pupils' world views, values and attitudes. Everington & Sikes (2001) conclude that RE teachers should resolve tension between their personal and professional beliefs and goals, and that in order to effectively contribute to reducing prejudice and promoting intercultural understand-

understanding of and a positive view of religious and cultural diversity'. On the Norwegian side, there was a different tendency: 'Oline' (NS3-T), for example, made one comment on the aims: that the first – giving pupils thorough knowledge of the Bible and Christianity as cultural heritage and the evangelical Lutheran faith – was 'quite important actually'. This is consistent with Haakedal's (2004) typology that the two older teachers were more focused on traditional content and values. 'Ingunn's' (NS2-T) sole remark was that learning about *other religions* and promoting respect for *Christian and Humanist values* are perhaps especially important. This could be explained with reference to her local context where active members of the Norwegian Humanist Association had made their voices very clear (see chapter 5, 7). This is, however, also consistent with Haakedal's (2004) finding that a younger teacher would be more focused on global issues.

The aims of RE as defined here are quite similar but, while English teachers saw promoting harmony between diverse societal groups as essential, the Norwegian teachers tended to see learning about 'our cultural heritage' as more central.[275] It is an interesting contrast that the Norwegian teachers did not see addressing plurality as equally central, even if this was *the* new element in the 1997 reform and has been at the heart of the debates (including the legal cases) and the various curricula since (see chapter 4). An important aspect of these debates has, of course, been resistance to this change, and disagreements over what it means to say that Norway is now a plural society (see chapter 3). In the English case, other aims of RE, for instance promoting a cultural heritage perspective (Christianity *in Britain*), was not seen as central by the teachers, even though this perspective also exists on the English side (see chapter 3 and 4).

6.5 The importance of RE

Here, also, there was a tendency among the English teachers to see the importance of RE in relation to plurality, while, on the Norwegian side, there was more of a cultural heritage perspective. Again, the age of the teachers could be seen as a factor as two of the Norwegian teachers were older[276], but in relation both to the curricular and legal texts (institutional level of curriculum see chapter 4) and differences in the debates about RE at the societal level (chapter 3), this can be interpreted as demonstrating different ideas of plurality and integration within the different *national imaginaries* (Schiffauer et al. 2004).

> (...) *Especially now I think we are moving into a religious age. People are much more aware of religion because of the media. A lot would say that people are less*

---

ing, pupils must be given the opportunity to explore their own world views, values and attitudes.
275 This was less true for the youngest Norwegian teacher 'Ingunn' (NS2-T).
276 Of the Norwegian teachers 'Ingunn' (NS2-T) had a more pluralistic approach to what the importance of RE was: for example, that it gives pupils opportunity to discuss things that are important to them, for instance in relation to culture, and understanding other cultures: 'They 'chat' online, they have contact with many different young people, and it is important in relation to tolerance to have knowledge both about yourself and the world you are in.' (NS2-T)

> *aware of religion because there is much bias and that things are incorrect in the media. For example like the September 11th attacks, that is full of ... um, you know, anti-Islamic feeling, and kind of lots of, you know, lots of people's misconceptions about what Islam is. And I mean I think we need to counteract that in school.* (ES3-T)

'Ruth' (ES3-T) had the broader debate about religion in society from the societal level (see chapters 2 and 3) as her frame of reference for formulating what she saw as the importance of RE. 'Ruth' (ES3-T) saw RE as an important aspect of education because 'if you can't tolerate and understand people who are different, then I think education is a little bit pointless really'. 'Ruth' (ES3-T) displayed in her answers her own interpretation of the debate about what goes on around her in society, and, in a sense, she participated directly in the debates at the societal level.[277] She could also be seen as referring to the general educational aims of RE as contributing to citizenship and social cohesion, which also relate to societal debates.

'Ruth' (ES3-T) was teaching in the most plural school in the English sample. For her, RE had an immediate importance for her pupils for two reasons. The first is tolerance and understanding, and the second is to acknowledge the expertise of those who bring a lot of religious experience to the school.[278] The English teachers all saw religious plurality among pupils as a strength for RE, providing good conditions for doing RE well.[279] Where the school's populations were more 'monocultural' (schools 1 and 2), the lack of actual plurality in the pupil population was seen as a challenge, but also as a factor making RE important. For example, 'Sally' (ES1-T) stressed that widening pupils' experiences and understanding of other people was especially important in her school since many of its pupils had little first-hand experience of the mix of cultures and religion in society at large. In all the English cases, RE's importance was seen in relation to education for living in a plural society. This is consistent with findings in Everington & Sikes (2001), and Everington (2009).

By contrast, the Norwegian teachers tended to see plurality as more of a challenge to RE, although when I asked leading questions about how plurality could be seen as an asset to RE, they did see this point. However, the totality of their answers, and the way the pupils answered as well (chapter 7), indicate that the positive way of thinking about plurality as an asset to RE is not established as the *main* reason for the importance of RE among these Norwegian teachers. For example, 'Oline' (NS3-T), the teacher in the most plural of the Norwegian schools (NS3), said:

> *It has got to do with, I would say, having some knowledge of one's own background, and most of the pupils are still members of the State Church. (...) I also*

---

277 Her noting that we are moving into a religious age is related to ideas formulated for example by Berger (1999) (resacralisation) and even Habermas (2006) (religion in the public sphere), see chapter 2.
278 I think we owe it to our pupils, if they're coming in with lots of religious knowledge and understanding (...) who have never had the opportunity to express these beliefs in an academic way through examination (...) I think we owe it to our pupils to build on that. And I think we are lucky that we can do that. (ES3-T)
279 Also consistent with findings in Everington (2009).

think those who come from other cultures should know a little about things that are happening in this country, like why we celebrate Christmas and Easter, and things like that. (NS3-T)

Oline (NS3-T) did think that KRL was an important subject, but she emphasised the cultural heritage perspective, which at the institutional and the societal levels can be found alongside the aim that RE should address the plural context. This is consistent with findings in Lund Johannessen (2009: 104): 'But more than that, they value KRL as a subject that serves the goal of making students more reflective and aware of their own faith, opinions and tradition.' However, when 'Oline' (NS3-T) said 'one's own background' the *subject* in this sentence was a State Church member. In exemplifying knowledge which *all* need, she pointed to those 'from other cultures' needing to have knowledge about Norwegian customs, for example 'why *we* celebrate Christmas and Easter': but her *we* is one which includes mainstream Norwegian Christians, and excludes, for example, both those belonging to other religions or life views and Christian immigrants – who might celebrate Christmas and Easter in different ways but largely for the same reasons. 'Oline' (NS3-T) was not inclusive in her choice of words[280]:

> *NS3-T: Some (pupils) think the subject is OK, some find it interesting, and some say that: 'No I am not a Christian so I do not want it'. You have all shades, and some say 'OK, that is fine, this is something I do not really want to know about, but I am still a Muslim'.*
> *O: Yeah? That is ...*
> *NS3-T: And I say: fine, we do learn about Islam as well.*
> *O: Yes!*
> *NS3-T: And then there are the most eager secular humanists that would rather we stopped teaching Christianity altogether.*
> *O: Mm.*
> *NS3-T: Especially if we are reading from the Bible. I try to tell them that, listen to me, well, what this is actually is also cultural history, it is not just religion.*

Even though it is stressed in the curricular texts that teaching about 'other' religions and life views on equal terms as Christianity is a part of Norwegian RE, there is a feeling here that these 'others' are somehow an addition to that which is the main focus, namely teaching about Christianity/ the Norwegian tradition. One factor forming 'Oline's' (NS3-T) answer above was the presence of critical secular humanist voices: something which we have seen consistently through all the curricular levels (chapter 3, 4, 7) on the Norwegian side. Her approach to secular humanist critics here is, however, not that of inclusion, for instance in her use of *'we'*: rather, it is trying to convince *them* that knowledge of the Bible, for example, is useful for *them* too. 'Jon' (NS1-T) also expressed a very traditional view of the importance of the subject, leaning heavily on a cultural heritage perspective:

---

280 'Ingunn' (NS2-T) has a broader and more inclusive *we* than 'Oline' and in my interpretation relates to the same kind of grand debates about religion, society and plurality as 'Ruth' (ES3-T) above.

> *(NS1-T) Well, it has got something to do with 'barnelærdom' (childhood learning), and deeply ingraining in, or the confidence in these things, or the deep rooting in these things, 'barnetroen' (childhood faith) and things like that.*
> *O: Oh, really?*
> *(NS1-T) Of course, yes, well, yes it is, I guess it is, well I think it is natural that this has its place in school, frankly, and ...*

It is difficult to translate the concepts of 'barnelærdom' or 'barnetro' adequately. A direct translation of the first would be 'childhood learning' and the frame of reference is from very traditional Christian RE: to nurture children into religion, as a means of creating a deep-rooted sense of religious identity. 'Barnetro' could perhaps be translated as 'childhood faith' or 'childlike faith' or a 'child's faith', referring to Christian nurture.[281] However the concept 'barnelærdom' ('childhood learning') has been generalised in the language so that it does not necessarily refer to religious learning, but rather to something essential that is learned in childhood. With reference to the Norwegian unitary school tradition, it could be understood as a common base of knowledge that we share, and that forms a basis for living together in society (social cohesion). The concept *social enculturation* perhaps covers it (see above). 'Barnelærdom' (childhood learning) could also be seen in relation to *formation*: 'buildung' or 'social cohesion' in society. 'Barnetro' includes the word faith ('tro') and has a more direct reference to religion, but both concepts are very common and have a varied use in the language. One should therefore perhaps not over-emphasise the religious reference.[282]

However, seen together with 'Oline's' answers above, these two teachers' answers form an interesting contrast to what the English teachers saw as the importance of RE. This contrast is also consistent with differences between findings reported in Everington (2009) and Lund Johannessen (2009). In the English case, the view of RE as contributing to intercultural education already has a long tradition, and is a well established and even dominating aspect of RE for teachers. On the Norwegian side this is not equally true, and this difference is reflected in the other levels, for instance in the societal level (see chapter 3). However, while 'Oline' (NS3-T) and 'Jon' (NS1-T) leant on the aspects of the societal debate that enhance the importance of Christianity as part of Norwegian cultural heritage, 'Ingunn' (NS2-T), like the English teachers, leant more towards the 'plurality' end of those debates. I can't really know what I would find if my samples were larger and more representative, so here further research into teachers' understanding of the subject would be useful.

However, my case studies suggest that interpretations made by teachers at the instructional level of curriculum reflect different perceptions of plurality. Despite participating in many of the same supranational processes, the differences which come from the national processes, the different styles of the debates on the societal level, the difference in specific national history, or the perception of this in the *na-*

---

281 Or to the special kind of faith that children have, and that Jesus values especially according to the Bible (for example in Mark: 10: 14-15).
282 Perhaps he just never really thought about it, and, when he was asked, this is what comes to his mind. Perhaps the answer would be different had I come back the next day. His pupils said that they learned a lot about different religions from him, see chapter 7.

tional imaginaries, seem to me to be decisive in explaining how similar aims are interpreted in the different national contexts. The examples reflect slightly different civilities. English and Norwegian teachers depend on different views of the role of multifaith RE in relation to plurality in the societies at large and in the schools. Schiffauer et al. (2004) found that *integration of immigrants* takes on different styles in different nations; and my findings indicate that multifaith RE, too, takes on different *national styles*, even where the formal aims for RE are quite similar.

6.6 National aims and local adjustments

At both the English and Norwegian institutional level, there is a dynamic between centralised national aims for RE and adjustment to local contexts, but this is structured very differently. The 'middle level' of local adjustments in England consists of the system which includes Standing Advisory Councils for Religious Education (SACREs) and local agreed syllabus conferences (see chapter 4).[283] In Norway, it is clear in the core curricula (KUF 1996)[284] that adjustment of the teaching should be done in the local area and could be done also in individual schools. On page 68 of the 1997 National Curriculum (KUF 1996), for example, there is a model demonstrating how much of the curriculum should be decided by the central document and how much should be decided locally. In the 1997 KRL Curriculum (KUF 1996), this point was only concretised by a recommendation that local religious communities be visited. However, the 2002 KRL Curriculum (LS 2002), which the teachers formally were following at the time of interviews, made the following point about local adjustment:

> *(...) the centrally decided learning material increases during the school years and is most extensive in the 'Ungdomsskole' (Lower Secondary school). In 'Barneskolen' (Primary school) the centrally decided material and the locally decided material constitutes equal parts* (KUF 1996: 13).

At the time of my interviews with the English teachers, the Non-Statutory National Framework for RE (QCA 2004) had been recently published. The centralising tendency associated with this document (see chapter 4) made the system a little more like the Norwegian, with its National Curriculum. However, all the English teachers in my sample defended the system of producing RE syllabuses locally. For instance, 'Ruth' (ES3-T) praised the richness of the competence of the people on the local SACRE, and both 'Ruth' (ES3-T) and 'Sally' (ES1-T) saw the way their

---

283 SACREs are, as the name implies, a standing council, while the agreed syllabus conference which actually agrees the local syllabus, is convened especially for this purpose. It will usually consist of SACRE members but this may vary and other members might be co-opted. A agreed syllabus conferences have four committees: a Church of England committee, a other Christian denominations and other religions committee, a teachers representative committee and a local authority committee. At the same time, there are also the national GCSE examinations which in English secondary schools represent a different authority influencing what is taught. See http://www.gcse-coursework.com/res_bor.html (Accessed 11.05.05).
284 This part has been kept on in revised curricula.

teaching reflected the faiths of the local communities as important; that RE is 'finely tuned to the area you live in'. When 'Ruth' (ES3-T) was asked to make a comment about the Norwegian system, she said:

> I wouldn't want to be personally responsible for teaching or not teaching my pupils something. (That is) the job that SACREs do; they have so many kind of important devotees, kind of respected religious individuals on there, I think that they can come to a better understanding about what needs to be taught, because they're a step back. (ES3-T)

Even as a qualified RE teacher, she considered that she could not have done the job of local adjustment equally well, and suggested that this might possibly have led to some teachers choosing not to comply with the local adjustments as required. I find reason to ask if this might actually be the case with the Norwegian teachers in my sample. In Norway, the schools/ teachers were formally responsible for the local adjustments, but it seemed that these Norwegian teachers were either not fully aware of this opportunity/ obligation or felt they did not have the possibility of doing it.

When I rephrased from asking how they *did* adjust locally to *if they would have wished for* more opportunity to adjust the teaching locally, 'Jon' (NS1-T) said he was quite content with the way it was, and that he generally had most experience with following the textbook. 'The Norwegian teachers understood 'local adjustments' in a rather narrow way, mostly referring to opportunity to visit places of worship. However, 'Oline' (NS3-T) was in the process of asking the Imam from the Mosque in the city to come and speak to the class, but she did not mention this in relation to my question of how she contextualised her teaching.[285] Maybe it was a question of vocabulary and of how things were understood and conceptualised. It could be the case that the teacher did not have awareness of the ways in which her own teaching was contextual, which could be seen as consistent with Leganger-Krogstad's (2007) point that *all* teaching as such *is* contextual.

In the comparative perspective, it is reasonable to take the view that the work of local adjustments in Norwegian RE could have gained from using local expertise and authorities in a manner similar to that of the local agreed syllabus conferences.

The difference in the size of the populations in England and Norway does also mean differences in terms of available resources for RE. For example, the city of Birmingham is very multicultural[286], and has therefore many potential religious experts from various faith communities who can be involved in the SACRE/ local Agreed Syllabus Conference. There are also quite a number of experts in religious education who could be co-opted on to the SACRE and local Agreed Syllabus Conference from the four universities in the area.[287] One would not find a parallel to

---

285 This was revealed later in the interview.
286 In terms of having in its population a wide range of different religious views and cultural backgrounds
287 Aston University, University of Birmingham, Birmingham City University and Newman University College, http://translate.google.no/translate?hl=no&langpair=en|no&u=http://www.birmingham.gov.uk/GenerateContent%3FCONTENT_ITEM_ID%3D93043%26CONTENT_ITEM_TYPE%3D0%26MENU_ID%3D15392&prev=/translate_s%3Fhl%3Dno%2

this in Norway: even if some areas would have a richness of potential resourses, in other areas such resources would be scarce. However, the amount of available resources would, of course, vary in England as much as it would in Norway. In most Norwegian regions there are a range of local experts and representatives of religious and non-religious organisations who could have been involved in a process of local adjustment in cooperation with local school authorities. This would also have ensured wider representation as more different experts and representatives of Churches and other organisations could have been involved.[288] Norwegian RE would probably gain from engaging a broader range of representatives both locally and nationally. At the same time, there should also be an awareness of the further question of representation: how far are religious leaders and authorities representing individual children in schools regarding their life views?

6.7 Text books and schemes of work

The text book ('læreverk') in the Norwegian context and *schemes of work* in England represent another layer in between the institutional and the instructional level of curriculum (see chapter 2). In the Norwegian sample, the text book ('læreverk') is very decisive for the content of the lessons.[289] In the English cases, text books were also used, but here these were seen as a resource among others to draw from in teaching.[290] On the English side, it seems that teachers relate to their school's locally produced *schemes of work* in a similar manner to the way in which Norwegian teachers relate to their 'text book' ('læreverk'). A Norwegian text book, called 'lærebok/ læreverk', is more of a general scheme of work for lessons to be followed during a whole year,[291] and therefore perhaps more a parallel to English schemes of work than to English text books. A difference is, however, that English schemes of work are produced locally by teachers, and therefore also relate to how Norwegian teachers plan to deliver lessons, often based on the textbooks.

6q%3Duniversities%2Bin%2Bbirmingham%26tq%3Duniversities%2Bin%2Bbirmingham%26sl%3Dno%26tl%3Den (Accessed 12.05.09).

288 An odd kind of precedence has been established in Norway in that the same handful of people represent the different religions and life views in many different contexts (Egil Lothe of the Buddhist organisation, Lena Larsen of Islamic Council of Norway, Bente Groth for the Jewish community and Bente Sandvik and Hans Christian Nes for the Norwegian Humanist organisation, for example). With regards to professional expertise, there has also been a tendency that political authorities ask persons from the same limited group of people.

289 I see this in my sample and it is also the same conclusion in studies of Norwegian KRL textbooks, for example Winje (2008).

290 I see this in my sample and this is also confirmed in the 'Materials Used in Schools to Teach World Religions project': a government-funded research project carried out by the WRERU unit at the University of Warwick in 2008-2009, http://www2.warwick.ac.uk/fac/soc/wie/research/wreru/research/current/dcsf/ (Accessed 11.05.2009).

291 The Norwegian textbooks ('læreverk') would include texts for students to read, assignments and tasks for them to do following a pattern of pedagogy which will vary between different textbooks (Winje 2008). In addition to the pupils' books, there will also be a manual for the teachers containing central principles for teaching the subject with additional resources for the lessons, like, for instance, crossword puzzles or additional stories which could be told during lessons.

As my research interest was concerned with finding out about the relationship between the levels of curriculum, I asked the Norwegian teachers if they would use the curriculum text in addition to just following the textbook. 'Jon' (NS1-T) answered 'No, just the textbook (...) and occasionally clips from newspaper or magazines to actualize the teaching'. There did not seem to be any reflection on this on his part; he obviously regarded this as a normal and correct way to go about his teaching. Since the textbooks used in 'Jon's' (NS1-T) school related to the 1997 National Curriculum (KUF 1996), this means that the 2002 KRL curriculum (LS 2002), which was in legal effect at the time, was not being followed in his school. This means that the relationship between the institutional and the instructional level, in this case, is dependant on similarities between the 1997 and the 2002 curriculum. Thus, the changes made in 2002 (see chapter 4) would be of no consequence for the practice of the subject. This answered in a very direct way my question about what the relationship was to the institutional level of curriculum.

'Jon' (NS1-T) did not seem to be aware that there was a new KRL curriculum in 2002. How representative this is I can not say, but all three schools in my sample used textbooks that followed the 1997 curriculum. 'Oline' (NS3-T) and 'Ingunn' (NS2-T) were aware of the new curriculum from 2002, but said they had not taken the time in their schools to implement it. 'Oline' (NS3-T) admitted this was not a satisfactory situation but in her mind she had to use the textbooks that the school had bought for the pupils.[292] However, they are only obliged to follow the law and the National Curriculum; there is nothing formally that says they have to use a textbook. It would be possible, for example, to use the new textbook even if there were not copies for all pupils. For example, the schools or the local authorities could have made a plan based on the new curriculum and teachers could have used textbooks as one resource among others without following the book's scheme in a precise way. However, 'Oline's' (NS3-T) understanding of her situation was that she was dependant on using these 'textbooks' ('læreverk') from 1997.

The publishers in their turn depend on teachers' and schools' choice in order to sell their books, and could therefore produce books that they based on surveys of potential purchasers.[293] The different Norwegian publishers' textbooks ('læreverk') have slightly different approaches to the subject, but all follow the National Curriculum closely (Winje 2008). Textbooks are, in other words, interpretations of the National Curriculum. Using a textbook would therefore also normally ensure that even non-specialist teachers follow the curriculum. However, the frequent changes in the National Curriculum for RE has made publishers hesitant to produce new

---

292 The school wish to buy new ones but this had not yet been prioritised in the budget.
293 In the spring of 2008, I participated in several meetings at the publisher (Aschehoug Forlag) where a possible new textbook following the 2005 curriculum was being discussed. This made me realise more than before how important the textbook is for the Norwegian school, and to what degree teachers selecting a textbook actually decide the profile through their choice. On the other hand, once a textbook is chosen, the school can not buy another one for a while, because it would not be prioritised in the school budget, so then the textbook decides for the teachers. At these meetings, a publisher told an anecdote of how they had once produced a really innovative new textbook for a certain subject, while their competing publisher had gone for a much more traditional and in his words 'boring' solution. The one that sold was the traditional one, because this was what the teachers wanted. The moral was obvious: because they rely on sales, they have to publish traditional textbooks.

textbooks and schools equally hesitant in buying them (Winje 2008: 75). This makes it plausible that my finding that schools used outdated textbooks for RE was part of a general trend. In this case, schools are not following the curriculum as they are legally obliged to because they follow the outdated textbook.

As inspection[294] does not exist in the Norwegian system, there is nothing to ensure a 'standard' of teaching except trust in the professionalism of teachers and school leaders. If the teachers (or school leaders) are not aware of or do not have the resources (or the will) to deal with the actual National Curriculum or changes in it, then I would say that the textbook ('læreverk') in the case of Norway fulfils the function of both SACREs and local agreed syllabuses and schemes of work produced in English schools. This means that a huge responsibility and a great deal of power over what actually goes on in practice lies with the publishers of textbooks. Publishers have a great responsibility in both countries, but more so in Norway where the structures supporting local adjustment by other means than choice of textbook is weak (or, in fact, non-existent).

Regarding the question of the relationship between levels of curriculum, in this section I have found that in England this relationship relies on a number of well-established processes such as the activities of the SACREs, local agreed syllabus conferences and the production of schemes of work in schools and inspections. In the Norwegian sample, however, I found indications that changes in the National Curriculum at the *institutional level* made no difference to practice (the instructional level of curriculum) because the implementation of change depended on textbooks that were not updated. Seen together with findings from other investigations into the question of the use of textbooks in Norwegian RE (Winje 2008), I found it likely that this would be the case in many Norwegian schools. If I combine this with findings in chapter 4, that changes in the curriculum have been a main tool used by central authorities to respond to international lawsuits[295], this is remarkable because it indicates that these changes which should represent a certain development in Norwegian RE since 1997, may in practice have had little effect on teaching in schools.

6.8 Content of teaching

One of the important similarities between English and Norwegian RE is that, in both countries, Christianity and 'other' religions are taught. My approach to the question of the content of the teaching was whether teachers emphasised the national contexts or had a more global perspective.

The formulation *Christianity and 'other'* signals a difference between 'Christianity' and the 'others'. At the institutional level (see chapter 4), the English 1988 Education Reform Act refers to Christianity and the other *principal religions represented in Britain*. This can be taken to mean that the focus should be on the British

---

294 In any form similar to what Ofsted does (see chapter 5).
295 Which has ruled that Norwegian RE is in violation of Human Rights.

context, but it could also simply mean that the substantial presence of a religion in Britain legitimates its inclusion.

The Norwegian education act[296] does not say explicitly that it is religions *in Norway*, but the curriculum wording reflects a traditional Norwegian outlook in that the first point refers to (thorough) knowledge of the Bible and Christianity both as cultural heritage and Evangelical-Lutheran faith, then secondly it refers to (knowledge of) *other* Christian denominations. Then follow the points with regards other religions, world views, etc. (LS 2002: 11, see chapter 4). The order in which the topics are listed is not coincidental.

Regarding whether teachers emphasised the national contexts or had a global perspective; on the English side, 'Ruth' (ES3-T) denied that her teachings of *Christianity* would be linked to a British context: 'No, international context'. She stressed that they 'try to look at Jesus from an international perspective, and often I find we turn things on their head'.[297] When I put the same question about other religions, whether that would be linked to a British context or set in an international perspective, Ruth (ES3-T) said:

Well it's funny actually, because I suppose on the flip side: if we talk about (...) Hinduism or Islam I try and relate it to (the local area) more than the rest of the world, because I don't want people to think oh well Hinduism is this strange religion that only happens in India and (...). Yeah, the danger is that people teach Christianity as a white middle class British religion, with, you know, Jesus, really, white British middle class, you know, and he is not, so I suppose as a teacher, I suppose to teach Christianity effectively you have to teach it as a world religion that, you know, people all over the world follow, while I suppose when you talk about Islam and Hinduism, I suppose you try and bring it closer to home, and say it is not something that people do on the other side of the world. (ES3-T)

In the middle of 'Ruth's' reflection over this, a colleague in the RE department entered and this topic was discussed at length[298]. A main point was how they saw their teaching as aiming to counter the idea of Christianity as a British phenomenon. In the other two English schools, this tendency was less clear since they said they taught Christianity both in an international perspective and through different denominations in Britain. The *other* religions would also be both about, for example, Muslims around the world and specifically about British Muslims.

---

296 The version from 2002 which was the one which was legally in force at the time of the fieldwork.
297 In her classroom there was a poster with different pictures of Jesus from different cultures (see chapter 5).
298 'We bring the other religions home, because that makes it relevant, but we take Christianity abroad because it is irrelevant if it is taught as a white middle class religion', 'Ruth' (ES3-t) explains. They say they 'are thought' not to teach Christianity as a British 'thing', '(...) because it is an international thing.' Her colleague (among other things) brings in that 'Religion is not something that belongs within a border, to which 'Ruth' (ES3-T) replies: Yes. It's not cultural is it, it is international. But then it is cultural, isn't it, it's dependant on your culture.' To which her colleague answers 'Yes of course!' They also have a very interesting discussion about the difference between 'White and Black Christianity' and how some African Christians now see Britain as an evangelical field: 'It is really interesting when you look at people who are coming from abroad, and they see England as a mission field, as a place where people need to hear the gospel. You know, yeah, it's gone completely full circle.'

On the Norwegian side, all the teachers said that teaching about Christianity would be linked mainly to the Norwegian context, but they would also emphasise the Norwegian context in their teaching about other religions. Both the teaching of Christianity and 'other' religions would also sometimes include international perspectives. For instance, 'Ingunn' (NS2) had recently taught about different Christian denominations in Norway, but her class had also placed religions on the world map. 'Oline' (NS3-T) and 'Jon' (NS1-T) often picked up events from the media, for example the recent death of the Pope,[299] or that it had been Ramadan. This would make their teaching both contextual and international, as it refers to pupils' personal relationship to international events. When I asked if they also linked teaching to a Norwegian context when it was about other religions, 'Ingunn' (NS2-T) said: 'Mm, yes I guess I do, without necessarily being very conscious about it. I guess it has developed a bit like that, yes, that we talk about others, people with other types of backgrounds who come to Norway (…)' (NS2-T). 'Jon' (NS1-T) said:

> *Yes, (…) and it is not difficult to base it within a Norwegian context now, because we have so many with other backgrounds now in Norway, (…) so that is an OK context to have as a starting point, really. I think it is easier to work with this now than many years ago when we did not have that many with different ethnic backgrounds.* (NS1-T)

In the way they express themselves, immigration is represented as a more recent phenomenon than with the English teachers. Also, the impression is that it is a less conscious choice to link their teachings to present plurality. I believe that it might be linked to the pedagogical idea about starting with that which is known. In Lund Johannessen (2009), six Norwegian teachers' evaluation of diversity varied from enthusiasm to 'a more down to earth and neutral acceptance of plurality as a fact of life'. The Norwegian teachers in my study would fit into the latter category. Linking the teaching to present plurality in society was more something which seemed logical given the changing social context of increasing religious plurality rather than a result of idealism, which was perhaps more the case with the English teachers (see also Everington 2009).

6.9 Social enculturation gives nationally distinctive patterns in teaching?

The pattern that emerged in relation to their description of the content of the teaching was consistent with the way English and Norwegian teachers understood the aims of multifaith RE (see above). In the case of the English teachers, the emphasis was on the plural societal context, while the Norwegian teachers tended to emphasise a cultural heritage perspective.

The idea of England as plural seemed more established than the idea of Norway as plural. This is consistent with my findings in chapter 3 that English RE is nego-

---

299 Jon Paul II: 'Jon' (NS1-T) said his health; 'Oline' (NS3-T) said his death.

tiated on the basis of *difference* as essential to the English [British] National Imaginary while developments in Norwegian RE are negotiated on the basis of *sameness* as an essential idea in the Norwegian National Imaginary.

In a publication from the REDCo project (van der Want et al. 2009: including Lund Johansen 2009 and Everington 2009), 'sameness' is put forward as a distinguishing characteristic for how RE teachers in Norway respond to religious diversity while individuality and inclusion (diversity/ heterogeneity) is put forwards as characteristic for the way English teachers respond to diversity. I see this as strengthening the theory that in my samples this tendency represents nationally distinct patterns, and a difference. While more research is needed to find out about the validity of this finding, a methodological point is that the identifiable differences on the institutional and societal levels are a source of explanation for differences in the way these particular teachers' answered my questions.

6.10 Learning about and from religion

In the case of England, learning 'about and from' refers to explicit goals for RE described in the Non-Statutory National Framework for Religious Education (QCA 2004) and in many local agreed syllabuses. It also refers to a debate on the societal level of curriculum which has been generalised from the English context and made international (see chapter 4). The Norwegian National Curriculum (LS 2002)[300] did not use the exact terms of 'learning about and from' but said, for instance, that pupils should get both knowledge and experiences ('opplevelser') in the subject. I see this as a parallel:

> *In all age groups the pupils should get both knowledge and experiences in their encounter with the content of the teaching. Variation in approaches are emphasised, including for instance repeating what they have learned, play, drama, artistic activities, music, work in projects and dialogue adjusted to age stage. Making connections to local events should contribute to making the subject more alive.* (LS 2002:14)[301]

Seeing this as a parallel depends on an argument that the word 'experiences' ('opplevelser') includes the possibility for pupils to *learn from* religion. 'Experiences' ('opplevelser') need to be interpreted as not just happening 'outwardly', but rather as having an 'experience' from, for example, reading a text that makes you think of something new, or analysing a picture which provides the student with new insights into its symbolism – in other words an experience that offers the learner something on a personal level.

I find support for the idea that learning *from* religion is an aspect also of Norwegian RE in the mention of dialogue and also in other parts of the curriculum (see

---

300 Or any of the other curricula since 1997, see chapter 1, 4.
301 My translation into English.

chapter 4).³⁰² I see the aims of learning *from* and not just *about* religion as connected to aims that RE should promote spiritual, moral, cultural and mental development (England) and contribute to understanding, respect and dialogue (Norway). It is hard to imagine any teaching as meaningful without aiming at developing pupils in some way. I see no reason why this should not also be an aim in RE, but there are issues of parents and others being afraid of pupils learning things that go against their religious or non-religious convictions.³⁰³

Against this backdrop in the institutional level and societal levels of curriculum, the question is raised regarding the instructional level: how did English and Norwegian teachers understand the ideas of 'learning about' and 'learning from', or having knowledge and experience (Norway) in RE? From these teachers' perspectives, how were pupils *influenced by* RE teachings, and what in RE teaching would contribute to pupils' personal development?

The English teachers all knew the concepts of 'learning about' and 'learning from' religion, and gave examples of this. They were basically convinced that their pupils were learning *from* religion as well as learning about it.³⁰⁴ For example, 'Ruth' (ES3-T) said:

> *'I think it is important that they feel it is related to their lives, because (...) a lot of our pupils are not interested in the academic study for the sake of academic study; we are looking for how the academic study can help you.'* (ES3-T)

'Vicky' (ES2-T) said that the 'about bit' was 'the bit that the pupils like the best. And that's the bit that generates all the conversations and discussions'.

The Norwegian teachers did not immediately understand 'having knowledge and experience' as learning *from* religion. The Norwegian teachers tended first to understand it in relation to exciting methods of teaching, especially excursions.³⁰⁵ However, when I explained what I meant, they all did think that their pupils were also learning *from* religion and got personal gains from RE teaching:

> *We talk about things; that this gives them something which, which ... they feel are engaging them and make them want to share their own points of view about it and, that they have experienced something in that lesson, and ... that it was valuable in a way. (...) I often say that I see KRL as a place to draw your breath in the hectic everyday life in school, where we can lean back a little and have awe and wonder.*
> *'Jon'* (NS1-T)

---

302 The concepts learning about and from does exist on the societal level of the Norwegian Curriculum, but are not used explicitly in the National Curriculum; see also Lund Johannessen (2009: 104). Implementing the terms learning about and from ('lære om og fra') in the Norwegian curriculum would in my view help make this point clearer.

303 This is of course reflected in the national and international legal cases against Norwegian KRL and a reason why there need to be opt-out rights (see chapter 4).

304 But they were equally convinced that their pupils would not be able to answer the question about what the difference between learning about and from would be, and they were right: see chapter 7.

305 'Oline's' (NS3-T) first response is representative of how they first understood the question. When she was saying that the great 'experiences' may be far apart, she was referring to 'outwardly' types of experiences that they might get from working with art in the religions, like Islamic calligraphy, or the rose window of the cathedral in town.

One of the English teachers also talked about wanting to inspire awe and wonder because she did not think the children got much opportunity for that kind of experience in other learning contexts. 'Ruth' (ES3-T) claimed the children sometimes experienced awe and wonder from their encounter with each other's religion.[306] She connected the issue of 'learning from' with promoting positive attitudes to other people, and thought this was especially important in her school as it was so religiously plural. Related to the multicultural makeup of 'Oline's' (NS3-T) school, she said that she had never seen any cultural conflicts or any racism. This was a positive statement, but still a very different perspective from that of the English teachers who strongly put the multicultural makeup of the school forwards as an asset for RE.

When I asked the Norwegian teachers whether they thought pupils were *influenced by* what they learned in KRL, my reference was an understanding of RE as pluralistic and aiming to influence pupils to a better understanding of different religions. The teachers' primary reference was, however, of a different kind. 'Oline' (NS3-T) first got defensive and stated that they were not proselytising! When I explained what I meant – as, for instance, to learn to have respect for others – she did not at first 'connect' to this idea.

It appears that this was not in accordance with 'Oline's' (NS3-T) understanding of the central aims of the subject, namely to pass on the (Christian) cultural heritage and inform those who come from another background about that (see above). The debate in Norway over whether children get too much of a religious/ Christian influence through KRL or too much influence from the 'wrong' religion also makes whether pupils are *influenced* by the teaching in KRL a sensitive issue. 'Jon' (NS1-T) very hesitantly replied that it would depend on whether I meant influenced in a good way or in a bad way. When I explained I meant the latter he said he did try to influence them positively and saw a good opportunity in KRL to work with attitudes.

When *influenced by* the teaching was understood positively, the Norwegian teachers did think RE contributed to pupils' personal development. For 'Oline' (NS3-T) this was connected to her belief that respect would be a result of knowledge: 'the more you know, the less dangerous the unknown would seem. (…) and I assume that at least some would get some more respect'.[307]

'Ingunn' (NS2-T) said she liked to think that KRL contributed to pupils becoming respectful of other people. She saw pupils' participation in discussions as contributing to this, but, like the English teacher 'Vicky' (ES2-T), 'Ingunn' (NS2-T) also stressed that influences outside of the school from homes, peer groups and other school subjects (Norwegian language and Social Studies) would also be important. 'Jon' (NS1-T) also saw it as an ideal aim that KRL should contribute to

---

306 "I think they are sort of having that respect for each other. They are kind of in awe of each other about things. We watched a video, you know, Michael Palin when he went to The Golden temple recently (…) and then when we watched it the kids were like 'oh wow, have you been there? Oh what is it like?' and I think it does create respect." (ES3-T)
307 The teachers in Lund Johannessen's (2009: 103) study also believed that knowledge about is important for making pupils more tolerant and open-minded.

developing respect for different people, but was unsure whether it would have this effect. On the English side 'Sally' (ES1-T), for example, said:

> *We have a saying here, you can take a horse to water, but you can't make it drink. It's the same here: you can introduce all these ideas to the kids, but if they don't want to accept it, then you're not going to develop them spiritually. They'll just know about things without ever taking it on board.* (ES1-T)

One similarity was that in both countries teachers did think RE promoted the positive development of pupils, but were modest about how much of an influence (positively understood) they thought they had. This is interesting because Anker (2011, who investigated respect and disrespect in practice in a Norwegian school, found that RE lessons were not very relevant for the practice of respect and disrespect.

Both English and Norwegian teachers mentioned RE as one of few opportunities to discuss important life issues related to religion, life views or ethics. In the findings of the EC REDCo Project, too, the opportunity to discuss and to have training in expressing one's opinion (dialogue) were seen as key elements that could contribute to the personal growth/ development of pupils through RE (Dietz et al. 2009). As a result of this, there is now a new focus on RE as a "safe space" where pupils can talk together about religion and differences.

6.11 Reflecting on multifaith RE as integrative RE

Alberts (2007: 328) has called Norwegian multifaith RE '(…) a halfway house between traditional Christian instruction on the one hand, and a multifaith study programme on the other'. Her use of the term *integrative RE* approximates to how I refer to multifaith RE: teaching that includes pupils with various religious or non-religious affiliations in the same physical space, and including teaching about 'all' the religions and life views (see chapter 1). However, I would argue that 'integrative' could also be understood *normatively*, referring to a desired function of multifaith RE.

In both England and Norway, aims for RE in state schools include that it should aid integration and thereby strengthen social cohesion in class, school and/ or society. In other words, in both England and Norway teaching is seen as integrative in a normative sense. But what kind of normativity is implied by this integrative function?

We have seen a tendency that older Norwegian teachers especially accentuate a cultural heritage perspective while there is more awareness among English teachers of the potential of RE to work within the plural context. I first found this surprising since Norway has had a multifaith 'integrative approach' since 1997. This does, however, become understandable in that the senses in which the national contexts as plural are different: negotiated on the bases of 'difference' in the case of England and on the basis of 'sameness' in the case of Norway (see chapter 3).

The English and Norwegian teachers seemed to have different ideas about integration. The Norwegian teachers did not have a very conscious idea of RE contributing to intercultural (or multicultural) education.[308] Were they still contributing to RE as having an integrative function for all, or did they actually rather reproduce stereotypes which could be seen as constructing some pupils as 'others'? Were they, through their teaching, constructing 'culturally Christian' Norwegian citizens? And is this a (more or less hidden) agenda in Norwegian RE? For the sake of balance, the question must also be asked as to whether the English teachers on their part reproduced any stereotypes.

Differences in the way RE was seen by teachers as having an integrative function became especially apparent when I compared the teachers from the two most 'multicultural' schools (English school 3 and Norwegian school 3). There were some similarities, which came from the similar social settings, and some differences which came from different understanding of what were the main aims for RE. Regarding 'other' religions, a similarity was that both said it was natural to start with their own class. For example 'Oline' (NS3-T) said: '... and then one of them could share that his father had recently been to Mecca'. If there had not been any Muslim pupils in the class, teaching about Islam would have been more theoretical. She thought pupils did better on a test because there were Muslim pupils in that class. This point made by 'Ruth' (ES3-T) is similar:

> (...) you know, here we are talking very first hand about different faiths, different religions and if I say 'Who's been to Mecca?' five hands go up, and 'Who's been to The Golden Temple?' five more hands would go up, and we're not talking about these strange far off unrelated religious people who do these things; we're talking about, you know, people who we know, people we can relate to who have done these things. (ES3-T)

Both 'Oline' (NS3-T) and 'Ruth' (ES3-T) saw it as an asset to teaching that their pupils brought in experiences from different religions, but 'Ruth' (ES3-T) expressed herself more enthusiastically, while it was more just an interesting observation in the case of 'Oline' (NS3-T). Also, while 'Oline's' (NS3-T) focus was that this made them perform better in tests, 'Ruth' pointed to the instrumental usefulness of it. This perspective on the instrumental was lacking on the Norwegian side. Being respected for being religious was not equally taken for granted in the Norwegian plural school (NS3). At the same time, the potential of RE to contribute to a tolerant school ethos was less recognised.[309]

When it comes to contributing to social cohesion, to RE's potential integrative function, in the English case this was done with reference to an 'imaginary' multicultural (intercultural) England/ Britain while, in the Norwegian case, it was more linked to 'our' shared cultural (Christian) heritage. Norwegian teachers even men-

---

308 Although multiculturalism can be understood differently, as group plurality (McIntyre 1978, Gravem 2004) whilst others have more flexible and malleable ideas of multiculturalism (Baumann 1996, Jackson 1997, 2004, Hylland Eriksen 1993, Davie 2007). In current political rhetoric in the UK (and in the White Paper on Intercultural Education from the Council of Europe), multicultural education is seen in a negative light as something to leave behind in favour of *intercultural education*, which allows more easily for cultural change and cultural interaction.

309 This impression is strengthened if one also takes the pupils' perspectives into consideration (see chapter 7).

tioned learning about this heritage as a reason why it would be important for 'others' with a non-Norwegian ethnic background to have RE (see above).

6.12 Is RE creating otherness?

Critically, one could remark that this would leave some pupils in a state of 'otherness'. In the study done by Schiffauer and his co-researchers (2004), a finding was that in Germany the (idea of a) shared past of the 2nd World War was so strong in the German *national imaginary* that it was difficult for immigrants to be fully integrated because they could never share this past. Is the idea of 'Norwegianness' also such that it is difficult to be integrated into, if the case is that the idea of a certain religious tradition as cultural heritage is strong, for example?

In terms of the English material, a parallel question could be whether the idea of 'Englishness' is so plural that indigenous English pupils are alienated or marginalised. For example, in the recent 'white season' on the BBC and in studies such as Dench, Gavron & Young (2006) it has been pointed out that an emphasis on global links in the classroom can lead to indigenous white children thinking that they are boring and 'from nowhere' (see also Rudge 1998, May 1999 and Maylor & Read 2007). This relates interestingly to the English teacher 'Ruth's' discussion on the teaching of Christianity above: that she tried not to teach this as a white middle class British religion.

This brings out a contrast between the English and the Norwegian contexts. It makes me think about a widely used metaphor from the Norwegian debate, printed in KUF (1998).[310]

> *I have a different relationship to my own house than to a house where I am a guest. In both places my conduct is respectful and reflects devotion and engagement. Both what is mine and that which belongs to those who welcome me into their house, concern me. I can get impulses from others which can enrich me and my house.*[311]

> *That which is mine is still not the same as that which belongs to the others. I am a participant and a co-owner in my own house but only a guest or a spectator in the houses of the others. To be a guest in another's home provides possibilities to learn about what it is like to live in a place where you yourself do not live. In the same way, one can relate to one's own and others' traditions: I am a participant in my own tradition, but merely a spectator to the others* (KUF 1998).[312]

This metaphor reflects a static idea of traditions as bounded, and also an idea of identities being firmly grounded in one tradition. This has a clear resonance in *Identity and dialogue* (NOU 1995: 9), which was an important background docu-

---

310 This was the first circular from the Department of Church, Education and Research that came after the 1997 KRL curriculum (KUF 1996) was released.
311 This could be understood as 'learning from'.
312 My translation.

ment for the introduction of KRL in 1997. Here, firm identities rooted in one's own tradition were seen as a platform from which to have dialogue.

This view reflects 'group pluralism'; it describes society as plural but on a group level more than on an individual level (see chapters 2 and 3). This metaphor indicates that ready-made 'houses' exist for individuals to choose, while a different perspective taking account also of modern plurality (Skeie 1995) would be that these houses are constantly constructed, negotiated and reconstructed both by residents and visitors, who perhaps both come and go.

This group plurality metaphor would be challenged by the discussions of plural identities and identities in a plural society (for example Østberg 1998, Skeie 1995, 1998, Jackson & Nesbitt 1993, and Jackson 1997). However, based on this case study, I raise the question whether this metaphor may reflect a general *idea of* the multicultural (a multicultural imaginary) in society, which is reflected in these teachers' answers. If, in this idea of plurality (multicultural imaginary), group plurality is preferred over individual plurality, what is the consequence of this for RE's integrative function?

The problem with this in relation to RE's potential integrative function is that individual variation, and variations outside or between, in RE – the 6 defined 'houses'[313] – are not captured. Thus some could be described as 'homeless', conceptualised as 'others'. There is also a danger of forcing young people into 'houses' they would like to escape from, or live in but on their own terms. From the position of one of the indicated groups, the Church of Norway for example, this may be seen as ensuring continuation of their traditions within a multifaith approach to RE.

6.13 How is 'Norwegianness' and 'Englishness' imagined?

Both 'Norwegianness' and 'Englishness' can be imagined in different ways, some more plural, others less so. The above reflects these particular teachers' imagery of the 'English' or 'Norwegian'. One question which I am left with regards differences between (Norwegian) regions. Would a sample of teachers from multicultural Oslo schools, for example, bring out more similarities to those views on plurality as expressed by English teachers? Another is how much the age of the teachers is an important variable within the national context. Having analysed a non-representative sample, this raises a number of questions which would need further attention in future empirical school research.

It might well be that a different sample could have given a different result. However, I now turn my attention to how these answers can be explained?

I see the differences between these particular teachers' imagery of the 'English' or 'Norwegian' as related to different *national imaginaries*.[314] In Norway, no doubt the history of nation-building and the traditional strong standing of the State Church are important in this imaginary (see chapter 3). In England, being part of a heterogeneous Great Britain with several strong religious traditions could be sug-

---

313 Judaism, Christianity, Islam, Hinduism, Buddhism, and Humanism (in Norway): in England it would be Judaism, Christianity, Islam, Hinduism, Buddhism, and Sikhism (see chapter 4).
314 This reflects ideas of historic events for the nation, see chapters 2, 5.

gested as central components (Schiffauer et al. 2004: 35). The debates on issues of shared history and nationalism are connected to the way *plurality* (and integration) is understood and negotiated in England and Norway.

It is possible to see the debate in Norway regarding whether those who did not belong in any of the 'houses' were *homeless* as parallel to the debate in England about the indigenously white English children being *from nowhere*. However, a difference is that in Norway it is not the indigenous Norwegian pupils who are from 'nowhere' or 'homeless'. The idea of the Christian cultural heritage is much stronger in the Norwegian case than is the idea of an English cultural heritage, which may have been challenged in a different way (see chapter 3). Sharing this cultural heritage is still a strong feature of being Norwegian (Norwegian national imaginary), and this is reflected in these teachers' answers. I see being a multicultural (intercultural) society as a stronger feature of the imaginary of being English (English national imaginary), as illustrated in the debate about 'whiteness'.

However, neither with the English alleged privilege of the ones who are not ethnically English, nor with the Norwegian apparently privileging those who share the indigenous cultural heritage, does the teaching become normatively *integrative* in a non-discriminatory way. In both cases, it keeps on (re)producing certain kinds of 'otherness' (distinctions/ categories). What *imaginary* – one may ask – would facilitate normatively integrative RE in the sense of 'inclusive on equal terms for all who participate'? (See chapters 7 and 8).

6.14 Summary and conclusion

In this chapter I have discussed teachers' perspectives on RE in England and Norway comparatively. I have looked at how different contextual factors affect their ability to describe their schools, and their views on the aims and importance of RE. I have discussed similarities and differences in how national aims are filtered through to the level of practice, and looked for explanations for differences and similarities in the teaching. Some main conclusions are as follows:

Firstly, with respect to subnational processes, there are differences between schools within a country, reflecting the local context of the schools. For example, a school could be dominated by strong humanist viewpoints (NS2) or be situated in a socially challenging environment (ES2, in part NS3), or be ethnically homogeneous with mostly ethnically English (ES1) or Norwegian (NS1) pupils, or ethnically heterogeneous (ES3, NS3). Sometimes there are more similarities between schools within one country and sometimes there are quite strong similarities between schools in similar settings in the two countries – for example, the most ethnically diverse schools in England and Norway.

Secondly, there are important differences between national processes, in the way that the plurality of society is discussed at societal level and formulated on the institutional level, for example.

Thirdly, there is also the issue of how supranational processes affect teachers' practice (see chapter 2).

Regarding the relationship between levels of curriculum, we have seen that there are in England some well established structures to support this, which have historical roots in times when the educational system in England as a whole was less centralised. We have seen that changes at the institutional level of curriculum do not automatically lead to changes in practice. In Norway the structures to ensure cohesion between levels of curriculum are weaker than in the English case. It is well understood from other research that changes in the institutional level of curriculum do not automatically lead to changes in practice (Goodlad 1979, see chapter 8), but this might not always be sufficiently considered by policy makers.

This disconnection becomes especially evident on the Norwegian side as some changes at the institutional level caused by formal supranational processes – the international legal cases (see chapter 4) – have not filtered through to the instructional level. This raises the question of why implementation has not been ensured and whether the changes in the national curriculum are perhaps not primarily aimed at practice, but rather at the debates on the societal level.

The societal level is also important, but the main aim of curricular change is to change practice, in which case practice needs to be addressed explicitly. Taking Goodlad's point that practice is the most important curricular level, and also Afdal's (2006) point about the communication between domains[315], I would also argue that changes at the institutional level should be made based on a thorough understanding of the field of practice. This could ensure a closer relationship between the levels of curriculum.

When it comes to the question of how English and Norwegian teachers understood their practice, it became clear that English teachers' way of conceptualising RE teaching reflected an English context, while the Norwegian teachers' understandings and practices reflected a Norwegian context. Even when aims at the institutional level were quite similar, they were understood differently in the two national contexts. There was, for example, a clear contrast in the way in which RE was seen to have an (integrative) function in relation to intercultural learning and integration. My suggestion is that the teachers' understandings of plurality were different in the two national settings.

For example, the English teachers tended to see a plural local setting as an asset to RE, while the Norwegian teachers did not immediately think in this way. One reason for this difference could be that society's plurality is conceptualised differently, reflecting differences in *national imaginaries* (Schiffauer et al. 2004, see chapter 3, 5). This view is supported by the REDCo research where findings indicated that different perceptions of diversity existed between nations. In case of Norwegian teachers, they tended to over-accentuate sameness: 'a result of a desire to treat everyone equally and to avoid drawing attention to difference unless a student chooses to do so' (ter Avest, Bakker & van der Want 2009: 118); in the case of England, 'All the English teachers valued the potential of cultural and religious difference in the classroom.' (ter Avest, Bakker & van der Want 2009: 115), and

---

315 I.e. levels of curriculum, should be better and that '(…) the multicultural classroom is not a place for teaching tolerance, but for finding out what tolerance is all about' (Afdal 2006: 350), see chapter 5.

'In England (...) teachers preferred to approach all students in an appropriate and unique manner' (ter Avest, Bakker & van der Want 2009: 118).

Further evidence that multifaith RE can take on *different national styles* is provided by other sources. In the English case, for example, RE teachers saw their role as promoting tolerance. This can be related to the English tradition which relates RE to anti-racist and multicultural education. Everington and Sikes (2001: 80) point out, for example, that 'for the past forty years RE has been viewed as a major contributor to the battle against racism and the promotion of intercultural understanding and respect'. By contrast, there seemed to be a lack of understanding of the possible contribution of RE to intercultural education among the Norwegian teachers[316].

The understanding of KRL as traditional RE is consistent with these Norwegian teachers' views and may be a reason why they considered RE to be inconsistent with contributing to intercultural education.[317] It is important to point out that this finding is not representative, but it is nevertheless significant that, in my sample none of the English teachers made any references to an English tradition similar to that found in Norway, where Christianity was seen as connected to Norwegian cultural heritage. A larger sample would be needed to judge the degree to which this is representative. In this particular sample, however, the idea of Christianity as British is only represented as something that needs countering in order to make Christianity relevant.

Regarding the *supranational dimension*, I found examples that some of the teachers participated in supranational debates, while others were more locally oriented. All the teachers from both countries referred to the new plurality in the national dimension, which is in fact the internationally shared challenge of the growing religious plurality in societies. The degree to which they see religions as global or national phenomena varied. The international connections are there as both Christianity and the 'other' religions are international phenomena, but the degree to which they are represented as national or supranational differs.

A central concern of Schiffauer et al. (2004: 10) was 'How do Nation State-schools manage to maintain and update their old links with the national imaginary despite there being so many school pupils who are not nationals or else not ethnically recognizable as such?' In view of individual (modern) plurality (Skeie 1995), everyone potentially has global links, through belonging to a religion or through experiencing travel or internet chat, for example.

From the perspective of these aspects of globalisation, distinctions between natives and those who could be recognised as non-natives in a country by certain criteria, such as mother tongue or own or parents' country of origin, becomes blurred. From this perspective, all are global citizens, and the national consists of all individuals and groups which are actually there. But this might not be how societal plurality is imagined by teachers and pupils as well as others who participate in societal debates.

---

316 This is also reflected in the interviews with the pupils (see chapter 7).
317 An alternative explanation is that civility as perceived by the teachers in Norwegian school 3 is so secular that they dismiss religion as such as a less important factor – despite a strong likelihood that religion is a very important factor in some of these pupils' lives.

As we have seen, however, links to traditional ideas of the national – the *national imaginaries* – are still being maintained. It is maintained in debates at the societal level, in the wording of curricular documents at the institutional level of curriculum, and also at the instructional level. But the imaginaries are also evolving, and it is perhaps the domain of practice which continues to challenge the levels 'above' rather than the other way around.

In the next chapter (7), I will explore pupils' perspectives on English and Norwegian multifaith RE, focusing on the final and most important level of curriculum as conceptualised in the thesis (see chapter 2, 5, 8): the experiential level.

7. Experiential Level: Pupils' Perspectives

7.1 Introduction

I understand the *experiential level* of curriculum to mean the curriculum that is internalised and made personal: this level reveals the effects of the curriculum on the individual learner.[318] Within my theoretical framework (see chapter 2), it becomes logical to consider the societal (see chapter 3) and institutional level (see chapter 4) as the context of the case studies (see chapter 5). In chapter 6 the focus was on how the societal and institutional levels were reflected in teachers' practice. In this chapter the focus will be the pupils' learning.

The pupil's perspective is here represented mainly through six semi-structured group interviews with pupils in year 10 in three English and three Norwegian schools, but I will refer to other sources when required. I am fully aware that this is not a representative sample, and will take notice of this in the analysis (see chapter 5).

As with the interviews with the teachers, the interview schedule (see appendix 1) had four main sections related to: *aims for RE, the content of the teaching/learning, learning about and from religion*, and *respect and personal growth*. The latter two sections are seen to cohere in the analysis. The questions were largely similar to those used in the interviews with the teachers, and were designed to capture relationships between the instructional and experiential levels of curriculum.

Using concepts from Schiffauer et al. (2004), I have suggested in the preceding chapters that multifaith RE takes on different styles in the two countries, reflecting different school and research traditions, but also different *national imaginaries*. Is this also the case with the pupils' learning? Schiffauer and his co-researchers (2004) claim that *social enculturation* is nation-specific.[319] My main focus will be on national processes, but the cases will also illustrate subnational processes, as well as providing an opportunity to discuss the influence of supranational processes (see chapter 2).

For this part of the research, my key research questions were:

- *What are similarities and differences in the English and Norwegian curriculum's experiential level as expressed by pupils in this sample?*
- *How do we account for these?*
- *How do we account for these with reference to the other levels of curriculum?*

---

318 The levels of the curriculum according to Goodlad & Su (1992): societal, institutional, instructional and experiential.

319 *Civil enculturation* is defined as 'the process by which an individual acquires the mental representations (…) and patterns of behaviour required to function as a member of (civil) culture, (…) taking place as a part of the process of education' (Schiffauer *et al.* 2004: 2). Further, as they define *civil culture* to include *civil society, civic culture* and norms of civility and a *social imaginary*, and define *social imaginary* as 'the dominant national self representation of a nation state', also called *'national imaginary'*: this makes social enculturation depending on *national imaginaries*.

I will proceed to describe the pupils and their contexts, and analyse how questions of religious affiliation were answered. This will be seen in relation to REDCo research, especially Dietz et al. (2009) which reports the main findings in the country-specific qualitative (Knauth et al. 2008) and quantitative (Valk et al. 2009) studies of the EC Framework 6 REDCo project on religion, education, dialogue and conflict.[320] These studies look into teenage perspectives on religion, interreligious dialogue and/ or conflict in eight European countries.[321] Further I will look at pupils' responses to questions about the aims of RE, the content of their learning, and what they have learned *from* religion in RE. I will consider pupils' answers in relation to how their teachers answered similar questions (instructional level), as well as in relation to the institutional and societal levels.

7.2 The pupils and their context

The context of the pupils includes personal issues, such as religious affiliations and influence from parents and peers, subnational factors, such as their school environment, national contexts, including *national imaginaries*, and international links. Examples of international links are when pupils have memories of living in other countries, or have identity tied to parents' or grandparents' country of origin, or when pupils take part in supranational processes through media or travel (globalisation).

In chapter 2 I distinguish between subnational, national and supranational processes affecting RE and, in the way I see this as the context of these individuals, it starts to resemble Jackson's (1997: 67) model of membership groups. My intention is to capture the relationship between individuals, specific groups to which a person belongs and the wider context. I see the context of these pupils in a similar way: that they are affected in their views by individual choice, by various local factors, like peers and the school environment, but also by their national context and their international links.

The pupils were interviewed in groups of four; they were from the classes that I observed (chapter 5), and their teachers were the ones I interviewed (chapter 6).

English school 3 and Norwegian school 3 were the schools with the largest proportions of pupils with ethnic and religious minority backgrounds (see chapter 5). In English school 3, the interview was with two girls and two boys. Both boys (ES3-PB1, ES3-PB2) said they were Muslims; one girl (ES3-PG1) said she was Hindu and the other Christian[322] (ES3-PG2). The two boys and the Hindu girl were of Asian background, while the second girl was of mixed race, her father being of Caribbean origin. In Norwegian school 3, the interview was with four girls. Two were indigenous Norwegian (NS3-PG1, NS3-PG2), one was a Bosnian Muslim

---

320 http://www.redco.uni-hamburg.de/web/3480/3481/index.html
321 I will refer only to the English and Norwegian studies. (Qualitative: Ipgrave & McKenna (2008), and von der Lippe (2008), Quantitative: McKenna, Neill & Jackson (2009), and Skeie & von der Lippe (2009). The sample in the English study included 109 students in the qualitative study and 402 in the quantitative, and in Norway it involved 154 students in the qualitative study and 707 in the quantitative.
322 Catholic: her mother being Irish.

(NS3-PG3), and one a Kurdish Muslim (NS3-PG4). The Muslim girls were both first generation immigrants, and the Kurdish girl had memories of living in other countries before coming to Norway.

English school 2 and Norwegian school 2 were both schools with a predominantly indigenous English/ Norwegian pupil population, with just a few pupils from other backgrounds (see chapter 5). In English school 2, there were two girls (ES2-PG1 and ES2-PG2) and two boys (ES2-PB1 and ES2-PB2), all indigenous English. In Norwegian school 2, there were two girls (NS2-PG1, NS2-PG2) and two boys (NS2-PB1, NS2-PB2), all indigenous Norwegian. In English school 2, and Norwegian school 2, all but one girl (NS2-PG2) said they were not religious.

English school 1 and Norwegian school 1 were both rural schools, and here too the pupils were indigenous white. In English school 1, there were two boys (ES1-PB1 and ES1-PB2) and two girls (ES1-PG1 and ES1-PG2) and in Norwegian school 1, the interview was with two girls (NS1-PG1 and NS1-PG2) and two boys (NS1-PB1 and NS1-PB2). All the pupils in both the English and Norwegian rural school identified themselves as Christians, but all of them also said that they were not *very* Christian.

An interesting pattern occurred across the country borders as all the pupils in schools 3 (ES3, NS3) self-identified as religious, whereas all but one pupil in both schools 2 (ES2, NS2) self-identified as *not* being religious. All pupils in the rural schools (ES1, NS1) self-identified as Christian, but all in addition mentioned that they were not *very* Christian. In English school 3, both the teacher and the pupils talked about how normal and accepted it was in this school to have different religions, and to be respectful of each other's religions. The *Christian* girls in English and Norwegian schools 3 also said they were not *very* Christian. Perhaps a school context where religion and religious issues are seen as normal and respected encourages pupils to have the confidence to reveal their religious identity.

Even though, in Norwegian school 3, the pupils had a religious identity, this was not revealed as enthusiastically; the religious diversity was under-communicated by the Norwegian pupils compared with the pupils in English school 3. It is as if the civility around Norwegian school 3 was more secular in tone than in the English case. Their religion was accepted as part of their individuality, but tuned down in the discourse.

Lund Johansen (2009) writes about under-communication of difference among Norwegian teachers, and how *sameness* is a recognised value (see also chapter 6). It was said explicitly by pupils in Norwegian school 2 that it was 'taboo' to talk about each other's religious backgrounds and that it was never addressed in class. This adds to the impression that difference was under-communicated in the Norwegian schools.[323] However, pupils in Norwegian school 2 said it would have been better if they could have talked about religious differences and been able to hear about the religions from someone who actually believed in them. In other words,

---

323 The Norwegian teachers (NS1-T, NS2-T) were largely unaware of their pupils' religions, not seeing this as relevant to how they would teach. In Norwegian school 3 the teacher knows what religions her pupils are connected to, but does not seem to take notice of it in the planning of her teaching. The understanding that the pupils' backgrounds are an important factor to consider was more integrated in the English side of this sample.

from the pupils' perspective, this taboo could very well be broken. They did not reject addressing religious plurality more directly.[324]

In English school 2 and English school 1, there was not an equally strong acceptance of religiosity and diversity as in English school 3, so it is important to consider how the sub-national contexts of the schools vary. In the REDCo Project (Dietz et al. 2009), researchers found that discussions of religious issues and personal belief was problematic for the indigenous white English pupils in more rural areas where they face a climate of youth apathy and negativity towards religion. I think this is relevant with regard to English school 1 in my sample, and probably also to English school 2, which was set in a predominately white suburban area.

In English school 1, pupils talked as if there was a danger of being bullied if one showed too much interest in religion outside of lessons, and similar tendencies are reported also by Ipgrave & McKenna (2008: 143) and Ipgrave & Bertram-Troost (2008: 383). The pupils self-identified as Christians but excused this by adding that this was 'because of their upbringing and the influence of their parents'. While a difference between the schools 3 (ES3, NS3) was that there was more acceptance of religion in the English plural school than in the Norwegian, there was more openness and acceptance for religiosity (Christian) in Norwegian school 1 than in English school 1. Pupils showed more embarrassment about their Christian connection in English school 1.

This relates interestingly to findings in chapter 6 showing that, in English RE, promoting tolerance for different religions is emphasised more by these pupils' teachers, while in Norway promoting the understanding of Christianity as cultural heritage is emphasised more. In other words, in my particular English sample, it is in the plural setting that religiosity is seen as normal and accepted, while in the Norwegian sample, it is in the least plural setting that religiosity (being Christian) is seen as normal and accepted. I can not conclude that this finding is representative nationally; but further investigation into this question would be interesting. This particular finding can however be explained with reference to differences in the nation-specific documents and debates.[325]

A possible explanation for this pattern is that pupils will adapt to what in their environment is regarded as normal. This suggests an interesting supranational pattern between similar social settings. In some instances, local social context will be more important for young people's religious choices than, for example, national processes. Then again, this cross-national pattern can also be explained through supranational impositions: forming 'similar' multicultural or monocultural settings in the two countries. While there will be variations between types of social environments in one country, there will also be similar settings in different nations.

I take the point regarding in which schools religion was seen as most normal to supplement the argument stated in chapter 6: that plurality is understood (imagined)

---

324 In the REDCo research, young people did not see religion as a factor which would contribute to conflict in the classroom, see Dietz *et al.* 2009.
325 It would be interesting to investigate differences between regions with regards to acceptance of being religious: I would, for instance, hypothesise that in regions near Oslo where there has been more focus on different religions, in some schools which have pupils with many different religions I would have found more acceptance of being religious compared to my one example of a plural school, which was from the Mid-Norway region.

differently in England and Norway. On the other hand, the question is raised as to whether society and its plurality are imagined differently in rural areas on the one hand and multicultural city centres, for example, on the other, forming supranational patterns? These will be different subnational contexts, but supranational patterns.

7.3 Which modernities?

In his reflection on western modernity's defining cultural formation, Taylor (2004) argues for the idea of 'multiple modernities'. He remarks:

> *Western modernity (...) is inseparable from certain kinds of social imaginary, and the differences among today's multiple modernities need to be understood in terms of divergent social imaginaries involved* (Taylor 2004: 1-2).

His idea is that different social imaginaries form different coexisting modernities, and he digs deep into western history to trace the ideas that formed our main ideas about ourselves. He does this in order to counter the idea that modernity is a single process that occurs in the same form everywhere (Taylor 2004: 195). To understand other cultures as civilised and modern, he begins with 'provincializing' Europe which he hopes can contribute to (a new) order and peace (Taylor 2004: 196). On the basis of what the pupils in my sample said about 'what religion if any they felt themselves connected to', what can be said about which modernities these pupils occupied?

The main 'labels' (identity markers) the pupils chose are indicated above,[326] and I have indicated that schools may be set in local contexts which reflect different variations of modernity. Included in these variations are different ideas about what views about religions are normal. Further, there is a tendency in *my* sample for the English pupils to answer this question mainly by referring to pre-existing 'labels' such as "I am a Hindu" or "I am a Christian",[327] while the Norwegian pupils were triggered by this question to have lengthy reflections on their personal world views. For example:

> *I feel I am kind of in the middle, I feel there is much that sounds right or things that I can take with me from many different religions and you can have opinions and thoughts from all the religions, and make your own religion* (NS2 – PG1).

It is a characteristic of late (or post-) modern western religiosity to be free to pick and choose from various religious traditions in order to construct private individual

---

[326] For example, the non-religious children, three in Norwegian school 2, said that they had chosen a civil confirmation ceremony, arranged by the Norwegian Secular Humanist Association, as an alternative to confirmation in church. Which of the two alternatives they had chosen was a significant identity marker in the Norwegian sample and the reason for the second girl (NS2-PG2) in Norwegian school 2 to label herself 'Christian': but stressing this was mainly due to her grandmother's wish and that she was not *very* Christian.

[327] Except one girl (ES2-PG1) who nuanced the label she had chosen ('not religious') by saying she used to be church-going but was currently in a phase where she had not decided what to believe.

religiosity/ spirituality (for example Winje 1999, Heelas & Woodhead 2005, see chapter 2). This phenomenon was described by Bellah (1985: 221): a young nurse named Sheila whom he interviewed described her religion as 'Sheilaism': 'I believe in God. I am not a religious fanatic. I can't remember the last time I went to church. My faith has carried me a long way. It's "Sheilaism". Just my own little voice'.

Bellah claims that 'Sheilaism' is strangely representative of current religious life in America. Radically individualistic religion like 'Sheilaism' may seem very different from, for example, fundamentalist religion, which is also characteristic of our time, but they both emphasise personal religious experience (spirituality). 'Sheilaism' is rooted in an attempt to transform external authority to internal meaning. Some may prefer to choose a religion of external authority (Bellah 1985: 235) for this purpose. That religion in principle is a choice, is a result of the religious freedom gained in the western world through secularisation: a central trait of western modernity (Taylor 2004: 185, Taylor 2007, see also chapter 2).

The girl (NS2-PG1) quoted above had the same attitude towards religion as Sheila ('Sheilaism') (Bellah 1985). One of the boys (NS2-PB2) also said he picked up elements from philosophy and religions which in his mind sounded right, in constructing his own life view. One boy (NS1-PB2), who labelled himself Christian, as he was baptised and confirmed in church, first said he felt most connected to Buddhism. He did believe 'a little' in God, he said, but just liked the way of thinking in Buddhism. As he argued that position, one of the other pupils (NS1-PG2), also formally Christian, agreed that Buddhism was 'a bit cool'.

It is as if these pupils played out recently learned material without feeling committed to a particular religion, not even the one stated as their own.[328] This could be seen as part of a process of developing individual identity, as indicated in Skeie's (1995) concept of 'modern' plurality (see chapter 2). Much relevant existing ethnographic research demonstrates how young people draw from different sources in their construction of (religious) identity (for example Jackson & Nesbitt 1993, Jackson 1997, and Østberg 1998). Some pupils in my sample who labelled themselves as Christians also said that this does not necessarily mean that they had to believe *everything* in the Bible, like Jesus walking on water:

> NS1-PG2: (...) I do not have to believe that even if I am a Christian (...)
> NS1-PB1: But then you do not have to be a Christian!
> NS1-PG2: No, but I choose to be.
> NS1-PB2: Yes, I do too.
> NS1-PG2: You just got to respect that!

This girl (NS1-PG2) takes personal charge over what in Christianity she believes in, still demanding respect for her choice of labelling herself as a Christian. She has the right to choose to be a Christian even if she does not understand it all, and even if she does not believe it all. When I asked if she felt she could choose freely what in the Christian religion she wanted to believe, the whole group (NS1-P) agreed to

---

328 There is a hint of the same with the Hindu girl (ES3-PG1) in English school 3: 'I started to believe in the other religions as well', but in her case I would think her Hindu background must be seen as part of the explanation, along with the possibility that the modernity she is located within opens up the possibility to pick and choose.

this. When I asked if they also felt they could choose from the other religions she (NS1-PG2) said:

> *I do not know so much about the other religions, or I know a little bit, but I don't think that only Christianity exists and what I really believe is that religion can be very individual, that if it works for you, you ought to believe in it* (NS1-PG2).

This fits very well with religion in modern western religiosity/ spirituality, as described, for example, by Heelas and Woodhead (2005). In the EC REDCo Project, researchers also found that the relationship between belief and practice was not straightforward, as exemplified in the English material with statements like 'I believe it's possible there may be a God, but don't have a religion'; 'religion ain't very important to me, but God is important in my life': 'I am a Christian, but I am not really religious' (Ipgrave & McKenna 2008: 122). In my material, the Hindu girl (ES3-PG1) stood out as more open to individual religiosity and using elements from different traditions for her own life view, while the Muslim boys (ES3-PB1, ES3-PB1) stood out as having the least individual kinds of answers.

It seems that 'Sheilaism' or *playful constructions of personal beliefs* among the young could be found in both countries, and that it is representative of the way many modern western young people relate to religion, regardless of national context. They are, in other words, influences by supranational processes in the way that they relate to religion in this individualistic style. In summing up the findings of all eight countries in the REDCo qualitative research, Ipgrave and Bertram-Troost (2008: 376-377) distinguish between ten different ways in which pupils relate to religion.[329] They state that 'some approaches are more strongly represented in some countries than in others' (Ipgrave & Bertram-Troost 2008: 376) without specifying a pattern in this.[330] There are, in other words, also some nation-specific differences regarding individual choice of how to relate to religion.

Muslims stands out as more committed to their religion and holding strong theistic views (Dietz et al. 2009). They were more explicit about their religion than, for example, committed Christians, who would keep their religious identity more hidden (Ipgrave & Bertram-Troost 2008: 383).

Both in my material and in the REDCo material, many who labelled themselves as Christian added that they were not *very* Christian. Ipgrave & Bertram-Troost (2008: 383) suggest that 'the public nature of being Muslim coupled with negative images of Islam increase a sense of solidarity and pride'. This is interesting in my context because this also refers to supranational processes as an explanatory factor, but to processes other than those which would be relevant to explain a very individualistic way of relating to religion (Sheilaism). Christians may be influenced by another supranational process; namely, the secular critique of religion.

---

329 As personal faith, as spiritual experience, to seek comfort and support, to seek moral guidance, for communal belonging, as group classification, as factual knowledge, philosophical theory, as having a societal role, or as being irrelevant to their lives.
330 They do indicate some nation-specific factors, like the sharp distinction in France between learning about religion in school and religious learning as a private matter, whereas in England there is a more holistic approach as schools also aim to help develop pupils' spiritually (Ipgrave & Bertram-Troost 2008: 387).

One possible interpretation of the various ways in which pupils describe or talk about their relationship to religion is to see Muslims and Christians, for example, as referring to different modernities (Taylor 2004).

In both my sample and the samples in Ipgrave & McKenna (2008) and von der Lippe (2008), all the Muslims and some Christians in organised religion outside the mainstream established churches, such as Charismatic Christians (Norway) and African Christians (England), were less private and more collectively oriented. They were more oriented towards sharing the same religion and belonging to religious groups, meaning that they would not 'pick and choose' in the same individualistic manner. This could be seen as a process of developing identity with reference to what Skeie (1995) calls a traditional plurality. This Muslim girl in my sample, however, was hesitant to identify herself as religious and Muslim:

> *NS3-PG2: I am Muslim, but I am not the kind of Muslim who would wear a headscarf or the kind who prays every day. That would be real Muslims, but I am not. I am Muslim, but I am not like that ... No, I do not believe everything.*
> *O: No?*
> *NS3-PG2: but some things I believe. There are a lot of things I am wondering about, and I ask my mother and father. They help me explain what it is. It is a bit difficult* (NS3-PG4).

Even if she is more modest in her self-definition than the Muslims in my English sample, and in both the English and Norwegian REDCo samples, I see this girl's identity work as more oriented towards searching out what the content of her religion was than picking and choosing religious elements freely. I understand this girl's (N3-PG4) answers as an attempt to be similar to her 'not very' Christian'[331] peers ('I do not believe everything'). This would make subnational processes explanatory factors for her way of describing herself as a Muslim.[332]

Difference in *social enculturation* may explain differences between nations in how young people relate to religion. Thus, there may be differences in how, for example, 'Christianness' or 'Muslimness' is constructed in different countries. Pupils' answers could then be seen as attempts to situate themselves within a certain national sense of, for example, 'Muslimness'. Then again, as Christians and Muslims are obviously heterogeneous groups, there would have to be competing ideas of 'Christianness' or 'Muslimnness' as well.[333]

In this section, I have discussed some possible reasons for the way young people identified as religious or not, and the way they talked about their relationship to

---

331 In the sense that they self-identified as Christians but stressed that they were not very Christian.
332 In the case of this Muslim girl in my sample, I would suggest that circumstances like being first generation immigrants in a setting with strong secularist – or even traditional Christian 'Norwegianness' around her – forms her views. This may be why the two Muslim girls in my sample reveal their personal doubts and questions more than the Muslim students in both my English samples, and in Ipgrave & McKenna's (2008) English material and in von der Lippe's (2008) Norwegian material.
333 This has become very obvious lately in Norway, as some Muslims join in marches against extremism, while others have formed groups (for instance "The prophets Umma") which are quite outspoken in their extremist views.

religion. Some of those reasons relate to specific local processes, some relate to different national processes, and some relate to supranational processes, like secularisation, pluralisation and globalisation (see chapter 2).

In conclusion, it may seem that there may be different national 'styles' which will be challenged by sub-national factors. These styles may also be challenged by supranational factors, for instance if Muslim pupils share a sense of solidarity in a world where Muslims in the media are often portrayed as a threat to society (an international imaginary). Taking Taylor's (2004) point that many types of modernities coexist in today's world, I will argue that pupils within one school or class may in fact have different modernities as their frame of reference. This affects the way in which they relate to religion, which is relevant for the question of how religion should be taught.

7.4 Aims of RE

From the pupils' perspective: why did they think they were taught RE? Was RE seen to be important? What did they see as the importance of RE? I discuss this in relation to what their teachers said to be central aims of RE, and I am also interested to see if there are differences between English and Norwegian pupils' perspectives. Even if my sample is not representative, I can discuss this against the suggested characteristics of national styles indicated in chapters 5 and 6. Do pupils' perspectives reflect their teachers' views? How do they relate to the way aims are formulated at the institutional and societal levels?

The English teachers' views on the aims of RE could be summed up as promoting respect and understanding for different religions. They tended to see plurality in school and in society as a strength to RE. There was a great deal of harmony between this and what the English pupils believed to be the main aims of RE. They all persistently repeated how the main reason why they had RE was to learn about different people's viewpoints on certain topics, and to avoid being offensive to other people. For example, one girl (ES1-PG1) said that 'You know (in) the world that we live in now we can't be ignorant of everybody else so you just have to know what they believe and respect it'. In English school 3, pupils clearly related the importance of RE to their plural school context: '(…) this is a mixed race school, so we have to know about other people's religions so we don't say anything bad and not realise it' (ES3-PG1).

In Norwegian school 3, they thought that the reason why they had RE was 'probably because Norway is a Christian country'. The two multicultural schools (ES3, NS3) contrast in that in Norwegian school 3 RE is not seen as instrumentally important because they were a 'mixed race school'. This is consistent with the Norwegian teachers' views about aims of RE being to promote knowledge about religions, and especially Christianity as part of Norwegian cultural heritage.

On the Norwegian side, teachers were not equally explicit that promoting tolerance and respect was the primary aim, but said that they hoped this could be a result of learning about religions. The Norwegian teachers were also more ambivalent towards the present plurality in schools and in society, and did not immediately see RE as especially important in a plural school environment as the English teachers did.

Their teachers' perspectives were reflected in the Norwegian pupils' answers, but it was also challenged by them. In their answers they tended to say that a main point was to learn about 'our' cultural heritage and to learn about the religions as such. In this, their answers reflected their teachers' responses. However, they were also critical of RE as they had experienced the teaching of it.

This critique especially included a wish that RE should be more about plurality, and included a desire that the quality of learning about other religions should be better. For example, one girl (NS1-PG1) said the aim of RE was 'To learn about the different religions and not just our own Christianity'. She had a societal perspective when she added that 'It is important to understand religions in order to understand humans, sort of improving our social intelligence a little'. In Norwegian school 2, there was a strong secular humanist perspective among pupils in the group, and even if they shared the general perspective on what the aims were, they had a critical angle – with clear links to the Secular Humanist Association's official critique of KRL/ RLE at the societal level:

> *Even if many people are members of the Church of Norway, there are also many who formally leave the church and who might convert to another religion: or one will perhaps be working with someone belonging to another religion, and in Norway there are quite a few who have got other religions than just Christianity. So then it is OK to know about them (...) their habits and bad habits (...) what is sacred to them and things like that.* (NS2-PB2)

Pupils in the Norwegian schools use vocabulary which distinguishes very clearly between that which is 'our own' (Norwegian Christianity) and that which is 'other'[334]. This distinction reflects their teachers' views. I would say this is a different sense of 'otherness' to that in the English sample where I understand 'other' as 'others' related to oneself as an individual. This might be attributed to the shorter history of multifaith RE in Norway compared to England, but I also think a different understanding of society as plural is a factor (see chapter 6). In this respect, the English sample represents a more 'modern' view of plurality while, in the Norwegian sample, it is a traditional or group plurality which is reflected (Skeie 1995).[335] Despite the Norwegian pupils seeming to lack the vocabulary to talk about modern plurality (as 'others' tended to mean other than Norwegian Christians), they expressed positive views regarding the shift towards multifaith RE:

> *NS1-PG2: because old people are quite prejudiced and stuff, because they have not learned anything about it ...*

---

334 Including here even secular humanism: which at the institutional level is named in a similar manner to Christianity as part of our cultural heritage. For example, in the school law preamble (both the old and the new from 2008) it says, 'Our Christian and Humanist cultural heritage'.
335 But both views of plurality exist in both countries: and, in describing their religion, modern plurality was more reflected in the Norwegian pupils' answers in my sample: but could also be found in the English sample of the REDCo research (Ipgrave & McKenna 2008).

> O: So, you think that KRL actually works in that way then, at least for you?
> NS1-PG2: Yes, at least in this school with the teacher that we have, right, and... then I think that it does eliminate prejudice. ...
> NS1-PB2: Yes.
> NS1-PG2: ... it does help so much that I do think it is very important
> NS1-PG1: Yes, you become more open minded

There was a tendency that those pupils who liked their teachers most (for example English school 3 and Norwegian school 1) were also the ones who were most positive both with regards to liking RE and seeing it as relevant and important. However, pupils were also able to distinguish between whether they personally liked RE and whether RE as such was seen as important. For example, one boy (ES2-PB1) said he liked RE because it was interesting, but did not think it was important compared to science, English and maths which could ensure him a good job in the future. 'Oline's' (NS3-T) pupils were very critical of her, saying her teaching was boring[336], but they still expressed the view that it was good to learn about other religions.

While there was a great deal of harmony between what teachers and pupils said was the importance of RE, in the Norwegian sample some pupils enhanced the importance of learning about *other* religions more than their teachers, whereas there was a stronger similarity between teachers' and pupils' views in the English sample. Perhaps one explanation is that RE is seen more in relation to present plurality by the younger teachers, and seen more in relation to both traditional religion and traditional RE by the older Norwegian teachers.[337] Another plausible explanation for this difference is that the history of multifaith RE is shorter in Norway (since 1997) while well established in England (in some parts of the country from 1975 when the Birmingham agreed syllabus appeared, see chapter 4). The theory that plurality is perceived differently in the English and Norwegian *imaginaries* is yet another possible source of explanation.

Generally, all pupils spoke favourably about inclusive multifaith RE, the kind of RE that they (in principle) received. The same finding appeared for English and Norwegian pupils in the REDCo studies (Dietz et al. 2009). This could be taken to mean that young people in England and Norway favour a multifaith type of RE because this is seen as relevant for them with respect to their context (local, national and/ or international). However, the REDCo research indicates that pupils in general had a tendency to support the kind of RE that they experienced within their own education systems, a finding which is a consequence of the differences in *social enculturation* in the different countries. Here, school, through *social enculturation* as a process, is successful in instilling a certain (nation-specific) pattern of civility. In this perspective the explanation for young people in England and Norway

---

336 Because they rarely had discussions and it was mostly about listening to her talking.
337 Haakedal's (2004) findings suggests that younger *teachers* were more globally oriented than younger (see chapter 6), so it could be reasoned that young pupils would be more globally oriented while their older teachers especially would have a narrower national or local perspective.

supporting multifaith RE may be simply that this is what they have learned.[338] I would like to conclude that *both* perspectives can be combined in explaining these pupils' general support for multifaith RE: it's because it is relevant for them, and it is because this is what they know.

7.5 Content of learning

While the content of RE in some aspects could be seen as similar at the English and Norwegian institutional levels, there are also some significant differences (chapter 4). We saw that *teaching* about Christianity and other religions was understood differently (chapter 6). In the English case, efforts were made to present Christianity as an international phenomenon, while in Norway it was more acceptable to present Christianity as a Norwegian tradition. Teachings about the 'other' religions were in both cases tied to local or national context – to the religious plurality that had resulted from immigration, while globalisation was a less central aspect.

From the perspective of *pupils' learning*, the most immediate national differences in my particular samples was that the Norwegian pupils were much more able to answer factual questions about religions and Norwegian Christianity especially, while the English pupils struggled with factual questions about either Christianity or other religions, and were largely ignorant about what would characterise Christianity *in Britain*. For example, in Norwegian school 2 (NS2-P) pupils were actually at one point discussing the content of the book of Job critically,[339] and they had no problems saying, for example, what the central message of Christianity was. They had some knowledge of the Christianising of Norway,[340] and they could tell me, for example, that Catholicism is the largest of the Christian denominations worldwide and that Catholicism is dominating in South America while Protestantism is dominant in North America. By contrast, for instance in English school 2, I had to prompt in order to get pupils to say Christmas was Jesus' birthday:

> O: Do you know what the core message of Christianity is? What's the most important message in Christianity? ... Essential message in Christianity?
> (Silence)
> O: What do you think it's got to do with?
> (Silence)
> O: What's Christmas about?
> ES2-PB1: Jesus.
> O: Yeah. What's Easter about?
> ES2-PB2: Easter bunnies.

---

338 I find a similar explanation in McKenna, Neill and Jackson (2009: 61): 'Muslims, Christians and non-religious alike, had assimilated the multi-faith and inter-faith ethic promoted by the English model of RE'.
339 (...) I get angry when I see that it encourages people who are suffering to believe blindly that they will be rewarded later (...) preferably in an afterlife (...) this downright pisses me off (...) I believe you only live once (...) this goes against everything I believe in' (NS2-PB2). Later, he considered the point that the book of Job may also give poor people hope, but in his opinion this was obviously a false hope.
340 By sword, one boy (NS2-PB2) remarked ironically, 'that is not much of a choice'.

O: Easter bunnies? (Smiles) ...
ES2-PB1: Jesus again.
O: Yeah, so what happens at Christmas?
ES2-PB2: You get presents.
O: yeah, but I mean to Jesus?
ES2-PB1: Celebrating his birthday.
ES2-PB2: Yeah, his birthday.[341]

In English school 3, they discussed whether the dominant Christian religion in Britain was Protestantism or Catholicism. The two Muslim boys (ES3-PB1, ES3-PB2) were quite persistent that it was Protestant, but the Hindu girl (ES3-PG1) kept arguing that there were a lot of Catholics as well and was supported by the other girl (ES3-PG2). Eventually, she yields to it being 'mixed, really' but the one boy (ES3-PB1) points out that 'the Church of England is the main one', and it is Protestant. The discussion was civilised and mature (except for the level of their knowledge), confirming there was an atmosphere of respect for different viewpoints in this school, as their teacher claimed.

7.6 What can explain the difference in quality of factual knowledge?

Which factors can be identified as possible explanations for this difference in the quality of factual knowledge between English and Norwegian pupils in this specific (and highly limited) sample?

Obviously, I cannot say whether these findings were representative. The RED-Co research does not include a question about what is actually learned, so on this point there is not other research to refer to as far as I know. It would probably be difficult to establish good quality of knowledge about this in any representative manner. It is hard to imagine international knowledge tests such as PISA and SIMS in mathematics for the field of RE, because of the differences in curricula, and because aims for RE include developing pupils' identity and ability to reflect as well as gaining knowledge and understanding.

The English and Norwegian pupils' knowledge must be judged against what they had in fact been taught. An overview of what they should have learned should be found at the institutional level of their curriculum. This would be the local agreed syllabus, GCSE[342] syllabus and local schemes of work (England) and the National Curriculum for RE and text books (Norway). In addition, there is the question of the efficiency of the teaching and the pupils' personal abilities and interests. These would, of course, vary between schools and teachers within a single country.

---

341 The conversation goes on like this: O: So why is that important? Why do they celebrate that in Christianity? (Silence) O: Who is Jesus? ES2-PB2: He's a good man. O: He's a good man. What else is he? ES2-PB1: Jew. O: He was a Jew, that's true. Ah, when did he live? ES2-PB1: Ah, 2000 years ago. O: Yeah. Well, he's the son of God they claim in Christianity, right? ES2-PB1: (low voice) yeah.
342 The General Certificate of Secondary Education (GCSE), see chapter 5.

It is easier to establish the degree of direct links between the institutional level of curriculum and the experiential in the case of Norway because there is a National Curriculum in RE (even if it has changed frequently: which is a complicating factor).[343] On the English side, there are many local agreed syllabuses and, in the case of this sample, it refers back to two different ones. An additional complicating factor is that the local agreed syllabus has limited influence on work at public examination level. With regard to my sample, which was from Year 10, Key Stage 4, the main influence was the GCSE examination syllabus. GCSE syllabuses are organised on a national basis and have a greater determining influence on what is taught in class and the local syllabi tend to be sidelined at this level.[344]

We saw in chapter 5 that the main topics of the lessons I observed in the English and the Norwegian schools were different. In the English schools, it was Christians' (and Muslims') attitudes towards poverty and wealth (ES3), sex in and out of marriage (ES2) and abortion (ES1). The topics related to a life theme type of RE (GCSE) syllabus. Although these are very specific examples influenced by public examination syllabuses, I think they reflect the national RE research and policy traditions in England.

In England, a strand in the tradition for RE in schools has been the use of 'life themes', including an emphasis on ethical teachings seen as relevant to the lives of learners (consistent with Goldman, Loukes etc. [see for example Jackson & McGrady 2007]). It is possible that the emphasis on ethical teachings in the English examination syllabuses may have diverted attention from gaining a solid basic factual knowledge of each of the religions or denominations.

On the Norwegian side, topics in the observed lessons reflected a phenomenological approach: central issues in Christian belief in (NS3), 'humans and the holy' (NS2) and the world religions (NS1) see chapter 5. In Norway there is a legacy of a phenomenological influence in the RE curriculum with reference to Smart's dimensions which may be traced back to Rian & Kværne (1983) (see chapter 3). They imported some of these ideas from English RE. I see this as an explanation for the relatively solid and comparative knowledge of the religions that these Norwegian pupils have.[345]

---

343 In Norway, the National Curriculum and its local adjustment decides the content of the teachings. These teachers were formally following the 2002 curriculum (Læringsenteret 2002), but were using textbooks which had been made after the 1997 reform (Det kongelige kirke-, utdannings-, og forskningsdepartement 1996) (see details on curricular history in chapter 4, and discussion on the use of textbooks in chapter 6).

344 There are a variety of GCSE religious education syllabuses from which English teachers select the one they want to follow with their pupils. Some have a strong religious studies or comparative religions base, while others focus more on Christianity with biblical options, and others are more philosophical in content (see chapter 5). See http://www.gcse-coursework.com/res_bor.html (Accessed 11.05.05).

345 The critique of the phenomenological approach in English RE does not exist in the same form in Norway, even if, for instance, Østberg (1998b) refers to it.

7.7 Religion in Britain? Norwegian religion?

In English school 2, pupils hesitated when I asked whether they had learned anything about Christianity *in Britain*. They discussed among themselves before concluding that 'We haven't learned about that maybe'. At one point I revealed that The Church of England had a special history and that it was special to England, and this made the pupils so curious (ES2-P) that I was tempted to start telling them about it (but did not). After having asked the pupils in English school 2 about what they had learned about Christianity and other religions, there was an exchange of words between the boys about what they did and did not learn in RE, and one of them concluded that 'Yeah, we learned about the different views that different types of Christians have on euthanasia or abortion.' (ES2-PB1)

I was trying to find out something about English pupils' knowledge about religions when I asked about the content of Christian faith, or the history of the Church of England, for example. I believed this to be a reasonable interpretation of 'Christianity in Britain' in the wording of the 1988 Education Reform Act and the discussion about cultural heritage on the societal level (which has a parallel in Norway: see chapters 3 and 4). In hindsight, however, reflecting on my findings in chapter 6, I wonder if the reason why I was asking this was influenced by the strong position of the 'Christianity as a cultural heritage perspective' in Norwegian RE. Was this a 'Norwegian style' interpretation of 'Christianity *in Britain*'?

However, the apparent emphasis in the English sample on 'different people's views' and 'how not to be offensive' reflects the examination syllabuses rather than the agreed syllabus. For example, a closer look at the agreed syllabus which English schools 2 and 3 followed[346] revealed that there was no shortage of aims concerning learning *about* religion. Indeed 'providing accurate information about the main religions' (p. 2) is a main aim.

This is specified for each key stage focusing on five main areas (authority, beliefs and teachings, celebrations (including of course Christmas), relationships and worship. This thematic organisation gives this element of the syllabus a phenomenological feel. There is not much focus on historical questions, on the development of Christianity in Britain for instance, or any of the religions as traditions in their own right. This may explain the pupils' lack of ability to answer questions about what would characterise the Church of England, but not their lack of ability to say what the main ethos of Christianity is.

> *(...) you know we don't actually get told what the main ethos of Christianity is about (...) Basically it all comes down to not wanting to offend anyone and being politically correct (...) We've been told that in any essay we have to put 'some Christians', so that we don't offend anybody* (ES1-PB1).

Other main aims for RE for Key Stages 1-4 and Post-16 (p. 2)[347] in this agreed syllabus include offering means by which pupils can understand the influence of reli-

---

346 For reasons of confidentiality I cannot identify this 2007 syllabus.
347 Regarding Key Stage 4, this agreed syllabus says that pupils are seen to meet the syllabus requirements if they follow either of five alternatives which all include the study of Christian-

gion on people's attitudes to life and death, and 'help people to develop a positive attitude towards other people, respecting their rights to hold different religious beliefs and value systems from their own' (p. 2). These aims are in harmony with what these pupils said RE was about: so, in the case of these pupils' answers, there was a close connection between the levels when it came to the aims of promoting certain attitudes, but a weak connection regarding aims of learning factual information about the beliefs and teachings of the religions.

However, the child's mistaken view of saying 'some Christians', for example, is not connected with not offending anyone, but with accuracy; it would be inaccurate to say that 'all Christians' shared a common view on euthanasia, for example. Based on this small sample, I can only raise the question whether there is some slippage, in the teaching and in pupils' understanding, between 'respecting the rights of people to hold their chosen religious or secular beliefs' and fostering the attitude of not causing offence to anyone? This is something that maybe needs close attention in English RE.

On the Norwegian side, the aim of RE contributing to respect for others and their rights is less explicit at the formal level of curriculum, even if it is a strong subtext reflected, for instance, in the debates about multifaith RE on the societal level (see chapter 3). Until the 2005 curriculum (UD 2005, see chapter 4) the content was not formulated as aims for learning but rather as content of teaching, saying, for example, how teaching should include education about the history of Christianity (LS 2002, p. 12). There was much emphasis on storytelling in 'småskoletrinnet' (lower primary school), more emphasis on presenting each religion/ tradition and its history in 'mellomtrinnet' (upper primary), and on contemporary perspectives, comparisons and dialogue on 'ungdomstrinnet' (lower secondary) (LS 2002, p. 12-15).[348] On 'ungdomstrinnet' (lower secondary) the religions are not presented separately, but through themes: 'sacred texts' and 'present day plurality of religious and life views', so it could be characterised as more phenomenological at this stage while more historically oriented especially in the 'mellomtrinnet' (upper primary).

What seems to be the case then, in a comparative perspective, is that there is a very close link in the English case to the institutional level of curriculum as pupils' answers reflected recent work based on GCSE syllabuses. However, links to aims in the local agreed syllabus, indicating that they should have a good knowledge base about religions, were weak.[349] In relation to the Norwegian sample, a link to

---

ity and at least one other religion (p. 59). a) A GCSE Religious Studies course which is based on the study of Christianity and at least one other religion, b) A GCSE short course (which was not the case with any of the pupils I interviewed), c) A COEA (Certificate of Educational Achievement (which was not the case with any of the pupils I interviewed), d) An approved school-based syllabus or e) An approved combined or integrated GCSE course.

348 For more details about the relationships between types of schools in England and Norway, see chapter 5.

349 The non-statutory National Framework for RE (which now influences many local agreed syllabuses) recommends building a sound knowledge of the religions by the end of Key Stage 3, so that pupils can move on to broader topics at Key Stage 4. 'Christianity should be studied throughout each key stage (…) the other principal religions represented in Great Britain (here regarded as Buddhism, Hinduism, Islam, Judaism and Sikhism) should be studied across the key stages. It is important that ASCs and schools ensure that by the end of Key Stage 3 pupils

the institutional level of curriculum can be identified also, but this is more indirect because of the situation with textbooks (see chapter 6); however, aims of learning about religions were reflected more in these pupils' answers, so on this point there was a closer link in the Norwegian sample than the English.

In the search for connections to the instructional level, I have no basis to claim that the English teaching was of poorer quality than the Norwegian. On the contrary, judging from the school observations as well as the interviews with the teachers, the English teachers came over as more reflective and better oriented about formal levels of curricula than their Norwegian colleagues, so in this respect this result is an enigma.[350] However, it may be the case that it is the very explicit aim of the English teachers of promoting respect and understanding, which is so clear to pupils, that it overshadows the basic aim of learning *about* religions. As we have seen, this was less explicit in the Norwegian sample, where teachers' framing of aims more strongly reflected learning about religions as the principal aim. This actually reflects differences at the institutional level of curriculum as well. These may be factors explaining why Norwegian pupils in this specific sample were more able to demonstrate factual knowledge about religions.

The final area which may explain differences is the individual level, but I did not obtain details about pupils' backgrounds, including their home backgrounds and individual levels of ability, in this study. What I do know from the basic experiences of the interviews, school visits and general knowledge of the school systems is, for example, that in Norwegian school 2 some participating pupils were reading books which demonstrated an interest in topics regarding religion or philosophy. Also, the level of discussion in Norwegian school 1 was of high quality. The styles of teaching in the English schools were generally more rigid and achievement-based, most likely because of their forthcoming GCSE examination.

My case studies do not provide enough data to explain the difference in answers to questions about religions in a satisfactory way, but a main point here is that the difference between the English and the Norwegian material reflects the institutional levels in various ways, and the different understandings of teachers to some degree. Reasons are very likely to be found in the "middle layer" of learning material such as textbooks or schemes of work (see chapter 6). Teachers' and pupils' different understandings of society as more or less plural are also relevant: for example, having different ideas of the role of Christianity as cultural heritage, reflecting different *national imaginaries*, could be seen as an explanation for national differences.

Whatever the reason, it is the case that, regarding the content of learning about religions, I found significant differences between the English and Norwegian sam-

---

have encountered all of these five principal religions in sufficient depth.' (QCA 2004: 12), see http://www.qcda.gov.uk/libraryAssets/media/9817_re_national_framework_04.pdf
The responses from the pupils in schools show that this level of sound knowledge had not been reached.

350 It is an enigma how, in my sample, the English teachers were so well oriented and ready to answer questions about RE, while the Norwegian teachers were more hesitant and gave answers indicating they had not reflected much about their roles as RE teachers: and then in the interviews with their pupils it was the Norwegian pupils who had better knowledge of religion.

ples. What can be concluded with regards to my methodology is that these differences must be explained with reference to differences in what is actually taught and learned in practice. These differences were not obvious from reading documents alone (chapter 3 and 4). This finding made it necessary to re-examine documents at the institutional level of curriculum with a different and specific focus, and this is an interesting indication of how this methodology could be developed further in the future. It is an argument for the importance of including an empirical element in a comparative study, even if this also complicates the comparison.

7.8 Learning about and from religion

The English teachers were familiar with the concepts of learning about and from (see chapters 4 and 6). They predicted that their pupils would probably not be able to say what the difference between learning *about* and *from* religion would be, and they were right. Some of the pupils did try to reason what it could mean, and one of the Muslim boys (ES3-PB2) suggested this: 'Like if some religion says you should give money to charities, you learn from that and you give money to charities'.

On the Norwegian side, the teachers were not familiar with the concepts of learning about and from as such. Even if this is an aspect of Norwegian RE according to the institutional level of curriculum (see chapter 4), this is clear neither to the teachers nor the pupils. Like their teachers, the pupils understood the terms 'getting both knowledge and experience' as referring to outward experiences from excursions or interesting methods of teaching (for example drama), rather than personal growth resulting from encounters with learning material (see chapter 6).

Looking beyond the problems over how concepts were understood by pupils, I conclude from my material that, both in the English and the Norwegian samples, pupils were learning both about and from religion. For example, in English school 3 the pupils said they thought RE was special compared to other subjects, because 'RE's got to be contemplated (…) because you may get the religions mixed up, and people do get defensive. It isn't like maths or English, you might get defensive' (ES3-PB1). They also said that they could express thoughts and feelings in RE (ES3-PG1).

It was quite clear that they related RE learning to their own lives; because they said, for example, that RE made it easier to talk to their friends about their different religions and understand them better.[351] They expressed a first-hand experience of why it was important, much in accordance with how it was expressed by their teacher. They (ES3-P) also confirmed that they did think RE contributed to their personal growth. Also in English school 2, they seem to have learned from religion: 'Because before we were like laughing and everything about what they were doing and everything, but now we know more about what they're doing and why they're doing it. So, it's their life' (ES2-PG1).

---

351 In the REDCo research, it was found that RE lessons in school was the most likely place for pupils to engage in discussions (dialogue) between different religious viewpoints, while outside RE class students were more likely to discuss religion with those from similar backgrounds to themselves (Dietz *et al.* 2009).

The clearest indication of learning *from* religion in the Norwegian sample was found in Norwegian school 1: where they used information from their RE to construct personal life views (see above). They could not have done this, even if it might have been in a playful manner, if they had not been learning both about and *from* religion. They also explicitly agreed that it was contributing to their own life: 'I think we all develop a lot when we have KRL' (NS1-PG2).

In Norwegian school 3, the pupils first said they did not think KRL was an important subject and did not see that it had any relevance for their own life. However, as the questions of the interview revealed the aims for the subject according to the institutional level (the National Curriculum), it turned out they did think RE might be important 'because they learn more about *other* religions'. In other words, these pupils think RE might be important when the focus is *other* religions. What they have experienced in praxis is perhaps the opposite: that the main aim of the learning was learning about the Norwegian Christian tradition.[352]

The question as to whether RE was contributing to pupils becoming more respectful was answered explicitly in the case of the two girls' (NS3-PG3, NS3-PG4) who had the experience of giving a presentation about Islam[353]: 'We *get* more respect when we tell others about Islam'. Both the indigenous Norwegian girls (NS3-PG1, NS3-PG2) also agreed they gained respect through learning about different religions but were sceptical of whether it had that effect on their classmates. In English school 1, they also thought RE *promoted* respect for other people: 'this is the big thing (...) and the most important point', but they were also hesitant as to whether it had the effect of making them or their classmates more tolerant.

In both the Norwegian and the English cases, the 'learning from' aspect was an element that gave RE a different quality compared to other school subjects. In Norwegian school 2, they said they thought RE was an important subject, because 'the things we learn in KRL might be stocked at the back of our heads for later in life, while things we learn in maths for example will be forgotten'.

In this school (NS2-P), the pupils did see themselves as respectful of other people, but not because of their RE.[354] They (NS2-P) also distinguished between getting a better understanding and becoming more respectful. For example, one boy (NS2-PB2) was so critical of Christianity and religion in general that it was difficult for him to say he had respect for it. At the same time, this was also the boy who criticised textbooks for being biased and said it would have been better if someone who really believed in Islamic religion for instance, could have explained it.

Signs that pupils were learning from religion in RE were found both in the English and Norwegian schools, but in varying degrees. In the English schools, they all saw RE as promoting learning to be respectful, for example, but were, like their teachers, hesitant as to whether it actually had this effect on themselves or their classmates. Even in English school 3, they expressed doubt that it had the same

---

352 This bias comes through to them both through their teachers' understanding of the subject and through their textbooks.
353 The teacher and the two girls themselves (NS3-PG3 and NS3-PG4) said that they had recently prepared a presentation about their own religion – Islam – and presented this both in their own class and in other classes.
354 This was exactly what their teacher (Ingunn NS2-T) said they might say.

positive effect on everyone, saying that some would still be racist. On the Norwegian side, it is often the case that they say that they do gain respect through RE, despite this being a less explicit instrumental aim at the instructional level. Both English and Norwegian pupils were ambivalent as to what degree they or their peers do gain respect through RE, which harmonises with their teachers' modesty as to whether this was actually an outcome of RE teaching (see chapter 6).[355]

The relevance of RE for their own lives was immediate for the pupils in English school 3, but in all the other schools in both countries pupils tended to understand 'relevance for your own life' in a very concrete way. Some noted that it would only be relevant for people wanting to become priests, while others said it was interesting, but did not see what they could do with this knowledge, as they did not see its relevance for future jobs. This was, for instance, the case with the pupils in Norwegian school 3 (NS3 P) which is an interesting contrast to the immediate relevance of RE for the pupils in English school 3. When, in Norwegian school 3, I explained that 'having use for' could for instance mean helping them in forming their opinions, they did see the use of it.[356] In English school 1, we had this discussion:

> O: *But you never know what your life is going to be like, maybe you will be doing engineering in say Africa, and you need to know about African religion and maths...*
> ES1-PG1: *We don't do that.*
> *(Laughs)*
> ES1-PB1: *We don't.*
> ES1-PG2: *We never learned about African religion...*
> ES1-PB2: *There are only two religions during the whole ...*
> ES1-PG2: *There's Muslims...*
> ES1-PB2: *Islam and Christianity, they're the only two ...*
> ES1-PB1: *Really, yeah, that's about right,*
> ES1-PG1: *... we should do more ...*
> ES1-PB2: *They're the ones they teach us because they are the biggest, the biggest two.*
> ES1-PG2: *It would be interesting to know about other religions ...*

The largest religions in Africa are of course Christianity and Islam, but the point here, with regard to seeing the relevance of RE to their own lives, is that some pupils' lack the ability to see its relevance. I would suggest that the implication of this for teachers and policy-makers is that the importance of RE should be explained to and discussed with pupils.

According to Jackson & O'Grady (2007: 193), 'The principle that religious education needs to be existentially relevant has been prominent ever since Loukes' in

---

355 It may be that pupils have different understandings of certain concepts, like, for instance, *respect*. Anker's forthcoming PhD thesis will discuss pupils' ideas of respect and disrespect.
356 The Kurdish girl (NS3-PG4) said she might get use for it if, in the future, she would be involved in discussions about religion. She (NS3-PG4) said it might be important to learn, that she learned a lot that she did not know before and that it is good that they have KRL and can learn about religion. This girl did not have much schooling before she came to Norway as a nine year-old, and her teacher spoke highly of how well she managed in school despite this. I interpret her negativity as adjusting to class or school environment, but that she might in fact enjoy school learning more than it is socially acceptable to admit.

English RE. As the aims of RE in both England and Norway have shifted from traditional Christian nurturing RE, it might still not be so obvious to some teachers and pupils exactly what the point of RE is. This is perhaps not totally unexpected given the ambivalence in the societal and institutional level about what the main aim of RE is. However, it is important that the purpose of the subject is clear for the RE teaching and learning to become meaningful.

7.9 What kind of imaginary would be inclusive?

When it comes to learning about and from 'other' religions, the differences were less obvious in the two countries. Both in England and Norway 'difference' is tied to the national context of increased religious plurality. The Norwegian pupils' knowledge of the other religions was better than that of the English pupils, but of a poorer quality than their knowledge about Christianity. I was not able to detect clear differences in quality in the English sample between the teaching and learning about Christianity and 'other' religions. In both countries, however, Christianity was the religion with the strongest representation at the institutional level of curriculum (see chapter 4), and this was reflected also in the practice that I observed during my school visits (see chapter 5).

> *You remember these stories, like about the one on the mountain who had to ah, who were to sacrifice his son, and but then God came; you remember a lot of these stories that you have either seen on film or they have been read to you. It kind of remains in your head, like Abraham and a lot like that, but I can't remember anything like that from any of the other religions. Then it's kind of just 'they think this' and 'Islam kind of has him' and stuff like that. We know a lot about Christianity, but we kind of just know that which, well very little like that about other religions* (NS2-PB2).

This critique demonstrates that, despite the effort at the institutional level (the National Curriculum for KRL: see chapter 4) to say that all parts of the subject should be presented on equal terms, this principle had not filtered through to the experiential level. One reason is the teachers' dependence on textbooks, which have not been successful in translating this principle of equality in teaching about Christianity and *other* religions into pedagogical material. We saw in chapter 6 that textbooks do not necessarily get updated to reflect new curriculum reforms, and this principle of equal treatment of material from all the religions has been enhanced with every reform since 1997. Another reason is the quality of the teaching as the teachers could have made pedagogical choices to improve the teaching with regards to avoiding a different quality of teaching about Christianity and other religions, despite the situation with the textbooks.

That pupils reported such a difference in quality between learning about Christianity and other religions could be because they were aware of the critique on the societal level regarding this, for instance from the Norwegian Humanist Association. However, this was also confirmed through their answers. They knew facts about the 'other' religions, but did not reveal the kind of insights that would enable them to discuss topics on the same level, as for instance they did (NS2-P) about the book of Job or original sin. For example, pupils did not know that there is not a concept of original sin in Islam, or that Islam and Judaism share some of the stories.[357] Neither are they very well knowledgeable about other religions in Norway, nor about religion in the local area, like knowing the location of the mosque. While they had other important sources of information about the Christian religion – from novels that they had read, for example – what they knew about the other religions depended more on school learning.[358]

Norwegian pupils even expressed the criticism that Christianity as 'our' heritage is emphasised too much, as we have seen above. They seem to be interested in more and better quality learning about the 'other' religions. For example, one boy (NS2-PB1) said that he thought the other religions were explained from a Christian point of view, which he thought was not right. In his view, Islam should rather be explained by a Muslim, thinking it was wrong if Christians explained the other religions. In Norwegian school 1, (NS1) too, they said that their study of the 'other' religions was 'sort of done with Christian eyes' and said this might have been different if there had actually been Muslims in the class.

> *NS1-PG2: (teaching would have been) more interesting perhaps*
> *NS1-PB1: Yes*
> *NS1-PG2: Would have learned more*
> *NS1-PB2: We would have had more different viewpoints and perhaps been less judgemental of things than if one only hears of Islam as this strict religion which suppresses women and stuff.*
> *NS1-PB1: We see it through our eyes you know and not through theirs.*

Here, these pupils' concern was how to represent religions in school. It is the same kind of concern with which the pupils in Norwegian school 2 expressed criticisms of their textbooks' use of 'we' referring to 'we Christians' while it is 'they' and 'the others' when the reference was to a secular life view or other religious life views. In other words, the Norwegian pupils in general expressed the same view as the English pupils and English teachers, that having representatives of the different religions (in class or through visitors) would be a strength to RE. I take this to indicate that Norwegian pupils were more oriented towards the plural and the global aspects of RE than were their teachers.

But, in the English sample, pupils also expressed themselves critically about the way religion had been represented in school:

> *ES1-PB1: It's not a problem with religion and stuff; it's how you go about telling me about it. I suppose in primary school, that's when your opinion is being formed.*

---

357 Although how to handle the shared stories about, for example, Abraham, Moses, Jesus, has been a central topic in some parts of the societal level: among educators and scholars and also some textbook publishers.

358 REDCo researchers also found that religious pupils learn about their own religion at home, and about other religions in school, whereas pupils who labelled themselves as not religious (including some of the domestic Christians who were stressing that they were not very Christian, see discussion above) had school as their main source of information about religion in general (Dietz *et al.* 2009).

When you get to 16-17 you've got your own mind made up. So that's the really important thing (...)
ES1-PG1: In my primary school, I wish they would have given us all the options. Not just the ones that they thought were right, which is what they did, because now I have ideas based on those. And I am now learning that there are other ideas. And I agree with those more. But because I couldn't agree to them earlier, I sort of base whatever I do around that.

These 14 year-olds were reflecting on their own identity formation and how this could have been different. Their main criticism is that they did not like it when teaching was biased and too normative, much in accordance with Loukes' findings in the UK about teenagers and religion (Loukes 1966). Education is, by definition, a normative task. There is often a tension in education between, on the one hand, enculturation into a certain sense of civility, necessary for the coherence of a society (Schiffauer et al. 2004) and, on the other hand, instilling in pupils an ability to think critically, which is also an important democratic value. The pupils interviewed expressed points of criticism of various kinds, towards RE in general or RE as they have experienced it, including perspectives on how to improve it.[359] Independent of what system they were in or the quality of their teaching or learning, the pupils' ability to reflect is impressive, even on why their knowledge was poor. In several instances, pupils connected directly to debates on the societal level of curriculum.[360]

In the REDCo material, it was a conclusion in the English findings that the idea of a harmonious multifaith community was widely shared, and in the Norwegian findings that the pupils did not believe religion was a factor contributing to conflicts in classrooms (Dietz et al. 2009). In summing up some general trends in findings in the qualitative and quantitative studies of all the eight countries, the researchers mention, for example, that 'students wish for peaceful coexistence across differences, and believe this to be possible' (Dietz et al. 2009: 16).

This resembles a cross-national finding in the comparative study done by Schiffauer and his co-researchers (2004: 329):[361] that

> *their process of enculturation is not only marked by the nationally specific civil cultures, which limits this explanatory framework. (...) we encountered highly convergent phenomena concerning pupils' visions of what a just society would look like from the view of minorities providing cultural experiences other than those of the majority population. With their shared demands for a value-neutral*

---

359 For example, in English school 3 they discuss critically the pubic debate about headscarves, and the banning of headscarves in French schools: in English school 2 the point that RE should be optional is strongly made, and in English school 1 one boy who had gone to a Church of England primary school was critical of having had to participate in religiously affiliated morning assemblies. In Norwegian school 3, they would have liked to have the involvement of more pupils and more discussions in class. In Norwegian school 2, they had criticisms reflecting a secular humanist criticism on the societal level, first and foremost that RE is biased in favour of Christianity, including the textbooks. There was also criticism of the textbooks in Norwegian school 1.
360 For further reflections on such 'bypasses' of adjacent levels of curriculum, see chapter 8.
361 Their focus group was Turkish immigrants in four countries: how they were integrated in schools.

recognition of their being different and for equal access to the arena of achievement-based competition (...).

Based on my own and the above mentioned, much larger comparative studies, an idea of the existence of *shared supranational imaginaries* among *young people* emerges. Reflecting on globalisation as a supranational force affecting national and local contexts, this is also highly plausible. In chapter 6, I asked what kind of imaginary would be inclusive for all, and such an international imaginary shared by young people, exemplified by the statement from the summing up of REDCo findings that 'students wish for peaceful coexistence across differences, and believe this to be possible', could be seen as one example of this.

7.10 Summary and conclusion

In this chapter, I have discussed pupils' perspectives on RE in England and Norway. I have considered patterns in how they related to religion, what they saw as aims in RE and what they had learned about and from religion in RE.

The reality of what goes on in schools is a difficult subject because of its complexity, and – perhaps related to the first reason – the lack of research-based knowledge of it. Lately, however, the research done in the REDCo project (summed up in Dietz et al. 2009) contributes to improving our knowledge of teenage pupils' encounters with religious pluralism in school and society (Knauth et al. 2008) and teenagers' perspectives on the role of religion in their lives, in schools and society (Valk et al. 2009), and also on how teachers respond to religious diversity (van der Want et al. 2009).

It would be interesting to look more closely at some patterns which occur in this research and in my own, on another occasion. Regin (1987) points out that, while one can recognise patterns in complexity, explaining them is more difficult because there are so many possible single reasons in each case. Both subnational, national and supranational processes are relevant for how pupils experience RE, how they understand it, and what they see to be its relevance.

A pattern which occurred across national borders was that in the 'multicultural' schools pupils said they were religious, in the English and Norwegian schools 2 (the city/ city outskirt schools), pupils said they were non-religious, and in the rural schools pupils self-identified as Christian (but not very Christian). For mainstream pupils who labelled themselves as non-religious,[362] an individual pick-and-choose type of religiosity was most typical, while, for pupils with religious family backgrounds, it seemed more to be about exploring one's own religion. This could be seen as different pupils referring to a different sense of modernity, which must be understood as a supranational phenomenon.

A national difference was that it was in the multicultural English school (ES3) and the rural Norwegian school (NS1) that there were most acceptances of being religious. This is consistent with the idea of different *national styles* of multifaith

---

362 Including some who labelled themselves Christians, but stressed that they were not very Christian: see discussion above of some possible reasons why pupils self-identify differently.

RE where plurality is enhanced more in the case of England while the national tradition is more central in the case of Norway (see also chapter 6).

In English school 3 (ES3-P), pupils had a combined experience of having peers with different religions and an enhancement of positive aspects of this by their teacher. In Norwegian school 3 (NS3-P), pupils also experienced peers in school having different religions, but, in this school, there is not the same positive outlook on how this contributes to RE. That is not to say that this school (NS3) did not take the plural makeup of their school population seriously, but the focus was not on religion or RE. Jackson (2004a: 173) has made the point that many who are preoccupied with intercultural perspectives in education policy at a European level are unaware of the potential relevance of RE. The same seems to be reflected in practice in this 'multicultural' Norwegian school. They do not see religion as especially relevant in this context.

Regarding what pupils saw as aims for RE, the pattern also followed the national borderlines, as on the English side the aims were said to be learning to respect other people's opinions, while on the Norwegian side the aim was of learning about 'our' heritage and about religions as such. Again, this was consistent with teachers' answers, strengthening the idea of multifaith RE taking on different styles in different countries (see chapter 6). The emphasis on traditional Christianity was, however, also a point of critique from the Norwegian pupils. In some instances, their ideas of how it should have been is actually closer to the way it is formulated at the institutional level, illustrating how some processes may bypass certain levels (see chapter 8).

The English pupils were not able to say much about religions as such, and explained that what they had learned was different people's opinions on, for example, euthanasia, abortion and sex in and out of marriage, which was largely consistent with the GCSE syllabuses they were following. The Norwegian pupils were more able to discuss religion as such, but there was a difference in quality in their knowledge of Christianity and other religions. Again, findings indicate different *national styles*, and the empirical methods in this case brought out additional differences which were not immediately obvious from the reading of documents alone (see chapter 4).

In both countries, teachers' and pupils' answers indicate that they do learn *from* religion in RE, but both teachers and pupils expressed uncertainty regarding what can be achieved through RE. The question of what is actually learned about and from religion is not central to the REDCo research, so this might be suggested as a topic for further investigation.

Regarding the supranational dimension, I will refer to two points: firstly, that some new imaginaries among young people may emerge internationally, since so many young people interact and share each other's views through the internet, other media and/ or travel. Based on my research alone, I cannot conclude that this is the case, but based on this and other comparative studies, I can point out that the question of how globalisation is shaping youth is one of relevance for RE, and one which I would also like to suggest for further investigation.

The second point is related to the first: how do different international phenomena affect youth differently? For instance, Muslims and non-Muslims probably relate to debates about international terrorism differently, and European secularisation probably affects religious youth (Muslims and Christians) with roots elsewhere in a different way than indigenous European Christians. This relates to the point that many modernities coexist in today's societies.

This are more questions arising from my research than a finding, but it is a question which I think it would be interesting to explore further. For example: is only one kind of modernity reflected at the institutional level? And, if so, is this a source of constructions of 'otherness' in multifaith RE despite explicit aims to be inclusive – in other words: are the laws and curricular documents still ethnocentric?

If I take these points regarding supranational processes together with the critique of RE by the pupils in my study, it challenges the ideas of *national styles* of multifaith RE. Should the focus be less on religions *in Britain*, or religious traditions *in Norway* (although this may mean different things); and be more internationally oriented? Should multifaith RE take more account of globalisation as a factor affecting the young?

As, this methodology, the supranational with is conceptualised as part of the context, this could well be combined with contextual approaches to RE. At the same time, I do not think that either 'white British' or the 'Norwegian cultural heritage' should be ignored. To come back to Schiffauer et al. (2004) again, a finding of theirs was that integration is easier if cultural patterns are explicit rather than hidden, and where rules for civil conduct are transparent: '(…) it is definitely not as easy for newcomers to meet implicit norms of internalised civility as it is to submit oneself to an explicit outward regime of rules (…)' (Schiffauer et al. 2004: 204).

The teaching of Norwegian and English religious traditions could make it clearer where some rules come from; and also what could be negotiated. That way, the *national imaginaries* might be challenged, maintained and updated.

In the final chapter (8), I will sum up the findings in the chapters of this book and evaluate the method which was used (as outlined in chapter 2).

8. Concluding Discussion

8.1 Introduction

In this study, I have compared aspects of RE in England and Norway following the development of a suggested methodology for carrying out comparative research (chapter 2). I looked at comparative studies in related fields and pioneering works in comparative RE as a background. A basic principle which I adopted from comparative education was that comparative studies in religious education are about studying the impact of supranational processes on different national educational systems, i.e. national processes (chapter 2).

I suggested a template for comparative studies in RE which was a synthesis of two sets of ideas: firstly, that three dimensions should be considered: supranational, national and subnational processes (Dale 2006) and, secondly, in order to capture the complexities of national contexts, an idea of four levels of curriculum (Goodlad & Su 1992): A: the societal level, B: the institutional level, C: the instructional level and D: the experiential level.

8.2 A systematic approach to comparative RE

I have used Goodlad & Su's (1992) ideas of levels of curriculum to structure the thesis (see chapter 2), so that

A: the societal level is discussed in chapter 3
B: the institutional level is discussed in chapter 4
C: the instructional level is discussed in chapter 6, and
D: the experiential level is discussed in chapter 7

In each chapter I considered supranational, national and subnational processes. In chapter 5, I discussed how the use of field data is linked to the overall methodology, making use of the concepts *civil enculturation, civil culture and social and or national imaginaries* (Schiffauer et al. 2004). Chapters 2, 5 and 8 explicitly discuss the methodology: this systematic approach to comparative studies in RE.

A model

This combination of the two ideas can be presented diagrammatically in the following way:

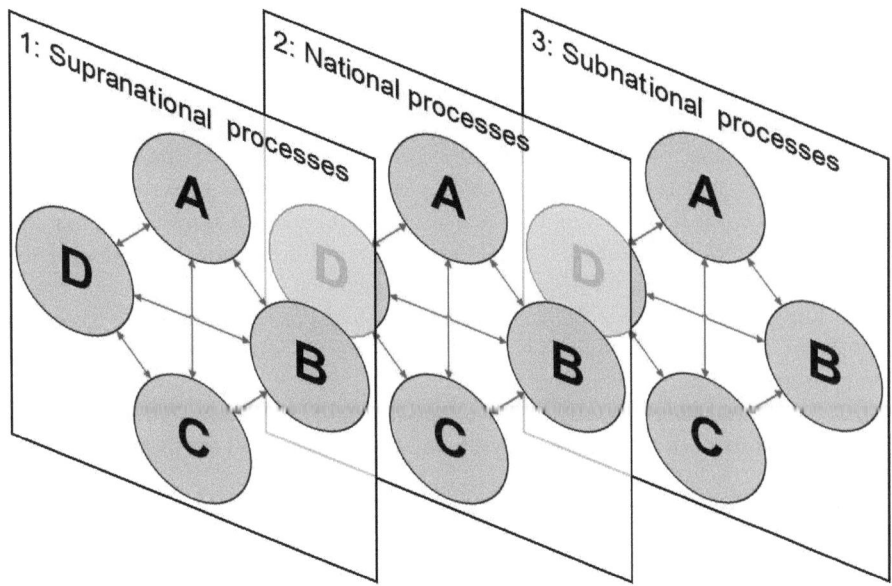

Illustration 2: Diagrammatical model of the methodology

This model counteracts any ideas of linearity or hierarchy between the levels, at the same time as preserving a sense of sequence through clockwise labels A-D. Goodlad (1979: 357) notes that 'the domain to domain transactions are not always between two adjacent domains', and that sometimes there may be more interactions between, for example, the societal and the instructional level, than between the institutional and the instructional level.

I found examples of this in my material (see chapters 6 and 7). In other words, arrows indicating mutual influence can, for example, bypass the institutional level, situated between the societal and the instructional levels. The model above catches these potential 'bypassing' influences between levels.

Afdal (2006: 82-85) also discusses whether the levels should be understood as linear and concludes by suggesting a cyclical model. His model does not, however, keep the sense of sequence and, since his is not an international or comparative study, it also lacks the supranational dimension. However, he distinguishes between school context and local context, both of which in my model form part of the subnational dimension.

8.3 Is this a general model, a template for comparative studies?

All of the levels A-D exist in one nation, and the concepts of societal, institutional, instructional and experiential levels of curriculum are tools to capture and analyse complexities in what goes on in school education in one country. For example: how are societal debates reflected in institutional curricula? What academic debates/ research, for instance, are reflected in the non-statutory guidelines for religious education (QCA 2004) in England or in the National Curriculum (UD 2005) in Norway?

Further, how are aims for RE at the institutional level reflected in the experiential level? What is the relationship between, for example, what the law says RE should be and what pupils in classroom experience and learn? Using this way of conceptualising RE reveals differences as well as coherences between the levels (see chapters 3-7). If, for example, we find that pupils do not learn that which the curriculum at the institutional level intends, this is a finding which is relevant for policy-makers as well as, for instance, teacher educators.

In today's world, however, it is not the case that processes of relevance come only from within the national contexts. Some of the main forces which have changed approaches to RE in England and Norway from traditional nurture to multifaith, are shared internationally. Hence, one needs to consider a supranational dimension; and this is a reason for carrying out international and comparative studies in RE.

With this model, the national traditions are conceptualised as processes, stressing their continuous and changing character. These internationally shared challenges are factors which develop and change RE in many countries today (see for example Jackson 2007, Willaime 2007). Therefore, this model might be considered a general model or a template for comparative studies in RE in today's world.

When I set out to compare two nations explicitly, the task raised the question of how England and Norway responded to internationally shared challenges. Was it a different response or a similar response? These supranational challenges come either from formal or informal supranational processes. Formal supranational processes are, for example, policy-making and informal processes are, for example, secularisation, pluralisation and globalisation, even if these in part unfold through international organisations (see chapter 2).

In each of the preceding chapters (3-7), the main emphasis is on national processes. This is because I wanted to explore the importance of the different national contexts in relation to how supranational challenges are met. Then, differences and similarities between England and Norway become evident, and it is possible to discuss reasons for them, using this comparative approach as an analytical device to look for explanations. If these challenges are shared, the question is raised as to why all the European nations do not respond by having multifaith RE? Why did England and Norway adopt this approach?

The same challenges are met in different ways, reflecting national traditions, and this becomes evident as the book chapters unfold. It was possible to suggest some of the national factors which determined how these international challenges were met in a particular country.

I discovered that the main sources for explanations of difference between English and Norwegian RE were found:

1. *within the domain of RE, for example in the different scholarly traditions of RE research, and traditional RE practice, and*
2. *outside the domain of RE, especially in the different school systems, but also in other societal factors (see chapters 1, 3 and 5).*

An interesting finding/ suggestion was, for instance, that the school and research traditions in England and Norway were initially so different that any direct parallels between the two countries' RE had to be considered coincidental (see chapter 4). The reasons for the type of RE which exists in England have to do with the English tradition meeting these challenges, and likewise in Norway. At the same time, the reasons for both countries having multifaith RE are a response to the same challenge of increasing religious plurality in society, which is a supranational process.

8.4 Obstacles and limitations

In this section, I will take the opportunity to reflect on obstacles and limitations that this study encountered. Firstly, finding arguments for doing comparative and international studies proved challenging. While it is easy to argue that comparative studies are interesting, it was less straightforward to find good arguments for its relevance (see chapter 2).

An additional challenge occurred as my aim was not only to identify differences and similarities, but also to explain them. However, through applying the above mentioned approach of supranational, national and subnational perspectives, this became possible.

The need to find a way of limiting what was to be compared and make the comparison systematic and valid was a huge challenge, resulting in the suggested methodology. It led to the decision to organise the thesis based on Goodlad & Su's (1992) idea of levels of curriculum. Also, finding theoretical perspectives and concepts (analytic tools) that fitted the purpose proved challenging, and several different perspectives are combined in the final chapters.

As I wanted this study to be contextual, this demanded a good knowledge of the contexts of both English and Norwegian RE teaching; including the school systems, societal debates and developments in research. It has been challenging understanding even the Norwegian context in sufficient depth, but especially the English and the wider international context as well.

Needless to say, there is always more that could have been investigated, or elements that ideally should be investigated more thoroughly. For example, I discovered how history and school systems were highly relevant for explaining how the supranational processes led to different national processes. At the same time, it would be beyond the scope of this project to also include a broad comparison of the school systems and their histories.

In addition to reasons why multifaith RE in English and Norwegian schools takes on different styles, related to history and national context, there are also differences in the traditions of research and academic studies in RE. I have addressed this issue in chapter 3, thus making it part of my discussion. However, being a Norwegian scholar doing an English PhD I might have occasionally made particular interpretations of the nature of the academic field, which is also part of the context of this text.

The evolving character of the field of *comparative studies in religious education* has also been a complicating factor. When I started out in 2002[363], few international and comparative studies existed, but during the course of the study several major comparative and international studies have emerged (for example, the RED-Co research and Alberts' (2007) thesis). This has been a strength, as it has provided additional studies through which to triangulate my own, and shown the wider relevance of my efforts. Some of their results and ideas or concepts have been considered in my own work, but it has been impossible to discuss fully the implications of these other studies for my own; such a discussion has been beyond what I could do in a one-person project working to a specific deadline.

Finally, being a one-person study has been a limitation, and my findings suggest many possibilities for further studies including developing the methodology further. However, the limitation of being a one-person project[364] has provided the opportunity to study selected issues in some depth, most importantly in developing a new approach, which can be seen as new a methodology for comparative studies in religious education (see above and in chapter 2).

8.5 Results: Examples of findings

An imperative for claiming the usefulness of this suggested methodology is that it did lead to some interesting results in my own research. In searching for explanations for similarities and differences, I looked for themes which emerged from the material in a grounded theory approach (see chapter 1). These include, for instance, how having a central curriculum or not affects the research traditions (chapter 3), how different school systems – including their traditional relationships to religion – are a source of explanations for differences (chapter 3, 4, 5), for example the different approach to rights of withdrawal (chapter 4). Other findings include the view that, while aims for RE may be to promote inclusiveness, the subject can also construct 'otherness', and perhaps even of different kinds in England and Norway (chapters 4, 6, 7).

Applying terminology from Schiffauer et al. (2004), I found that multifaith RE took on different styles in England and Norway (chapter 3, 5, 6, 7). However, expanding on this terminology, in view of the inclusion of supranational processes in my methodology, I suggested there would also be *supranational imaginaries* which may challenge the *national imaginaries*. This may, for instance, be the case when some relate to *international imaginaries* such as that of international terrorism, or of international youth cultures (chapter 7).

One question which could be raised from this is how globalisation, as opposed to pluralisation (although these are intertwined phenomena, see chapter 2), is affecting the young and their relationship to religion. Another question is how one particular supranational process, or phenomenon, may affect pupils with different

---

[363] Proceeding to a one-year maternity leave almost immediately, and, in 2006, I had another child, thereby delaying and prolonging the project an additional year.

[364] With some very good support and suggestions for correction from my two supervisors: R. Jackson and G. Skeie.

religious or non-religious affiliations differently if they have 'different modernities' (Taylor 2004) as their frame of reference (see chapter 7).

These emerging themes demonstrate, for instance, how some supranational processes are formed differently as they are filtered through the levels of national processes, and also how some may bypass the institutional national level altogether (see diagram above). This may, for instance, be the case when there are so called 'global links' in the classrooms, including pupils with 'international families'. Due to migration, particular pupils may have relatives in various parts of the world. Moreover, this can apply to pupils who participate in international fellowships online, through online games or twitter/ facebook for instance, or simply if they are connected to religions with a global spread.

It is not possible, in this final chapter, to reconsider all the themes that could possibly be identified because that would involve rewriting the whole thesis. Examples of such themes are: how concepts are understood differently – for example, how plurality is understood (chapters 2, 5, 6) – what the impact of the 'new' plurality in society is (all chapters), what considerations there are regarding how religions are represented (see chapters 3, 6, 7). Further themes are: what is seen as RE's relevance for pupils (all chapters), how educational versus religious goals are balanced (chapters 3, 4) and what the views on or contributions from 'secular' religious studies are as opposed to theology or other relevant fields (chapter 3), what concepts of civil religions could be identified (chapter 4), what are the concerns regarding Human Rights (chapter 4), and to what degree global perspectives are present in RE, including the suggestion that pupils in a class may have different modernities as their frame of reference which affects how they relate to religion in RE (chapter 7).

One way of applying this methodology in a different way (see chapter 7) would be to identify a question based on fieldwork and analysing this through examining the levels of curriculum. That would be using my methodology differently from the main approach in this study, and thus developing it further. For instance, one could examine such emerging grounded themes in relation to how they are reflected on each level A-D (see above), whilst taking account of supranational, national and subnational processes on each level.

In the present chapter, I will discuss two themes emerging from preceding chapters in this way:

1. The idea of different *national styles*, and
2. the question of inclusive RE and the construction of otherness.

Here, I will be focusing more on the supranational processes than in the previous chapters. This is also to experiment with possible further uses of the approach. I will in the following reconsider certain findings in the wider supranational context. This discussion, it is important to note, builds on the chapters 3-7 emphasis on the national contexts.

8.6 Different national styles

In chapters 3-7, I discussed whether multifaith RE takes on different styles in England and Norway, reflecting particular *national imaginaries*. In England, being part of the heterogeneous Great Britain with several strong religious traditions could be suggested as being central components of this national imaginary (Schiffauer et al. 2004: 35). In Norway, I suggested that the history of the nation-building project and the strong standing of the State Church are central (see chapter 6). School traditions are very different, among other things reflecting different relationships between state, religion and Church, and having different history and traditions with regard to the centralisation and unity of the school systems. In chapter 5, I found that certain classroom activities did reflect different *national styles* and that a number of differences went along national lines.[365] But what signs of different *national styles* were identified in the various levels of curriculum? And how are these challenged by supranational (and subnational) impositions?

If I consider first the societal level (chapter 3), we saw how academic traditions in the two countries reflected differences in the traditional relationship between state, religion and school. In England, for example, the dual system of shared responsibility for schools between state and school and the existence of several strong Christian traditions led to RE being non-denominational with reference to traditional Christian religious plurality. Combined with the decentralised character of the school system (until 1988), and the tradition of producing RE syllabuses locally, this made it possible to address the challenge of growing religious plurality on a local level first.

Change towards multifaith RE in some local areas was brought on by the actual challenge of plural classrooms. Scholars with a religious studies background were central initiators and participants in this process of change. In Norway, the strong centralisation of the school system and the tradition of having a National Curriculum made it necessary to make the policy change first. Relevant research did exist in Norway, but seemed to be irrelevant to political change. Because of the strong standing of the Norwegian state Church, in society as well as traditionally in the state school, there is less tradition for Christian religious plurality in Norway.

I would suggest that still, today, the contrast between centralised and decentralised systems for RE affects the academic debates in the two countries differently, forming part of different *national styles*. In Norway, much energy is expended in discussing and interpreting the changing 'text' which is the National Curriculum, while this is not so central to the English debate given the devolution of RE in community schools to the local level.

In both countries, however, national traditions are negotiated in meeting with supranational challenges, especially migration and pluralisation, and many of the debates can be found in parallel – but perhaps in slightly different *national styles*,

---

[365] Included wearing of school uniforms, division into ability groups, the way classrooms were used, the focus on subjects vs. well-being of pupils, ethical themes regarding different people's views vs. more phenomenological content about religions as such, more teacher-led activities vs. more pupils' initiative, a more formal tone vs. more informal through, for example, the use of teachers' surnames in the case of England and first names in Norway.

such as with the debate about Christianity as cultural heritage. At the same time, academic traditions are developing more and more as international fields with international networks, publication channels and research projects (see chapter 3). This challenges *national styles*, or they are challenged to various degrees depending on whether central national academic figures participate in the international scene. As the debates increasingly become international, they can increasingly be seen not only as parallel debates but also as the *same* debate where national differences are a factor to consider.

Moving on to the institutional level of curriculum (chapter 4), the question is what constitutes part of nation-specific styles? Again, the tradition of the school systems' relationship to traditional religion is a factor explaining differences. In England, for example, collective worship, which should be (wholly or mainly) of a broadly Christian character, is a traditional part of schools' activities, still sanctioned by the law. In Norway, the school law preamble until 2008 made Christian nurture the central object of schooling (while the new version from 2008 emphasises the Christian and Humanist tradition, the cultural heritage perspective). The point is that, both in England and Norway, the history of the Christian traditions is present still in contemporary laws and documents, and can be said to form part of the *national styles*.

The (traditional) relationship between state, school and religion is, therefore, considered to be a decisive factor in the nation-specific styles, determining what kind of multifaith RE is attempted. Again, having a central national curriculum (Norway), and a decentralised system of producing RE syllabuses locally (England), is perhaps the most important difference.[366] At the same time, these national traditions are challenged by supranational processes to introduce revolutionary new types of RE where educational aims are enhanced and traditional religious aims are reduced or removed. This has been possible both in the English and Norwegian systems, however different, and this is a similarity.

How are negotiations of national traditions reflected in relevant laws and curricular documents?[367]

To begin with the law, in England this was changed in 1988 to make it clear that the main religion in RE was still to be Christianity. The need to clarify this may be seen as created by the supranational challenge of plurality. But this law also included, for the first time, that other main religious traditions in Britain should also be taught. This change reflected the negotiation of the tradition for RE (still legally called RI[368] until 1988, although called RE in some local agreed syllabuses since the 1960s) in England which had been going on through some new and revolutionary locally produced syllabuses (for example Birmingham 1975). This changed the tradition for RE following what, in the vocabulary of this book is identified as a supranational challenge: the growing religious plurality in society. Actually, since the initiative was local, it could also be described in terms of subnational

---

366 Although the emphasis on local adjustment and centralisation shifts in national processes.
367 The documents which I chose to focus on were *the Non-Statutory National Framework for Religious Education* (QCA 2004) and *the KRL book 2005: Knowledge of Christianity- religion- and philosophies of life: Curriculum for $1^{st} - 10^{th}$ grade: Curriculum-guidelines and information* (UD 2005).
368 Religious Instruction, see chapter 4.

factors challenging the national style. Either way, this now became an essential part of 'the English style'.

In Norway, the same supranational challenges of growing religious plurality led to the change in the law and the National Curriculum in 1997 (and 2002, 2005 and 2008). In Norway, however, the challenges were also felt and reported from school practice. In other words, subnational factors formed part of the negotiation of the traditional Norwegian style of RE at the time with the two subjects 'Christianity' and 'Life views' (until 1997). While both English and Norwegian RE was challenged at the institutional level by *informal* supranational processes (pluralisation), in Norway the initial idea of what an inclusive multifaith RE was about in a Norwegian context was challenged further by *formal* supranational processes: through international legal cases, most importantly by the verdict in the European Court of Human Rights in Strasbourg (see chapter 4).

Examples of differences at the institutional level of curriculum are: the inclusion/ exclusion of Humanism but relative exclusion of Sikhism (Norway) versus the inclusion of Sikhism but relative exclusion of Humanism (England); different systems for bringing about change (in England, this is integrated into the system as local agreed syllabuses are scheduled to be revised regularly whilst, in Norway, change has so far been imposed by central reforms of the National Curriculum); and approaches to opt-out rights (England has full opt-out rights whereas, in Norway, these rights are limited).

Despite important differences, however, aims formulated for RE at the institutional level are surprisingly similar considering how different religious and school traditions in the two countries are. The main similarities are that they both include learning about and from[369] Christianity and other religions, and that they both attempt an inclusive, multifaith approach to RE as a response to societal religious plurality. The reason for this similarity is the shared supranational challenge of increased religious plurality in society.

Given the similar and converging debates at the societal level, and similar aims at the institutional level, where the challenge of growing plurality has been at the core of developments in both countries, differences in *national styles* appeared surprisingly clearly at the instructional level (chapter 6). The challenges of the new plurality *and* concerns to preserve a sense of cultural heritage are negotiated issues at the societal and institutional levels of curriculum in both England and Norway. However, it came out as a clear contrast that the plurality aspect was at the forefront of the English teachers' thinking about RE, while the cultural heritage perspective was more central for the Norwegian teachers.[370] Thus, in practice, it seems that multifaith RE with similar aims did take on different *national styles*.

While the English teachers all saw a plural classroom as a strength for RE, the Norwegian teachers saw this more as a challenge. That is to say, English and Norwegian teachers seemed to have different views of plurality. This was an issue which was also a concern in the EC REDCo Project research. Here, too, how plurality was understood differently was discussed (van der Want et al. 2009: 115-

---

369 In my interpretation, see chapter 6.
370 Which I found support for in the REDCo research: Everington 2009, Lund Johansen 2009, see chapter 6.

119). In the Norwegian case, I identified the main perspective as that of group plurality while, at the same time, toning down differences and accentuating 'sameness'. In the English case, the view that we are all different was accentuated more, reflecting an individual plurality.

While the English teachers were critical of a cultural heritage approach, the Norwegian teachers seemed to see this not only as a legitimate concern, but as the central concern of their teaching. This may have been coincidental to this particular sample, but this result can be explained with reference to differences in national styles and it does have a certain resonance at the societal level; in debates, for instance, on the critique of orientalism (England) and nation-building (Norway).

Even if these are common issues in both countries' academic debates, there is a difference regarding which perspectives are more dominant (see chapter 3). The different national histories provided different contexts for these issues. A concern about preserving the cultural heritage was a part of the debates around the 1988 reform in England, and is reflected in their law; on the Norwegian side, this has been a central aspect in laws and National Curricula since 1997, alongside concerns about 'the new' plurality. Criticism of this has, however, been stronger in England, and this permeates through to the instructional level of curriculum. In other words, this may be one example of issues from the societal level bypassing the institutional level but influencing the instructional level directly (see diagram above).

At the experiential level (chapter 7), we find a new twist to the question of *national styles*. On the one hand, the differences in style from the other levels, and especially from the instructional level (the understanding of their teachers), were reflected in the pupils' answers. For example, the English pupils stressed how RE was all about learning to respect other people's views while the Norwegian pupils' answers clearly reflected the emphasis on the Norwegian Christian tradition. In quite a direct way, this reflected how the plurality aspect was a central issue for the English teachers, whilst the cultural heritage perspective was more central to Norwegian teachers.

I also found that RE was different in the two 'multicultural' schools (Norwegian school 3, English school 3), reflecting different *national styles*. For instance, the English pupils saw the immediate relevance of multifaith RE to their own life and school environment while this was not the case in Norwegian school 3. Also, the finding that it was in the more plural of the English schools (English school 3) that being religious was most common or acceptable whilst, in Norway, it was in the rural school (Norwegian school 1) that being religious (in effect Christian) was most common/ acceptable, supports the point that practice was affected by different *national styles*.

However, the Norwegian pupils also expressed criticism of this emphasis on the Norwegian tradition, noting, for instance, how the other religions could be better represented from more of an insider's view, and that their textbooks should not distinguish 'us' from 'them' in the way they did. Also, English pupils were critical of some views being presented as more normative than others, although there was not an equally clear difference between 'us' English Christians and 'others' here (probably reflecting their teachers' views). We can again identify a 'bypass' as this can be seen as pupils participating directly in the critical debate on the societal level of curriculum. Thus, they can also be seen as participants in the negotiations of *'national styles'*.

Other elements which could be said to challenge the idea of *national styles* came from the subnational and supranational processes which, in some instances, converged at the experiential level of curriculum. A cross-national pattern which occurred was that:

> *in the two 'multicultural' schools (English school 3, Norwegian school 3), the pupils claimed to be religious,*
> *in the city/ city outskirts schools (English school 2, Norwegian school 2), all (but one) claimed not to be religious,*
> *in the two rural schools (English school 1, Norwegian school 1), all claimed to be Christians (but not 'very' Christian).*

I see this cross-national pattern as demonstrating how the supranational process of pluralisation provides similar local settings within different countries – and also different settings within countries (which has, of course, always been the case but in new ways reflecting immigration since the 1950s and 1960s). This provides for different contexts for doing RE where defining contextual factors come from supranational processes. This factor accentuates the question of contextuality in RE in a new way as global aspects can be seen as part of the local context also (see also Leganger-Krogstad 2007, Bråten 2013b). This should also challenge the ideas of *national styles*.

8.7 Inclusive RE and construction of otherness

Alberts (2006) used the term 'integrative RE' descriptively in approximately the same way that I use the term 'multifaith RE' (chapter 1). However, in chapter 6, I discuss whether the term 'integrative' could also be understood normatively as a desired function of multifaith RE.[371] Clearly, the mere collection of pupils within the same space does not ensure inclusiveness on equal terms. This is true even when RE intends to be inclusive, as in England and Norway. Multifaith RE does create an arena where integration and social cohesion in a plural society could potentially be brought about. However, it might equally create an arena for construction of otherness, counteracting the idea of its integrative function.[372]

I even found indications that the construction of otherness takes on different styles in the two countries, in a similar manner to Schiffauer et al. (2004) who consider that the integration of immigrants takes on different styles, reflecting different *national imaginaries*. Schiffauer et al. (2004: 60ff) also discuss how the construction of otherness is different in different countries.

How can this theme of inclusiveness or construction of otherness be traced through the levels of curriculum in my methodology?

---

371 Alberts does, however, set up very specific criteria for integrative RE, evaluating existing models in relation to those, which must be considered normative also. What she suggests is a study-of-religions approach.
372 Which Alberts also notes (Alberts 2006: 303).

How do supranational impositions influence the way in which multifaith RE is an arena for integration or construction of otherness?

If first we look at the societal level, the question of how multifaith RE can be inclusive and relevant for pupils in a plural society is central to recent debates. In England and Norway, it is generally agreed that attempts at inclusive multifaith RE are worthwhile, while some would still argue for separate RE[373]. This is a similarity between England and Norway which becomes evident in a wider comparative context, as, for example, the Netherlands, Germany, Spain and Italy have mainly retained separate RE. Here, the churches and religious communities have responsibility for the religious education of the young (see Jackson et al. 2007).

Furthermore, 'religious' RE can aim at being inclusive and integrative, but this would be on different terms from those cases where it is seen as an ordinary school subject with educational aims. The debates about what constitutes inclusive multi faith RE do take on different styles in England and Norway, as well as in other countries. The understanding of what inclusive RE constitutes is shaped in dialogue with the respective national research traditions, but challenged by supranational processes (see chapter 3).

Because of the decentralised system for RE in England, the debate has had a 'bottom up' character, since the move towards multifaith RE was first addressed locally and later sanctioned in national legislation. I see an educationally-focused research tradition connected to multifaith RE in England as important in developments at the societal level. This tradition (Loukes, Goldman, Smart, Hull, Jackson, Wright and others: 1997, Grimmitt 2000, Jackson 2004, Alberts 2007) has emerged based on questions coming from the school context, the level of practice.

The tradition for RE research in England can be described as an educational/ pedagogical tradition where a range of distinct *pedagogies* are suggested, some of which are more theologically based while others are more clearly based in a religious studies or social science tradition (see chapter 3). This is why, in my view, making a very clear distinction between theological and study-of-religions approaches, as Alberts (2006: 360) suggests, would be a step back in the English context. In the German, and perhaps also the Norwegian context, this might still be useful. In Norway too, however, I would say that the growing interest in RE research, especially since 1997, has been increasingly educational in its focus (se chapter 3).

In contrast to the English 'bottom up' style, the academic debates in Norway have had a 'top down' character. In Norway, the field of RE went from being Christian RE and an optional Life View subject to one subject and multifaith RE 'overnight' as a result of a political decision. At that time, the professional field was dominated by theology.[374] Scholars from a religious studies background were in some cases only reluctantly drawn into the field of RE, often primarily as a source of information about the 'other' religions, and not, for instance, as partners in developing pedagogy for the new multifaith RE. Among other things, this resulted in different approaches in textbooks (see chapter 6) between those parts which

---

373 Teaching religion separately according to religion, as for example in Finland.
374 And the tradition for Christian religious education which was more pedagogical but still based in theology, see chapter 3.

concerned the other religions (often phenomenological in their approach) and those parts which concerned Christianity (which continued in Christian subject tradition, see chapter 3).

In Norway, a battle at the societal level immediately broke out over how the subject KRL[375] should be understood and what it meant for practice. The early debates are summed up in a particular way by Gravem (2004) (see chapter 3). Concerns that RE should be inclusive for those from 'other' religions and for each person as individuals have been important in the academic debates in both countries. This is, for example, reflected in the ethnographic research done at the University of Warwick. The Shap Working Party has also throughout its history been inclusive of different religions and beliefs, well outside the six which are usually included (Hayward 2009). In Norway, the question of how to deal with the new element of 'other' religions was high on the agenda of the KRL network that emerged after the introduction of KRL (see chapter 3).

Meanwhile, concerns about how Christianity is represented in multifaith RE also exist in England – in the research of Trevor Cooling (2000), for instance, while in Norway I think there could also be more debate about how RE as a multifaith subject should affect the way of presenting Christianity. Concerns that 'liberal' RE promotes certain values which are contrary to deep religious convictions have also been raised (Wright 1993: 39, see Jackson 2004a: 78). Lately, the discussion about 'whiteness' (see chapter 6) includes the criticism that white English pupils are turned into 'others' as everyone else is from somewhere, while they are 'from nowhere' (Rudge 1998).

In Norway, it seems to still be those from 'other' religions who are 'others' faced with the strong tradition of presenting Christianity mainly as Norwegian cultural heritage. However, it may be that this development in England is a preview of what could also happen in Norway if attention is not paid to the different qualities in presentations and representations of Christianity and other religions and worldviews.[376] Members of the Secular Humanist Association in Norway still see themselves as 'others' despite all the changes which attempt to include them on a more equal basis (see chapter 4).

Seen from different perspectives, all these examples listed above can be said to concern how or to what degree RE can be inclusive or integrative. In other words, the question of inclusiveness is central to debates about multifaith RE, but it is an issue which apparently is not easily solved in either national context.

At the institutional level, in both England and Norway, Christianity is specified as the main religion to be taught. Christianity is to be included at each key stage in England, whereas the inclusion of other religions varies (QCA 2004).[377] According to the Norwegian National Curriculum (UD 2008), Christianity is still the main content of RE and is expected to be given one third of the time devoted to the sub-

---

375 As presented in the 1997 National Curriculum.
376 As my sample is not representative, it may well be that I could have found examples of white mainstream Christian Norwegians feeling alienated as well.
377 I have chosen this particular document to represent general developments at the Institutional level in England, but it needs to be noted that local agreed syllabuses do not have to follow the national framework (although most do): it is the 1988 law which is legally binding (see chapter 4).

ject. This leaves 'other' religions and secular life-views one third to share between them, with the last third concerning ethics and philosophy. The dominant role of Christianity as subject content is justified by its central role in the country's history, and in still being the majority religion. This is, in fact, another similarity between English and Norwegian RE which contributes to making minorities and non-religious people 'others' at the English and Norwegian institutional level of curriculum.

Despite Christianity being the most represented religion in the societies and also in terms of curricular content, the teaching of this religion in England and Norway is non-confessional (and non-denominational).[378] It is stressed in both countries that multifaith RE should be inclusive in its approach, and that its aims are to educate pupils about religion and not nurture them into any particular religious faith. In the case of Norway, it has been repeatedly stressed that the emphasis on the (Norwegian) Christian tradition should be quantitively rather than qualitatively different. This ideal, which is expressed in all the Norwegian National curricula since 1997, was, however, challenged in the critique of KRL given by the UN's Human Rights Committee[379] and the verdict in Strasbourg (see chapter 4).

In the two documents featured in chapter 4, inclusiveness is stressed but there is still ambivalence between wanting to open up and be inclusive on the one side, and, on the other, a wish that elements from the time of Christian instruction in school continue. This includes, for example, the perspective that Christianity has a special importance in Norwegian society as part of its cultural heritage. There are reasons to ask if this intended inclusive RE is still ethnocentric (see chapter 7), as the sense that some are 'others' is retained.

Skeie (2006b: 24) has, for example, suggested that 'Norwegian RE runs on two tracks: on the one hand there is an intention to counter relativism through promoting a certain set of values. This can be seen as an intention to counter the (imagined) problems with 'modern plurality'.[380] On the other hand there is the countering of conflicts among religious and ethnic groups. This can be seen as an intention to counter (imagined) problems with 'traditional plurality'.[381] The Non-Statutory National Framework for RE (QCA 2004) and the National Curriculum for KRL (UD 2005) both reflect the ambivalence of 'wanting to maintain and update old links to the *national imaginaries*' (Schiffauer et al. 2004: 10; see also chapter 6) on the one hand, and wanting to address plurality on the other. This ambivalence is, as we have seen, also evident at the societal level, in academic debates for instance, so here there is cohesion between adjacent levels of curriculum (see diagram above).

At the instructional level (chapter 6), teachers' responses to what they saw as the importance of RE revealed how similar aims at the institutional level of curriculum were understood differently. The English teachers emphasised the RE curriculum's relevance to the plural context and expressed the need to counter stereotypical ideas of Christians as 'white, middle class and British', for example. This was a

---

378 See chapter 1 for the different meaning of these concepts in the two countries.
379 http://www.regjeringen.no/nb/dokumentarkiv/Regjeringen-Bondevik-II/ufd/233191/251920/Human-Rights-Committee-Communication-No-11552003.html?id=422478 (Accessed 27.01.09).
380 See also Skeie 1995, see chapter 3.
381 I added the term 'imagined' referring to a possibility that this is part of a national imaginary.

clear contrast to the Norwegian teachers' emphasis on the importance of learning about religions and especially the Norwegian Christian tradition. The Norwegian teachers saw this as important to immigrants (in their wording)[382] as a means of being able to integrate into Norwegian society, or rather perhaps the Norwegian *national imaginary*. Thus, it seems that, in the construction of 'Norwegianness', sameness was more dominant, while, in the idea of 'Englishness', difference (plurality) was more central to teachers' thinking.

This emphasis relates interestingly to the more pluralistic religious history of England (relationship between state and religion), and its non-denominational RE in schools since 1870, and in Norway to the monocultural religious tradition, where up till 1845 not even other Christian denominations were allowed into the kingdom ('dissenterloven', see Haraldsø 1989), and confessional RE continued until 1969, denominational RE until 1997.

It seems that the traditional history of the relationship between religion, state and school still influences *national styles* of RE today, even after the shift to multifaith approaches. Further, I think an important factor in the different *national imaginaries* which inform these different styles is the different character of the critique of colonialism in each country. England has had a need to deal with its past as a colonial power, while this would be less pressing in Norway. But the questions raised regarding modern-day cultural imperialism, for example, are also of concern to Norway as part of modern western culture. However, Norway, as a small and relatively new nation (from 1814) has a different need to construct an idea of the national, justifying its nation-building project, in which the unitary school tradition has been central (Engen 2005).

When it comes to RE's potential integrative function, this was pursued, in the case of England, with reference to an imaginary of multicultural English culture, while, in the case of Norway, it was done more through a desire to integrate 'others' into 'our shared cultural heritage'. This was a rather surprising finding, as the spur to changes at the institutional level in Norway, as in England, has been the need to address plurality.

From a Norwegian perspective, it could seem a bit strange that the English teacher in my (small and limited) sample did not emphasise the cultural heritage perspective at all, because this is an aspect of the institutional level in England too. In chapter 6, I asked if 'Norwegianness' (national imaginary) is difficult to be integrated into, if it includes sharing 'our cultural heritage'. A parallel question in the English case was whether the idea of 'Englishness' is so plural that indigenous English pupils are alienated or marginalised. From this a question emerged regarding what kind of imaginaries would aid multifaith RE's integrative function when integrative is meant normatively to mean inclusive on equal terms for all who participate.[383]

---

382 This according to Oline (NS3-T), who had in her school and class a number of first generation immigrants, see chapter 6.
383 Even if I cannot conclude from my empirical research that these findings are representative, I can still raise the question, especially as I find resonance for it in the levels above (A-B) and a degree of support in the REDCo publication van der Want *et al.* (2009).

On the experiential level (chapter 7), the English pupils were clear that integration, or promotion of tolerance for *others*, was not only an aim, but the major aim of RE. Like their teachers, however, they were modest as to whether they thought RE actually had this effect. It was not equally clear to the Norwegian pupils that learning to respect *others* was the main aim but, when I pointed out to them that it *was* an aim, they did see this as a potential function of learning about different religions. However, they were hesitant as to the degree to which RE would have this effect.

It was rather consistent in the Norwegian pupils' language that 'others' meant other than Norwegian Christians, even though they were critical of this view. In the way English pupils spoke about 'others', the main impression was that they were referring to 'others than themselves'. In other words, pupils' language use could be said to reflect different senses of otherness, referring to group plurality in the Norwegian case and a more individual idea of plurality in the English case.

This was to a certain degree contradicted in the way in which pupils related to the question of their own religious affiliations. Regarding this, there was a tendency in my sample for the English pupils to answer this question mainly by choosing a pre-existing 'label' (group plurality), while I found the Norwegian pupils offering lengthy reflections about what they actually believe on a personal level (individual plurality/ 'Sheilaism'). Triangulated with the EC REDCo Project research, we see that similar types of individual responses are also found in English pupils' accounts of their relationship to religion.

I see this individual way of relating to religion as reflecting a certain brand of modernity, namely modern western modernity, whereas other kinds of modernities may be the reference point for some pupils (Taylor 2004, see chapter 7). For instance, it was an interesting similarity in my material, and that of the REDCo research concerning English and Norwegian pupils' relationship to religion (Ipgrave & McKenna 2008, van der Lippe 2008), that all the Muslims and some Christians outside the mainstream established churches (Norway, Charismatic Christians; England, African Christians) were less individual and more collectively oriented towards their 'groups' in the way in which they related to religion. This made me raise the question of whether those who may relate to different senses of modernity than the modern western (which is what is reflected in the institutional level of curriculum) are constructed as 'others'.

8.8 Summary and conclusion

There is always a relationship between religion and society, but what that relationship is will change over time and be different from place to place. In this study, I have set out to examine and compare two 'places': or, rather, the *national imaginaries* of two 'places'/ countries in relation to the choice of attempting a multifaith approach to RE in their state schools. The timeframe has mainly been from the time when multifaith approach to RE was sanctioned in law; in England in 1988 and in Norway in 1997 to 2009. A complicating factor has been the evolving nature of RE as many significant changes have occurred in this period in all levels of curriculum.

As it turned out, the suggested methodology, or approach (chapter 2), grew to be a key element of this study. The starting point was that I wanted to investigate RE in England in comparison with Norway, as both had developed multifaith approaches (see chapter 1). English RE research has often been referred to in the Norwegian context (see chapter 3), and vice versa, but, from my point of departure, an interest I had was to understand the context of English RE. This is, indeed, also one result of my work, *but equally important is the increased understanding of the Norwegian context, which is a direct result of the comparative perspective and this methodology.*

To sum up, in chapter 1 I set the scene by doing some initial points of comparison and by explaining the basic rationale of the book This included the choice of structure which was based on exploring a suggested template for comparative studies in RE.

In chapter 2, I discussed literature on comparative studies, especially from the field of comparative education and comparative religious studies, but also some pioneering work within comparative religious education. This became the background for suggesting this template, which is a combination of two sets of ideas. The first idea is that three dimensions must be considered in comparative education: supranational, national and subnational processes (Dale 2006). A main perspective was that comparison in religious education is about the study of the impact of supranational processes on national processes. The second set of ideas regards levels of curriculum: that there are societal, institutional, instructional and experiential levels (Goodlad & Su 1992). Combined together, these ideas capture both the complexities of the national dimension whilst taking account of the impact of all the supranational formal and informal processes on national processes (see chapter 2).

The book's chapters explore these levels, looking at how they are affected by supranational, national and subnational processes. The main emphasis in the chapters has been on the national dimension because I saw exploring the particular national context as important for the comparison to be valid, but supranational and subnational processes have also been considered in chapters 3-7.

The rationale for the way that the book was structured was to explore this suggested methodology, and thus, in chapter 3, I went on to explore *the societal level of curriculum*. This was done by focusing on two main themes in academic debate:

1) *The role of academic disciplines in the development of multifaith approaches to religious education in England and Norway; and*
2) *analysis of two 'power texts' that I considered characteristic examples of academic debate in England and Norway.*

Towards the end of chapter 3, I discussed briefly the supranational dimension in academic debate in RE in England and Norway today, by addressing some issues related to the internationalisation of research.

In chapter 4, I proceeded to explore *the institutional level of curriculum*. This was done by comparing relevant legal texts and two representative curriculum documents, *the Non-statutory National Framework for Religious Education* (QCA 2004) and *The KRL book 2005: Knowledge of Christianity- religions- and philos-*

ophies of life: Curriculum for 1st – 10th grade: Curriculum-guidance and information (UD 2005).

In chapter 5, I explained how empirical field data can fit into a comparative research design, thus setting the scene for exploring the two last levels of curriculum, the levels of practice (chapters 6 and 7). These chapters were mainly based on my own fieldwork in three English and three Norwegian schools. Here, I designed questions to reflect aims at the institutional level but also to be as similar as possible in my approach to teachers and pupils in England and Norway in order to look at relationships both between levels of curriculum and between the nations. However, I also triangulated findings with other research, especially findings from the EC REDCo Project which included perspectives on both teachers and pupils in England and Norway (see chapters 6-7).

In chapter 6, I considered the *instructional level of curriculum* by exploring teachers' perspectives on aims and content of RE, including the *learning from* aspect, while, in chapter 7, I discussed the *experiential level of curriculum* through exploring pupils' perspectives on aims and content of RE in parallel with teachers' perspectives.

In chapter 8 – this present chapter – I have offered a diagrammatic representation of the methodology in a visual model (see beginning of this chapter), which helped me in some final comparative discussions. Further, I reflected briefly on some aspects of the process of the study, and gave some examples of findings.

I wanted to take the opportunity briefly to explore ways in which this methodology could be developed further: for example, through focusing on selected themes which had emerged through the chapters. These were, firstly, the question of *'different national styles'* in RE in England and Norway and, secondly, the question of *'inclusive RE and construction of otherness'* (see above). As the main focus in the chapters 3-7 was the national dimension, I wanted here to focus more on the supranational (and subnational) dimension(s).

Finding myself at the end of this journey – that has been this study – I want to conclude that something was accomplished. It was not exactly what I set out to do, because the journey led me to places that I could not have foreseen or even imagined when I started the research. Some even claim the journey is the aim. However, I do consider the main task of doing a systematic comparison of RE in England and Norway, as being accomplished. I also hope that the methodology or approach that was developed in order to accomplish this will be of help to others who want to conduct comparative research and who see its usefulness in this increasingly globalised world.

Appendix 1: Interview Schedules

The following are the interview schedules used in the English schools. The ones used in the Norwegian schools were close to identical, except what came from the use of a different language and where questions of aims and content of the subject had to be formulated a little differently.

Schedule for interviews with RE teachers

Introduce myself if necessary.
Are you familiar with my reasons for this school visit and this interview?
The main reason is to get first-hand experience of RE in England, and to learn about and from teachers' and students' experiences with RE, to inform my comparative study of RE in Norway and England. It is the systems that are going to be compared, not the material from the schools. Examples from the material might be used to illustrate each system.
The schools and all participants will be anonymous in the study.
Do you have any additional questions you want to ask before we proceed? Please feel free to ask me questions during the course of the interview if you want to.

Questions

Backgrounds

Can you describe your school and its position within the English school system?
What characterises this school compared to other secondary schools? What are the students like here? Are they good achievers?
What background do the students come from?
What religions, if any, are the children connected to? Do they have different ethnic backgrounds? What are their ethnic backgrounds? What are the backgrounds of the teachers? Does the school have a policy regarding issues like anti-racism, tolerance etc.?
What are your qualifications as an RE teacher?
What training did you have as an RE teacher?

Aims

In your opinion, what is the importance of RE in school?
Is it important to have RE? Why do you personally think RE in school is important? Do you think RE actually has an effect on students? Do you think RE is important to your students? Why? Why not? In what way?

Do you agree with the present legal requirements for RE?
Do you agree with the requirements of RE as formulated in the 1988 Education Act, that
1. it you should teach about Christianity and other principal religions in Britain?
2. teaching should be non-denominational?
3. the spiritual, moral, cultural and mental development of pupils should be promoted?
Do you agree with aims in the RE syllabus which says RE should help students in promoting a positive attitude towards other people? That they should learn both *about* and *from* religions?
What do you think of the system of local agreed syllabuses?
Is it a good system? What are the benefits of the system? What are the downsides? Would you prefer a National Syllabus? Does your syllabus come with support materials? Do you use those? What sources do you use?
Can you describe what RE is like in this school?

How do you relate to the legal requirements for RE; the 1988 Education Act and the local agreed syllabus? How does this impact on your teaching? How does inspection influence what you do? How do public examination syllabuses influence what you do?
In what ways do you feel that you, yourself, influence what you do in RE lessons?
To what degree can you influence the guidelines, through, for instance, the local agreed syllabus? To what degree are you free to choose method, content, or in what order things are done?

Contents

Could you give a description of what RE lessons usually are like?
What methods are frequently used? How would you work with central topics? Do you read in class? Write? Do you have a lot of discussions? Do you go out on excursions, or have visitors in your class? Would you use art in any way?
When the topic is Christianity, would it typically be related to a British context? Would it, for instance, be linked to British church history? The Church of England? Other denominations in Britain? Would the topic Christianity be linked to Christianity internationally? In what ways?
When the topic is one of the other principal religions, would it be primarily linked to a British context?
Would it, for instance, be linked to colonial history? To recent history of immigration? To the religions in the locality of this school? What local resources do you have? To what degree would you look at these religions in an international perspective?

Learning from and about

Do you think your students would know the difference between learning about and learning from religion?
Why not? Why?
Do you think your students are learning both about and from religions?
Why not? Why? In what ways? How do you know?

Respect

Do you think RE makes the student more respectful of people who are different from them?
Do you think RE in general would contribute to them having better understanding of different people with different faiths or different opinions about faith and religion? Why? Why not? In what way? Do you have examples? Do you think that RE has made them more willing to accept people who are different from themselves? Do you think your own teaching promotes tolerance?

Personal growth

Do you think RE contributes to the students' personal growth?
Why? Why not? What is contributing to this? Does it make them reflect more on topics related to religion, like life and death, the meaning of life, how to behave with others, contribute to society? What do you think influences students' behaviour and their sense of right and wrong etc.? Would you convey to them your personal views? Why? Why not? Do you think they know anyway? Do you think this influences them in any way? How?
Do you have any additional points you want to make before we finish?
Thanks so much for your time.

Interview schedule for group interviews with pupils

First, I want to thank you for participating in my project.
My name is Oddrun. My job is training teachers in Trondheim in Norway.
Do you know anything about Norway?
Do you know the reason I want to interview you?
I am doing a study in which I want to compare RE in Norway and England.
The reason why I have come to your school is to see for myself what RE can be like here in England, and I would like to learn from you. When you answer, it would be great if you could think not only about the RE that you have now, but also about RE in earlier years.
No one other than me will know your answers, so don't be afraid to state your opinions, whatever they are.

Do you have any questions for me before we go on?

If you feel like asking me a question later, please feel free, and you can also put questions to each other if you want.

First of all, I would like you to say your first names, and just a few words about yourself, so that I can get a picture of who you are.

Questions

Aims

Why do you think you have to study RE in school?
Can you think of reasons for having RE in school? What are they? How is RE different to other subjects? How is it similar?
How do you feel about RE in school? Do you like it?
Why? Why not? What's good about it? What's not so good?
Do you think RE in school is important?
Why? Why not? In your view, should you have RE in school? Why? Why not? What do you think it should be like?

Contents

Could you tell me what you do you when you're having RE?
What methods are used? Do you read, write, have discussions, draw or paint? Do you visit temples or other religious places? What do you do?
Can you give me an example of something that you have experienced in RE that stands out, that you remember especially?
What makes this special; why do you remember that especially? What did you learn from it? Could you expand on this?

Learning from and about

The syllabus requires you to learn about Christianity in RE. What have you learned about Christianity?
Can you give examples? Do you think any of the things you've learned are important? Why? Why not? In what way? Have you learned anything about English history in RE? What have you learned about English history? Have you learned about Christianity in other countries?
The syllabus requires you to learn about different religions in RE. What have you learned about different religions?
Can you give examples? Do you think any of the things you've learned are important? Why? Why not? In what way? Have you learned about other religions in Britain? Or in your own town or neighbourhood? Have you learned about religions in other countries?

The syllabus also requires you to learn *from* religion. What do you think is meant by learning *from* religions?

Respect

The syllabus says that RE should promote respect for different people. Do you think that RE has made you more willing to accept people who are different from you?
Do you think it is important that people are allowed to have different opinions? Has RE made you more tolerant of people who you disagree with? Why not? In what way? Do you think that things that you've learnt in RE have made you understand people with different religions more? Why? Why not? Do you think that RE in general contributes to making people more respectful? More tolerant?

Personal growth

What religion, if any, do you feel yourself connected to?
What makes you feel connected to this religion? Do you feel like you belong to this religion? Do you have an opinion about religion or philosophy of life? What influences the way you live, or the way you behave? What do you consider important in life? Who do you learn important things from? How do you learn about what is right and wrong?
Do you think RE relates to your own life in any way?
Is it relevant to your own life? Why? Why not? How does it relate to your own life? The syllabus says that RE should contribute to your own personal growth. In your experience, has it? Has RE helped you to form your own opinions on issues related to religion? Do you think it might have contributed to your fellow students' religion, spirituality or views about important issues? Why not? Why? In what ways?
Do you have any additional points you want to make before we finish?
Thanks so much for your time.

Appendix 2: Norwegian Legal Texts

The law on KRL prior to the change in 2005

The first law that described Norwegian multifaith RE, the subject of KRL, is from 1997. The legal text from 1997 is quoted in Afdal et al. (1997: 109). In 2002, there was a revised National Curriculum for RE, but § 2-4 of the Norwegian Education Act as it was formulated in 1997 was unchanged except for the name of the subject but only in such a way that the abbreviation KRL could be kept. The exact text of the law is now quoted in the text of the curriculum (LS 2002: 11).

The text of the law in its 2002 version (my translation):
'Teaching in the subject Christian Knowledge and Religious and Ethical Education[384] shall:

- provide a thorough knowledge of the Bible and Christianity both as cultural heritage and Evangelical-Lutheran faith,
- provide knowledge of other Christian denominations,
- provide knowledge of other world religions and philosophies of life, ethical and philosophical topics,
- promote understanding and respect for Christian and humanist values, and
- promote understanding and respect and the ability to carry out a dialogue between people with different views concerning beliefs and philosophies of life.

Christian Knowledge and Religious and Ethical Education is an ordinary school subject that shall normally be attended by all pupils. Teaching in the subject should not involve preaching.

Teachers of Christian Knowledge and Religious and Ethical Education shall present Christianity, other religions and philosophies of life on the basis of their distinctive characteristics. Teaching of the different topics shall be founded on the same educational principles.'
(Quoted in Afdal et al. 1997: 109, LS 2002: 11).

Christian object/ purpose clause – the school law preamble before 2008

This act related to the Primary and Secondary Education (Education Act), Chapter 1, Section 1-2. The object of education: as translated into English on the Norwegian government's official website: http://www.regjeringen.no/upload/KD/Vedlegg/Gru

---

[384] Here, I use the name as it is translated in English versions of these documents, since it is a quotation, but in my view translating it as 'Knowledge of Christianity, Religions and Life' is closer to the Norwegian title, and explains how the name was changed without its acronym changing, see chapter 1.

nnskole/Opplaeringsloven__engelsk_(sist_endret_2005-06-17).pdf (Accessed 29.01.09).

Section 1-2 of the Norwegian Education Act is the school law preamble, called 'formålsparagrafen': ('Christian object/ purpose clause').

'The object of primary and lower secondary education shall be, in agreement and cooperation with the home, to help to give pupils a Christian and moral upbringing, to develop their mental and physical abilities, and to give them good general knowledge so that they may become useful and independent human beings at home and in society.

Upper secondary education shall aim to develop the skills, understanding and responsibility that prepare pupils for life at work and in society, and assist the pupils, apprentices and trainees in their personal development. Upper secondary education shall contribute to increased awareness and understanding of fundamental Christian and humanist values, our national cultural heritage, democratic ideals and scientific thought and method.

The primary, lower secondary and upper secondary schools shall further the equal status and equal rights of all human beings, intellectual freedom and tolerance, ecological understanding and international co-responsibility. Teaching shall provide a foundation for further education and for lifelong learning and provide support for a common foundation of knowledge, culture and basic values, and a high general level of education in the population.

Teaching shall be adapted to the abilities and aptitudes of individual pupils, apprentices and trainees. Emphasis shall be placed on creating satisfactory forms of cooperation between teachers and pupils, between apprentices, trainees and training establishments, between the school and the home, and between the school and the workplace. All persons associated with the school or with training establishments shall make efforts to ensure that pupils, apprentices and trainees are not injured or exposed to offensive words or actions.'

Kirke-, utdannings- og forskningsdepartementet (Ministry of Education, Research and Church Affairs) (2000)

The Bolstad Committee's suggestion for a new school law preamble

In NOU 2007: 6 Formål for framtida: Formål for barnehagen og opplæringen (Purpose/ object for the future: purpose/ object of kindergarten and education) the preamble of the school law is reviewed (see above) and the suggestion made that it should be replaced by (my translation):

'Education in school and enterprises[385] which takes trainees shall open doors to the world and the future and gives the pupils historical and cultural insights. It should be grounded on respect for human dignity, on intellectual freedom, love of one's neighbour, equality and solidarity, in the manner that these values are expressed in Christian and Humanistic tradition, in different religions and life views, and the way that they are anchored in Human Rights. The education should promote democracy, gender equality and scientific rationality.

The pupils shall develop knowledge, ability, and attitudes so that they can manage in their lives and participate in work and fellowship in society. They shall be given opportunity to have scope for their joy of creating, engagement and their desire to explore. The pupils shall learn critical thinking, act ethically and take economic responsibility. They should be given responsibilities and opportunity to co-operate

The school and enterprises which takes trainees shall meet the pupils with trust and demands, and give them challenges which promote generic formation and a desire to learn. All forms of discrimination should be counteracted.
The school shall co-operate with pupils' homes.'

The issue of the school law preamble has been much debated in Norway, and was also criticised by the UN Human Rights Committee and the Human Rights Court in Strasbourg (see chapter 4). The suggestion from the Bolstad Committee also caused debate in the 'Stortinget', and was altered before it was passed and put into legal effect in 2008 (see chapter 4).

The new school law preamble as it was passed:
My translation, from the original text posted on the official website of the Norwegian government http://www.regjeringen.no/nb/dep/kd/tema/Grunnopplaring/formalsparagrafer-.html?id=542401 (Accessed 29.01.09).

The purpose of education: 'Education in schools and enterprises which take trainees shall, in cooperation and understanding with the home, opens doors to the world and the future and give the pupils and trainees historical and cultural insights and rooting.

Education shall be founded on fundamental values in Christian and Humanistic heritage and tradition, such as respect for human dignity and nature, intellectual freedom, love of one's neighbours, forgiveness, equality and solidarity, values which are expressed through different religions and life views and which are anchored in Human Rights.

Education shall contribute to expanded knowledge and understanding of the national cultural heritage and our common international cultural tradition.

---

385 Norwegian: 'bedrift': according to Kirkeby (1988): this translates to 'works; factory; *(=foretagende)* industrial undertaking; enterprise'.

Education shall provide insights into cultural plurality and show respect for the individual's convictions. It should promote democracy, gender equality and scientific rationality.

Pupils shall develop knowledge, ability, and attitudes so that they can manage in their lives and participate in work and fellowship in society. They shall be given opportunity to have scope for their joy of creating, engagement and their desire to explore. Pupils shall learn critical thinking, act ethically and take economic responsibility. They should be given responsibilities and opportunity to co-operate.

The schools and enterprises which take trainees shall meet the pupils with trust and demands, and give them challenges which promote generic formation and a desire to learn. All forms of discrimination should be counteracted.'

Appendix 3: The Teachers' Educational Backgrounds

The teachers' educational backgrounds reflect (changing) educational options for teachers in England and Norway. The difference in the number of universities (90 vs. 6) and number of teacher training institutions (58 vs. 30) reminds us of the difference in the size of populations.[386] Norway has more teacher training colleges than it has universities, as teacher training colleges are often part of University Colleges ('Høyskoler'), but there is a policy to turn more of the University Colleges into Universities. The Universities in Stavanger and Agder have, for example, recently changed their status from University Colleges to Universities (Stavanger from 2005, Agder from 2008). In England, what used to be teacher training colleges are now part of Universities, so on this point the educational systems as such are converging, as a result of general (and not specific RE) educational policy in the *formal supranational processes* (see chapter 2, 3).[387]

One-year university courses in 'Educational Science' exist in both countries. In England, they are called the Post Graduate Certificate in Education (PGCE). In Norway, until 2003, an equivalent to this was called 'pedagogical seminar' (Ped.Sem.), but since then has been called 'Praktisk Pedagogisk Utdanning' (PPU). In recent translation into English in the statistical documentation[388], the English term 'Educational Science' is used. In both countries, these courses build on degrees in different subjects, and some teachers would have an *RE* PGCE course in Educational Science, while others would have done the equivalent to RE in combination with another subject such as language, maths or science.

Some things regarding the sample teachers' educational backgrounds were unclear from their comments on this in the interviews, but I did not go back to investigate this in more detail, as I did not see it as very central to my purpose (see chapter 6). However, here is what I know:

---

386 http://www.axcis.co.uk/html/universities.html (Accessed 24.03.09).
387 This is a result of general international educational policy, for example (and especially) the Bologna process the explicit aim of which is that the systems of Higher Education should converge, see http://www.ond.vlaanderen.be/hogeronderwijs/bologna/. The Bologna process is an international juridical framework setting certain standards with regard to length of studies, degrees and quality control. In Norway, a main strategy to implement this is the so called Quality reform ('Kvalitetsreformen'). See http://www.regjeringen.no/en/dep/kd/Selected-topics/Higher-Education/Degree-structure-and-grading-system.html?id=491287 (Accessed 03.09.09).
388 http://udir.no/upload/Rapporter/Utdanningsspeilet_2007/The_Education_Mirror_2007_2mb.pdf (Accessed 05.05.09.)

Teacher training college	A first university degree	Higher university degree	PhD (subject)	PGCE/ Educational Science[389]	PhD in RE
'Ingunn Duesund' (NS2-T)	'Ruth Lakes' (ES3-T)		'Vicky Haley' (ES2-T) ?	'Ruth Lakes' (ES3-T)	Vicky Haley' (ES2-T) ?
	'Sally Fields' (ES1-T)			'Sally Fields' (ES1-T)	
	'Oline Gammelseter' (NS3-T)			'Oline Gammelseter' (NS3-T)	
	'Ingunn Duesund' (NS2-T)			'Jon Martin Sivertsen' (NS1-T)	
	'Jon Martin Sivertsen' (NS1-T)				

'Jon' (NS1-T) had a Cand. Mag. which is a first university degree consisting of two to three subjects. His degree included courses in history, Norwegian language and sociology of religion. 'Jon's' (NS1-T) Ped. Sem. could theoretically have been in RE.

'Ingunn' (NS2-T) had done some of her training in a teacher training college, including the compulsory RE course (before 1997 it was mainly Christianity), and teacher training in Educational Science, equivalent to the university Ped. Sem. 'Ingunn' (NS2-T) had taken additional university courses to complete her degree, but not in religious studies. Her main subject was Norwegian language.

'Oline' (NS3-T) had a Cand. Mag. degree and her initial subjects were in English, history and Norwegian language. Recently, she has done further education and taken a course in religious studies. 'Oline's' (NS3-T) 'Ped. Sem.' would be a half-year's course[390] based on one of her initial subjects.

'Sally' (ES1-T) said she had a degree in theology and religious studies, and her PGCE was in religious education.

'Vicky' said she has a degree in theology and a PhD; it was not clear whether this is an RE PhD or a PhD in another subject. Quotation from her answer: 'I did a degree in theology. At the end of the three years I really didn't know what I wanted to do. I knew I wanted to stay within my field, because I loved RE and I wanted to stay with doing something with RE. So, I thought I'd try a PhD for a year and see if I liked it, so I did my PhD'. Of course, she must have stayed for at least two years longer to complete the PhD.

'Ruth' (ES3-T) also said she has 'a degree in theology and religious studies'. Her PGCE is in religious studies.

---

389 One year courses in Educational Science in England called (PGCE), in Norway called 'Ped. Sem.': meaning 'pedagogical seminar'.
390 In the mid-1990s, it changed from a half-year course to a full-year.

References

Adams, D. and Keeves, J. P. (1994) 'Comparative Methodology in Education' in T. Husèn, and T. N. Postlethwait (eds.), *International Encyclopaedia of Education* (Oxford, Pergamon), 948-958.

Afdal, G. (2006) *Tolerance and Curriculum* (Münster, New York, München, Berlin, Waxmann).

Afdal, G., Haakedal, E., and Leganger Krogstad, H. (1997) *Tro, livstolkning og tradisjon. Innføring i kontekstuell religionsdidaktikk* (Oslo, Tano Aschehoug).

Alberts, W. (2006) 'European Models of Integrative Religious Education' in M. Pye, E. Franke, A. T. Wasim and A. Ma'sud (eds.) *Religious Harmony: Problems, Practice, and Education* (Berlin, New York, Walter de Gruyter), 267-278.

Alberts, W. (2007) *Integrative Religious Education in Europe: A study-of-Religions Approach* (Berlin, New York, Walter de Gruyter).

Alexander, J. C. (2006) *The Civil Sphere* (Oxford, Oxford University Press).

Alexander, R. (2000) *Culture and Pedagogy: International Comparisons in primary Education* (USA, UK, Australia, Blackwell Publishing).

Anderson, B. (1991) [1983] *Imagined Communities* (London, New York, Verso).

Andreassen, B.-O. (2008a) *Et ordinært skolefag i særklasse: En analyse av fagdidaktiske perspektiver I innføringsbøker I religionsdidaktikk*, unpublised PhD thesis (Tromsø, University of Tromsø).

Andreassen, B.-O. (2008b) 'Konfliktperspektiver i religionsundervisning og religionsdidaktikk – en bredere og bedre tilnærming til religion?' in *Acta Didacticae Norge*, 2 (1), 1-22.

Anker, T. (2011) *Respect and Disrespect: Social Practices in a Norwegian Multicultural School,* unpublished PhD thesis (Oslo, The Norwegian School of Theology).

Asheim, I. (1977) *Religionspedagogikk: En innføring* (Oslo, Universitetsforlaget).

Avest, I. ter, Bakker, C., van der Want, A. (2009) 'International Comparison – Commonalities and Differences of 36 Teachers Teaching Religion(s) in Europe' in A. van der Want et al. (eds.) *Teachers responding to Religious Diversity in Europe: Researching Biography and Pedagogy* (Münster, New York, München, Berlin, Waxmann), 111-126.

Avest, I. ter, Bakker, C., Bertram-Troost, G., Miedema, S. (2007) 'Religion and Education in the Dutch Pillarised and Post-Oillarized Educational System: Historical Background and Current Debates' in R. Jackson et al. (eds.) *Religion and Education in Europe: Developments, Contexts and Debates* (Münster, New York, München, Berlin, Waxmann), 203-220.

Baumann, G. (1996) *Contesting Culture: Discourses of Identity in Multi-ethnic London* (Cambridge, Cambridge University Press).

Bellah, R. N. (1970) *Beyond Belief* (London, Harper and Row).

Bellah, R. N. (et al.) (1985) *Habits of the Heart: Individualism and Commitment in American* (Berkeley: University of California Press).

Bellah, R. N., Hammond, P. E. (1980) *Varieties of Civil Religion* (San Francisco, Harper and Row).

Berger, P. (1969) *The sacred Canopy: Elements of a Sociological Theory of Religion* (New York Anchor Books/ Doubleday).

Berger, P. (1999) *The Desecularization of the World: Resurgent Religion and World Politics* (Michigan, William B. Erdmans Publishing Company).

Bible, the good News (1976) *The American Bible Society*, New York.

Birkedal, E. (2001) *"Noen ganger tror jeg på Gud, men ...?"En undersøkelse av gudstro og erfaring med religiøs praksis i tidlig ungdomsalder,* unpublished PhD thesis (Trondheim, Norges Teknisk Naturvitenskapelige Universitet).

Birmingham (1975) *The Birmingham Agreed Syllabus for Religious Education* (Birmingham, Birmingham City Council).

Bø, M. (2006) *Norsk skole og den etterlengtede helheten: En studie I et læreplanverks forsøk på å skape helhet I et differensiert samfunn og religionens tildelte oppgave I dette forehavende*, unpublised PhD thesis (Trondheim, Norges Teknisk Naturvitenskapelige Universitet).

Breidlid, H. and Nicolaisen T. (2004) 'Multi-Faith Religious Education in a religiously mixed Context: Some Norwegian Perspectives' in R. Larsson and C. Gustavson (eds.) *Towards a European perspective on Religious Education: The RE Research Conference March 11-14, 2004, University of Lund* (Sweden, Artos and Norma bokforlag), 69-79.

Bråten, O. M. H. (2006) 'Civil Enculturation: Nation State, School and Ethnic Difference in The Netherlands, Britain, Germany and France' Book review in *British Journal of Religious Education* 28 (2), 213-216.

Bråten, O. M. H. (2009) 'Mounting an Assault on complexity: Comparative Research Design in Religious Education' in G. Skeie (ed.) *Religious Diversity and Education – Nordic Perspectives* (Münster, New York, München, Berlin, Waxmann), 93-106.

Bråten, O. M. H (2010) *A comparative study of religious education in state schools in England and Norway*, Unpublished PhD Thesis (Coventry, University of Warwick).

Bråten, O. M. H. (2013a) 'Comparative Studies in Religious Education: The Issue of Methodology' in *Religion & Education*, Vol. 40 (1), 107-121.

Bråten, O. M. H. (2013b) 'The meaning of context when utilizing the comparative methodology' in G. Skeie, J. Everington, K. H. terAvest, S. Miedema (eds.) *Exploring Context in Religious Education Research: Empirical, Methodological and Theoretical Perspectives* (Münster, Waxmann), S. 227–248.

Buk-Berge, E. (2005) 'Komparativ og internasjonal pedagogikk i dag: Et overflødighetshorn for forskning og praktiske tiltak' in *Nordisk Pedagogikk* 3/2005, 273-281.

Burawoy, M. (1991) 'The Extended Case Method' in Burawoy (et al.*) Ethnography Unbound: Power and Resistance in the Modern Metropolis* (Berkley, Los Angeles, London, University of California Press), 271-287.

Cole, W. O. (1972) *Religion in the Multifaith School.*, 1st edn., Yorkshire Committee for Community Relations.

Cole, W. O. (1985) *Six Religions in the Twentieth Century* (Amersham, Hulton).

Cooling, T. (2000) 'The Stapleford Project: Theology as the Basis for Religious Education' in M. Grimmitt (ed.) (2000) *Pedagogies of Religious Education. Case Studies in the Research and Development of good Practice in RE* (Essex, Great awakening), 153-169.

Copley, T. (1997) *Teaching Religion: Fifty Years of Religious Education in England and Wales* (Devon, UK, University of Exeter Press).

Keast, J. (ed.) (2007) *Religious Diversity and Intercultural Education: A reference Book for Schools* (Strasbourg, Council of Europe Publishing).

Cox, E. (1966) *Changing Aims in Religious Education* (London, Routledge and Kegan Paul).

Dale, R. (2006) 'Policy Relationships between Supranational and National Scales; imposition/ resistance or Parallel Universes?' in J. Kallo and R. Rinne (eds.) *Supranational Regimes and National Education Policies* (Turku, Finland, Finnish Educational research Association), 27-52.

Davie, G. (1994) *Religion in Britain since 1945* (Oxford, Blackwell Publishing).

Davie, G (2007) *The Sociology of Religion* (London, Sage).

Delors, J. (1996) *Learning: The treasure within* (France, UNESCO publishing).

Dench, G; Gavron, K. and Young, M. (2006) *The New East End, Kinship, Race and Conflict* (London, Profile Books).

Department for Education (DEF) Circular 1/94.

Det kongelige kirke-, utdannings- og forskningsdepartement (KUF) (1996) *Læreplanverket for den 10-årige grunnskolen* (Oslo, Nasjonalt læremiddelsenter).

Dietz, G., Jackson R., Skeie G. (2009) *Work package 2 Theories and Methods: M 2.2 Triangulation of Theoretical and Empirical Results*, report in the EC REDCo Project, Unpublished Report.

Dybdahl, G. (2008) 'KRL-faget og fritak' in *Bedre Skole, 3,* 63-67.

Eliassen, K. O. (1996) 'Oversetterens etterord' in M. Foucault (1996) [1966] *Tingenes Orden: En arkeologisk undersøkelse av vitenskapen om mennesket* (Oslo, Aventura forlag).

Engen, T. O. (2003) 'Enhetsskole og flerkulturell nasjonsbygging' in P. Østrud and J. Johnsen (eds.) *Leve skolen: skolen i et kulturkritisk perspektiv* (Vallset, Opplandske bokforlag), 231-250.

Engen, T. O. (2005) 'Enhetsskole og flerkulturell nasjonsbygging' lecture held at a KRL conference in Trondheim, 05.11.05, published on the internet: (http://www.krlnett.no/konferanser/2005/Engen.swf)

Engen, T. O. and Kulbrandstad, L. A. Syversen, E. M (eds.) (2006) *Monokultur og multikultur: Nasjonsbyggende diskurser 1905 – 2005* (Vallset, Opplandske bokforlag).

Epstein, E. (1994) 'Comparative and International Education: Overview and Historical Developments' in T. Husén and T. N. Postlethwait (eds.) *International Encyclopaedia of Education* (Oxford, Pergamon), 918-923.

Evans, K. (1975) *The Development and Structure of the English Educational System* (London, Unibooks: University of London Press Ltd.).

Everington, J. (2009) 'Individuality and Inclusion – English Teachers and Religious Diversity' in Want et al. (2009) *Teachers responding to Religious Diversity in Europe: Researching Biography and Pedagogy* (Münster, New York, München, Berlin, Waxmann), 29-40.

Everington, J. and Sikes, P. (2001) 'I Want to Change the World: the Beginning RE Teacher, the Reduction of Prejudice and the Pursuit of Intercultural Understanding and Respect' in H. G. Heimbroch, C. Th. Scheilke and P. Schreiner (eds.) *Towards Religious Competence: Diversity as a Challenge for Education in Europe* (Münster, Lit Verlag), 180-202.

Flornes, K. (2007) *An Action Research Approach to Initial Teacher Education in Norway*, (Birmingham, PhD at the University of Birmingham).

Foucault, M. (1996) [1966] *Tingenes Orden. En arkeologisk undersøkelse av vitenskapen om mennesket* (Oslo, Aventura forlag).

Frances, L. (2004) 'Research in Religious Education: A Perspective from England and Wales 1960 – 2000' in R. Larson and C. Gustavson (eds.) *Towards a European perspective on Religious Education: The RE Research Conference March 11-14, 2004, University of Lund* (Sweden, Artos and Norma bokförlag), 279-295.

Gatherer, W. A. (2005) *Pioneering Moral Education: Victor Cook and his Foundation* (Edinburgh, Edinburgh University Press).

Germeten, S. (1999) *Evaluering av Reform 97 "På vei mot ny grunnskole i Oslo" Delrapport 1: Resultat av spørreskjemaundersøkelsen høsten 1998, HIO-rapport 1999 nr 5,* (Oslo, Høgskolen i Oslo).

Giddens, A. (1990) *The Consequences of Modernity* (Cambridge, Polity Press).

Giddens, A. (1999) *Den tredje vei: Fornyelse av sosialdemokratiet.* (Oslo, Pax forlag).

Glaser B. G. and Strauss, A. L. (2008) [1967] *The Discovery of Grounded Theory: Strategies for Qualitative Research* (USA/ UK, Aldine Transaction: A division of Transactions Publishers).

Goldman, R. J. (1964) *Religious Thinking from Childhood to Adolescence* (London, Routledge and Kegan Paul).

Goodlad, J. I., von Stoephasius, R. and Klein, M. F. (1966) *The Changing School Curriculum* (New York: Fund for the Advancement of Education).

Goodlad, J. I. (ed.) (1979) *Curriculum Inquiry* (New York, McGraw-Hill Book Company).

Goodlad, J. I. (1986) 'The scope of the Curriculum Field' in B. Gundem (ed.) *Om læreplanpraksis og læreplanteori:* Rapport Pedagogisk Forskningsinstitutt, (Oslo, Oslo University).

Goodlad, J. I. and Su, Z. (1992) 'Organization of the Curriculum' in P. W. Jackson (ed.) *Handbook of Research on Curriculum: A project of the American Educational Research Association* (New York, Macmillan Publishing Company), 327-344.

Gravem (2004) *KRL – ET FAG FOR ALLE? KRL-faget som svar på utfordringer i en flerkulturell enhetsskole?*, Published PhD thesis (Vallset, Oplandske bokforlaget).

Gravem, P. (2005) 'Religions- og livssynsundervisningen i skolen innenfor rammene av menneskerettighetene' in *Norsk Teologisk Tidsskrift*, 2, 67-81.

Grimmitt, M. (1987) *Religious Education and Human Development* (Essex, Great Wakening, McGrimmons).

Grimmitt, M. (ed.) (2000) *Pedagogies of Religious Rducation: Case Studies in the Research and Development of good Practice in RE* (Essex, Great awakening).

Gripsrud, S (2008) 'Vitner om et utdatert religionsbegrep' in *På Høyden, Nettavis for Universitetet i Bergen* (Accessed 13.04.08).

Groth, B., Halvorsen, P. B., Kværne, P., Vogt, K. (1997) [1985] *Levende religioner* (Oslo, Cappelen Akademiske forlag).

Haakedal, E. (1983) *Kristendomsundervisning, religionsundervisning, livssynsundervisning. En systematisk drøfting av problemer innen Engelsk religionspedagogikk i sammenligning med svensk religionspedagogikk*, Unpublished Masters Thesis (Oslo, Det teologiske Menighetsfakultet).

Haakedal, E. (1986) *Religionspedagogiske tendenser med hensyn til utviklingen av kristendoms-, religions- og livssynsundervisning i noen vesteuropeiske skolesystem under 1960- og 1970-årene,* Unpublished Report (Oslo, Det Teologiske Menighetsfakultet).

Haakedal, E. (1995) 'Religionspedagogikkens tverrfaglighet: tilbakeblikk, status og muligheter' in H. Leganger-Krogstad and E. Haakedal (eds.) *Religiøse og pedagogiske idealer* (Oslo: Norges forskningsråd, KULTs skriftserie nr. 42), 8-52.

Haakedal, E. (2001) 'From Lutheran catechism to world religions and humanism: dilemmas and middle ways through the story of Norwegian religious education in *British Journal of Religious Education,* 23 (2), 88-98.

Haakedal, E. (2004) *"Det er jo vanlig praksis her hos oss ..." Religionslærerrolle, livstolkning og skolekulturell ritualisering – en religionspedagogisk studie av grunnskolelæreres handlingsrom på 1990-tallet,* Unpublised PhD thesis (Oslo, Det Teologiske Fakultet).

Habermas, J. (2000) *Den postnationella konstellationen* (Göteborg, Daidalos).

Habermas, J. (2005) 'Religion in the Public Sphere', *Lecture presented at the Holberg Prize Seminar 28th November 2005,* Bergen.

Habermas, J. (2006) 'Religion in the Public Sphere' in *European Journal of Philosophy,* 14 (1), 1-25.

Hakovirta, H. (2006) 'Global Governance through Education Policy and Education' in J. Kallo and R. Rinne R. (eds.) *Supranational Regimes and National Education Policies* (Turku, Finland, Finnish Educational research Association), 353-372.

Hampshire (1978) *Paths to Understanding: The Hampshire Agreed Syllabus for Religious Education* (Winchester, Hampshire County Council).

Haraldsø, B. (ed.) (1989): *Kirke – skole – stat. 1739 – 1989* (Oslo, IKO-forlag).

Hayward, M. (2009) 'Shap – a brief History' at The Shap Working Party on World Religions in Education, *http://www.shapworkingparty.org.uk/history.html* (Downloaded 22.02.2013).

Heelas, P. and Woodhead, L. (2005) *The Spiritual Revolution: Why Religion is giving way to Spirituality* (USA, UK, Australia, Blackwell Publishing).

Høstmælingen, N. (2005) 'For sterk trospåvirkning: norsk kristendomsundervisning i strid med menneskerettighetene' in *Norsk Teologisk Tidsskrift,* 4, 232-248.

Hovdelien, O. (2011) *Den multikulturelle skolen – hva mener rektorene? Grunnskolerektorer, skolens verdiforankring og religions- og livssynsundervisning,* unpublished PhD thesis (Kristiansand, University of Agder).

Hull, J. M. (1978) 'From Christian Nurture to Religious Education: The British Experience', in *Religious Education,* 73, 124-143.

Hull, J. M. (1989) *The Act Unpacked: The Meaning of the 1988 Education Reform Act* (Birmingham, University of Birmingham and the Christian Education Movement).

Hull, J. M. (1998) 'Religious Education and Muslims in England: Developments and Principles', in *Muslim Education Quarterly,* 15 (4), 10-23.

Hull, J. M. (2005) 'Religious Education in Germany and England: The recent Work of Hans-Georg Zibertz' in *British Journal of Religious Education,* 27 (1), 7-19.

Hylland Eriksen, T. (1993) 'In which Sense do Cultural Islands exist?' in *Social Anthropology* 1, 133-47.

Hylland Eriksen, T. (1996) 'Kristendomsundervisning og menneskerettigheter' in L. G. Lingås and L. London (eds.) *Likhet eller likeverd? En kritikk av det nye kristendomsfaget i grunnskolen* (Oslo, Humanist forlag AS), 153-166.

Ipgrave, J. (2002) *Interfaith Encounter and Religious Understanding in an Inner City Primary School,* Unpublished PhD thesis (Coventry, University of Warwick).

Ipgrave, J. and Bertram-Troost, G. (2008) 'European Comparison: Personal Views and Experiences of Religion' in T. Knauth et al. (eds.) *Encountering Religious Pluralism in School and Society: A qualitative study of Teenage Perspectives in Europe* (Münster, New York, München, Berlin, Waxmann), 375-389.

Ipgrave, J. and McKenna, U. (2008) 'Diverse Experiences and Common Vision: English Students Perspectives on Religion and Religious Education' in T. Knauth et al. (eds.) *Encountering Religious Pluralism in School and Society: A Quantitative Study of Teenage Perspectives in Europe* (Münster, New York, München, Berlin, Waxmann).

Iversen, L. (2012) *Learning to be Norwegian: A case study of identity management in religious education in Norway* (Münster, New York, München, Berlin, Waxmann).

Jacobsen, K. A. (2005) [2001] *Verdensreligioner i Norge* (Oslo, Universitetsforlaget).

Jackson, R. (1990) 'Developments in Religious Education in England and Wales' in U. King (ed.) *Turning Point in Religious Studies: Essays in Honour of Jeffery Parrinder* (Edinburgh, T. and T. Clark Publishers, Ltd.).

Jackson, R. (1997) *Religious Education, an Interpretive Approach* (London, Hodder and Stoughton).

Jackson, R. (ed.) (2003) *International Perspectives on Citizenship, Education and Religious Diversity* (London, RoutledgeFalmer).

Jackson, R. (2004a) *Rethinking Religious Education and Plurality: Issues in Diversity and Pedagogy* (London and New York: RoutledgeFalmer).

Jackson, R. (2004b) 'Current Issues in Research in Religious Education' in R. Larson and C. Gustavson (eds.) *Towards an European Perspective on Religious Education: The RE Research Conference March 11-14, 2004, University of Lund* (Sweden, Artos and Norma bokförlag), 19-35.

Jackson, R. (2007) 'European Institutions and the Contribution of Studies of Religious Diversity to Education for Democratic Citizenship' in R. Jackson et al. (eds.) *Religion and Education in Europe: Developments, Contexts and Debates* (New York, Münster, München, Waxmann), 27-56.

Jackson, R. (2008a) 'Teaching about Religion in the Public Sphere: European Policy Initiatives and the Interpretive Approach' in *NUMEN*, 55, 151-182.

Jackson, R. (2008b) 'Contextual Religious Education and the Interpretive Approach' in *British Journal of Religious Education*, 30 (1), 13-24.

Jackson, R. (2009) 'Is Diversity Changing Religious Education? Religion, Diversity and Education in Today's Europe' in G. Skeie (ed.) *Religious Diversity and Education – Nordic Perspectives* (Münster, New York, München, Berlin, Waxmann), 11-28.

Jackson, R., Miedema, S., Weisse, W. and Willaime, J. P. (eds.) (2007) *Religion and Education in Europe: Developments, Contexts and Debates* (New York, Münster, Berlin, Waxmann).

Jackson R. and Nesbitt, E. (1993) *Hindu Children in Britain* (Oakhill, Trentham Books).

Jackson, R. and O'Grady, K. (2007) 'Religion and Education in England: Social Plurality, Civil Religion and Religious Education Pedagogy' in R. Jackson et al. (eds.) *Religion and education in Europe: Developments, Contexts and Debates* (Münster, New York, München, Berlin, Waxmann), 181-202.

Jensen, T. and Rothstein, M. (2000) *Secular Theories on Religion: Current Perspectives* (Copenhagen, Museum Tusculanum Press).

Johnstad, T., Klausen, J. E., Mønnesland, J. (2003) *Globalisering, regionalisering og distriktspolitikk*, Makt og demokaratiutredningens rapportserie, Rapport 76, august 2003.

Jørgensen, C. S. (2013) *Som du spør får du svar? En empirisk studie av hvordan ulike skriveoppgaver ivaretar et utvalg ungdomstrinnselevers anledning til å utvikle kompetanser med relevans for dannelse gjennom skriving I religions- og livssynsfaget*, unpublished PhD (Trondheim, Norwegian University of Sciences and Technology).

Kallo, J. and Rinne R. (eds.) (2006) *Supranational Regimes and National Education Policies* (Turku, Finland, Finnish Educational research Association).

Kandel, I. L. (1933) *Comparative Education* (Boston, Massachusetts, Houghton Mifflin).

Karlsen, G. E. (2005) Bologna-prosessen – en markedstilpasset standarisering av utdanning?, *Norsk Pedagogisk Tidsskrift*, 89, 263-268.

Karlsen, G. (2006) *Utdanning, styring og marked: Norsk utdanningspolitikk i et internasjonalt perspektiv* (Universitetsforlaget AS, Oslo).

Kirkeby, W. A. (2001) *Ordbok Videregående: norsk-engelsk engelsk-norsk* (Skedsmokorset, Kirkeby Forlag).

Kirke-, utdannings- og forskningsdepartementet (KUF) (1998) *Differensiert undervisning og avgrenset fritak I faget kristendomskunnskap med religions- og livssynsorientering* (Rundskriv F-03-98).

Kirkhusmo, A. (1983) *Akademi og Seminar: Norges Lærerhøgskole 1922-1982* (Trondheim, Universitetet i Trondheim).

Knauth, T., Jozsa, D.-P., Bertram-Troost, G. and Ipgrave J. (eds.) (2008) *Encountering Religious Pluralism in School and Society: A Qualitative Study of Teenage Perspectives in Europe* (Münster, New York, München, Berlin, Waxmann).

Knauth, T. (2007) 'Religious Education in Germany: Contribution to Dialogue or Source of Conflict?' in R. Jackson et al. (eds.) *Religion and Education in Europe: Developments, Contexts and Debates* (Münster, New York, München, Waxmann), 243-265.

Kuyk, E., Jensen, R., Lankshear, D., Löh Manna, E., Schreiner, P. (eds.) (2007) *Religious Education in Europe: Situations and current Trends in Schools* (IKO – Publishing House, Norway).

Læringssenteret (LS) (2002) *KRL – boka. Kristendoms-, religions,- og livssynskunnskap. Læreplan for den 10-årige grunnskolen* (Oslo, Utdannings og Forskningsdepartementet).

Larsson, R. and Gustavson, C. (eds.) (2004) *Towards a European Perspective on Religious Education: The RE Research Conference March 11-14, 2004, University of Lund* (Sweden, Artos and Norma bokförlag).

Leganger-Krogstad, H., Haakedal, E. (eds.) (1995) *Religiøse og pedagogiske idealer* (Oslo: Norges forskningsråd, KULTs skriftserie nr. 42).

Leganger-Krogstad, H. (2007) 'The Contextual Approach' in J. Keast (ed.) *Religious Diversity and Intercultural Education: A reference Book for Schools* (Strasbourg, Council of Europe Publishing), 99-112.

Lerheim, B. (2009) *Vedkjenning og gjenkjenning. Refleksjoner i snittpunkta mellom kyrkjetenkning og kyrkjepraksis*, unpublished PhD thesis (Oslo, University of Oslo).

Lied, S. (2004) *Elever og livstolkningspluralitet i KRL faget: Mellomtrinnselever i møte med fortellinger fra ulike religioner og livssyn*, Published PhD (Elverum, Høgskolen i Hedemark).

Lied, S. (2006) 'Norsk religionspedagogisk forskning 1985-2005', in *Norsk Teologisk Tidsskrift*, 3, 163-195.

Lijphart, A. (1971) 'Comparative Politics and the Comparative Method', in *The American Political Science Review*, 65 (3), 682-693.

Lingås, L. G, London L. (1996) *Likhet eller likeverd? En kritikk av det nye kristendomsfaget i grunnskolen* (Oslo, Humanist forlag AS).

Lippe, von der M. (2008) 'To believe or not to believe: Young People's Perceptions and Experiences of Religion and Religious Education in Norway' in t. Knauth et al. (eds.) *Encountering Religious Pluralism in School and Society: A Quantiative Study of Teenage Perspectives in Europe* (Münster, New York, München, Waxmann), 149-171.

Lippe, von der M. (2011) *Youth, Religion and Diversity. A qualitative study of young people's talk about religion in a secular and plural society. A Norwegian case*, unpublished PhD thesis (Stavanger, University of Stavanger).

Loukes, H. (1961) *Teenage Religion* (London SCM).

Loukes, H. (1965) *New Ground in Christian Education*, (London, SCM).

Lund Johannessen, Ø. (2009) "Sameness' as Norm and Challenge – Norwegian Teachers and Religious Diversity' in A. van der Want et al. (2009) *Teachers responding to Religious Diversity in Europe: Researching Biography and Pedagogy* (Münster, New York, München, Berlin, Waxmann), 95-110.

May, S. (ed.) (1999) *Critical Multiculturalism: Rethinking Multicultural and Anti Racist Education* (London, Falmer Press).

Maylor, U. and Read, B. (2007) *Diversity and Citizenship in the Curriculum: Research Review* (95-97 DfES).

McIntyre, J. (1978) *Multi-culture and Multifaith Societies: Some examinable Assumptions* (Occasional Papers, Oxford, Farmington Institute for Christian Studies).

McKenna, U., Neill, S., Jackson, R. (2009) 'Personal Worldviews, Dialogue and Tolerance' in P. Valk et al. (eds.) *Teenagers' Perspectives on the Role of Religion in their Lives, Schools and Societies: A Quantitative Study* (Münster, New York, München, Berlin, Waxmann), 49-70.

Mogstad, S. D. (1999) *Fag, identitet og fortelling: Didaktikk til kristendomskunnskap med religions- og livssynsorientering* (Oslo, Universitetsforlaget).

Mogstad, S. D. (2001) *Trostradisjon og livssituasjon: En systematisk teologisk analyse av hvordan etablere korrelasjon mellom fortelling og erfaring med utgangspunkt I Hans Stocks og Georg Baudlers bibeldidaktiske teorier*, Published PhD thesis (Trondheim, Tapir forlag).

Müller, F. M. (1873) *Introduction to the Science of Religion: Four Lectures delivered at the Royal Institution, with two Essays on False Analogies, and the Philosophy of Mythology* (London, Longmanns, Green and Co).

Murphy, T. (2000) 'Speaking Different Languages: Religion and the Study of Religion' in T. Jensen and M. Rothstein *Secular theories on Religion, Current Perspectives* (Denmark, Museum Tusculanum Press), 183-192.

Norges Høyesterett (2001): Dom 22. august 2001 I sak nr. 2000/1533, sivil sak, anke, Humanetisk Forbund m.fl. mot Staten v/ Kirke-, utdannings og forskningsdepartementet. (Norwegian High Court 2001: Sentence 22nd August 2001 in case nr. 2000/1533, civil case, appeal, the Humanist Organisation and others versus the State by the Department for Church, education and research.)

Norges Offentlige Utredninger (NOU) (1995): 9 *Identitet og dialog. Kristendomskunnskap, livssynskunnskap og religionsundervisning* (Oslo, Kirke – utdannings og forskningsdepartementet).

Norges Offentlige Utredninger (NOU) (2007): 6 *Formål for framtida: Formål for barnehagen og opplæringen,* (Oslo, Departementenes servicesenter: Informasjonsforvaltning).

O'Grady, K. (2003) 'Motivation in Religious Education: A Collaborative Investigation with year eight Students' in *British Journal of Religious Education*, 25 (3), 214 – 225.

O'Grady K. (2005) 'Professor Ninian Smart, Phenomenology and Religious Education' in *British Journal of Religious Education*, 29 (2), 157-168.

Organization for Security and Co-operation in Europe (OSCE) (2007) *Toledo Guiding Principles on teaching about Religions and Beliefs in Public Schools: Prepared by ODIHR Advisory Council of Experts on Freedom of Religion and Belief* (Warsaw, OSCE/ ODIHR).

Osmer, R. R., Schweitzer, F. (2003) *Religious Education between Modernization and Globalization* (Michigan, Wm. B. Eerdmans Publishing Co.).

Paden, W. E. (1994) [1988] *Religious Worlds: The Comparative Study of Religion* (Boston Massachusetts, Beacon Press).

Paulston, R. G. (1994) 'Comparative and International Education: Paradigms and Theories' in T. Husèn and T. N. Postlethwait (1994) *International Encyclopaedia of Education* (Oxford, Pergamon), 923-933.

Phillips, D. (2005) 'Policy Borrowing in Education: Frameworks for Analysis' in J. Zajda et al. (ed.) *International Handbook on Globalisation, Education, and Policy Research* (Netherlands, Springer).

Phillips, D. and Ochs, K. (2004) *Educational Policy Borrowing: Historical Perspectives* (UK, Symposium books).

Plesner, I. (1998) *'Frihet eller fellesskap?': et liberalt og sosialdemokratisk dilemma: sosiologisk analyse av debatten om det nye grunnskolefaget "Kristendomskunnskap med religions- og livssynsorientering"* Unpublished Master thesis (Oslo, Universitetet i Oslo).

Pye, M., Franke, E., Wasim, A. T. and Ma'sud, A. (eds.) (2006) *Religious Harmony: Problems, Practice and Education* (Berlin, New York, Walter de Gruyter).

Qualifications and Curriculum Authority (QCA) (2004) *Religious Education: The Non-statutory National Framework* (London, QCA).

Ragin, C. (1987) *Comparative Method: Moving beyond Qualitative and Quantitative Strategies* (London, England, University of California Press, Ltd.).

Rasmussen T. and Thomassen, E. (eds.) (1999) *Kildesamling til Kristendomskunnskap med religions- og livsorientering* (Oslo, Nasjonalt læremiddelsenter).

Rian, D. (1999) *Verdensreligioner I undervisningen* (Oslo, Universitetsforlaget).

Rian, D. and Kværne, P. (1983) *Religionshistorie og religionsundervisning: Noen fagdidaktiske synspunkter* (Trondheim, Tapir).

Robson, C. (2002) *Real World Research: Second Edition* (Oxford UK, Blackwell Publishing).

Rudge, L. (1998) 'I Am Nothing – Does it Matter? A Critique of Current Religious Education Policy and Practice in England on behalf of the Silent Majority', in *British Journal of Religious Education*, 20 (3), 155-165.

Sagberg, S. (2001) *Autensitet og undring. En drøfting av kristendommens plass i norsk barnehage: institusjonsetisk og personetisk perspektiv*, Unpublised PhD thesis (Trondheim, Norges Teknisk Naturvitenskapelige Universitet).

Said, E. (1978) *Orientalism* (London, Routledge and Kegan Paul).

Said, E. (1993) *Culture and Imperialism* (London: Chatto and Windus).

Sandvik, B.(1996) 'Fra katekisme til livssynsmangfold' in L. G. Lingås and L. London (eds.) *Likhet eller likeverd? En kritikk av det nye kristendomsfaget i grunnskolen* (Oslo, Humanist forlag AS).

SCAA (1994a) *Model Syllabuses for Religious Education: Consultation Document: Introduction* (London, SCAA and the Central Office of Information).

SCAA (1994b) *Model Syllabuses for Religious Education: Consultation Document: Working Groups reports* (London, SCAA and the Central Office of Information).

SCAA (1994c) *Model Syllabuses for Religious Education: Consultation Document: Model 2* (London, SCAA and the Central Office of Information).

SCAA (1994d) *Model Syllabuses for Religious Education: Consultation Document: Glossary of terms* (London, SCAA and the Central Office of Information).

Schiffauer, W., Baumann G., Kastoriano, R. and Vertovec, S. (eds.) (2004) *Civil Enculturation: Nation State, School and Ethnic Difference in The Netherlands, Britain, Germany and France* (New York, Oxford, Berghahn Books).

Schools Council (1971) *Working Paper 36: Religious Education in Secondary Schools* (London, Evans/ Methuen Educational).

Schreiner, P. (2007) 'Religious Education in the European Context' in E. Kuyk, R. Jensen, D. Lankshear, E. Löh Manna, P. Schreiner (eds.) *Religious Education in Europe: Situations and current Trends in Schools* (IKO – Publishing House, Norway), 9-16.

Schweitzer, F. (2004) 'Comparative Research in Religious Education: International-Interdenominational-Interreligious' in R. Larsson and C. Gustavsson (eds.) *Towards a European Perspective on Religious Education* (Stockholm, Artos & Norma), 191-200.

Schweitzer, F. (2006) 'Let the Captives speak for Themselves!: More dialogue between Religious Education in England and Germany', in *British Journal of Religious Education*, 28 (2), 141-151.

Schweitzer, F. (2013) 'Comparing Religious Education in Schools in European Countries – Challenges for International Comparative Research' in M. Jäggle, M. Rothgangel and T. Schlag (eds.) *Religious Education at schools in Europe. Volume 1 – Central Europe* (Vienna, Vienna University Press).

Selander, S. Å. (2004) 'Elisabeth Haakedal: 'Det er jo vanlig praksis her hos oss ..." Religionslærerrolle, livstolkning og skolekulturell ritualisering – en religionspedagogisk studie av grunnskolelæreres handlingsrom på 1990-tallet', in *Norsk Teologisk Tidsskrift*, 4, 219-222.

Sharpe, E. J. (1975) *Comparative Religion: A History* (London, Duckworth).

Skeie, G. (1993) *Referat fra: Nettverksseminar for forskere med interesse for flerkultur og religion*, Unpublished report from the first NEKRIF seminar at the University of Trondheim, 22.-23rd. March 1993.

Skeie, G. (1994) *Rapport om reisestipend*, rapport til Norges allmennvitenskapelige forskningsråd (NAVF).

Skeie, G. (1995) 'Plurality and pluralism: a Challenge for Religious Education', in *British Journal of Religious Education* 25 (1), 47-59.

Skeie, G. (1998) *En kulturbevisst religionspedagogikk*, Unpublised PhD (Trondheim, Norges Teknisk Naturvitenskapelige Universitet).

Skeie, G. (2003) 'Nationalism, Religiosity and Citizenship in Norwegian Majority and Minority Discourse' in R. Jackson (ed.) *International Perspectives on Citizenship, Education and Religious Diversity* (London, RoutledgeFalmer), 51-66.

Skeie, G. (2004) 'An Overview of Religious Education Research in Norway' in R. Larson and C. Gustavson (eds.) *Towards a European Perspective on Religious Education: The RE Research Conference March 11-14, 2004, University of Lund* (Sweden, Artos and Norma bokförlag), 317-331.

Skeie, G. (2006a) 'What do we mean by 'Religion' in Education? On Disciplinary Knowledge and Knowledge in the Classroom' in K. Tirri (ed.) *Religion, Spirituality and Identity* (Bern, Peter Lang AG, International Academic Publishers), 85-99.

Skeie, G. (2006b) 'Diversity and Political function of Religious Education', in *British Journal of Religious Education*, 28 (1), 19-32.

Skeie, G. (2007) 'Religious Education in Norway' in Jackson et al. (eds.) *Religion and Education in Europe: Developments, Contexts, Debates* (Münster, New York, München, Berlin, Waxmann), 221-242.

Skeie, G. and von der Lippe, M. (2009) 'Does Religion Matter to Young People in Norwegian Schools?' Valk et al. *Teenagers' Perspectives on the Role of Religion in their Lives, Schools and Societies: A Quantitative Study* (Münster, New York, München, Berlin, Waxmann), 49-70.

Skoglund, R. I. (2008) *Helklassesamtaler om livsspørsmål: en kvalitativ studie I KRL-faget på småskoletrinnet*, Unpublished PhD (Trondheim, Norges Teknisk Naturvitenskapelige Universitet).

Skottene, R. (1994) *Den konfesjonelle skole: debatten om den konfesjonelle profil i kristendomsundervisningen og grunnskolen i Norge fra 1870-årene til 1990 årene*, Unpublised PhD thesis (Oslo, The Norwegian School of Theology).

Skrunes, N. (1995) *Kristendomskunnskap for barn: en fagplanhistorisk undersøkelse av kristendomsfagets utvikling 1889 – 1939*, PhD thesis (Bergen, Norsk Lærerakademi).

Smart, N. (1968) *Secular Education and the Logic of Religion* (London, Faber and Faber).

Spreen, C. A. M. (2001) *Globalisation and Educational Policy borrowing: Mapping Outcome based Education in South Africa*, PhD thesis (New York, Columbia University).

Stausberg, M. (2006) 'Sammenligning' in S. E. Kraft and R. J. Natvig R. J. (eds.) *Metode i religionsvitenskap* (Oslo, Pax Forlag), 29-50.

Steiner-Khamsi, G. (ed.) (2004) *The Global Politics of Educational borrowing and lending* (New York and London, Teacher College press, Columbia University).

Telhaug, A. O. (1994) *Utdanningspolitikken og enhetsskolen: studier i 1990 årenes utdanningspolitikk* (Oslo, Didakta).

Thomassen, E. (1998) 'Teologi og religionshistorie – mot en ny tverrfaglig identitet?', in *Norsk Teologisk Tidsskrift* 99, 30-35.

Thomassen, E. (2006) 'Religious Education in a Pluralistic Society: Experiences from Norway' in M. Pye, E. Franke, A. T. Wasim and A. Ma'sud (eds.) (2006) *Religious Harmony: Problems, Practice and Education* (Berlin, New York, Walter de Gruyter), 257-266.

Taylor, C. (2004) *Modern Social Imaginaries* (Durham and London, Duke University press).

Taylor, C. (2007) *A Secular Age* (Cambridge Massachusetts, and London, England, The Belknap Press of Harvard University Press).

UK Government (1988) *Education Reform Act* (London, HMSO).

Utdanningsdirektoratet (UD) (2005) *KRL-boka 2005: Kristendoms-, religions-, og livssynsorientering* (Oslo, Utdanningsdirektoratet).

Utdanningsdirektoratet (UD) (2006) *Læreplanverket for kunnskapsløftet: Midlertidig utgave juni 2006* (Oslo, Utdanningsdirektoratet).

Utdanningsdirektoratet (UD) (2008) *Læreplan i religion, livssyn og etikk* (Oslo, Utdanningsdirektoratet).

Valk, P., Bertram-Troost, G., Friederici, M. and Bèraud, C. (2009) *Teenagers' Perspectives on the Role of Religion in their Lives, Schools and Societies: A Quantitative Study* (Münster, New York, München, Berlin, Waxmann).

Want, van der A., Bakker, C., ter Avest, I. and Everington, J. (2009) *Teachers responding to Religious Diversity in Europe: Researching Biography and Pedagogy* (Münster, New York, München, Berlin, Waxmann).

Webster (2003) *The New International Webster's Comprehensive Dictionary of the English Language: Encyclopaedic Edition* (Columbia, Trident Press International).

Weisse, W. (2007) 'The European Research Project on Religion and Education 'REDCo': An Introduction' in R. Jackson et al. (eds.) *Religion and Education in Europe: Developments, Contexts and Debates*, (Münster, New York, München, Berlin, Waxmann), 9-25.

Willaime, J. P. (2007) 'Different Models for Religious Education in Europe' in R. Jackson et al. (eds.) *Religion and Education in Europe: Developments, Contexts and Debates* (Münster, New York, München Waxmann), 87-102.

Wilson, B. (1987) 'Secularization' in M. Eliades *The Encyclopedia of Religion*, (New York, Macmillian), 159-165.

Winje, G. (1999) *Fra bønn til magi: Nye religioner og menneskesyn* (Kristiansand, Høyskoleforlaget).

Winje, G. (2008) 'Lærebøkene i KRL – hva har skjedd på 10 år?' *Norsk Teologisk Tidsskrift* (1), 72-87.

Winsnes, O. G. (1984) *Kristendomskunnskap – erfaring – kommunikasjon. En samling artikler om religionspedagogikkens emner* (Trondheim, Tapir).

Winsnes, O. G. (1988) *E' du rel'giøs, eller ...? Om konseptualisering og metodilogi i empirisk religionsforsknng*, Unpublished PhD thesis (Trondheim, Den allmennvitenskapelige høgskolen, Universitetet i Trondheim).

Wright, A. (2008) 'Contextual Religious Education and the Actuality of Religions' in *British Journal of Religious Education* 30 (1), 3-12.

Østberg, S. (1998a) *Pakistani Children in Oslo: Islamic nurture in a Secular Context*, Unpublished PhD Thesis (Coventry, University of Warwick).

Østberg, S. (1998b) 'Religionshistorie og religionsdidaktikk' in I. M. Ruud and S. Hjelde (eds.) *Enhet i mangfold? 100 år med religionshistorie i Norge* (Oslo, Tano Aschehoug AS), 239-261.